MORALS

OF A HAPPY LIFE, BENEFITS, ANGER AND CLEMENCY

MORALS

OF A HAPPY LIFE, BENEFITS, ANGER AND CLEMENCY

ANNAEUS LUCIUS SENECA

Translated by Sir Roger L'Estrange

WILDSIDE PRESS

MORALS

Borgo Classics of Greek and Roman Philosophy #1.
Series Editor: John Betancourt

CONTENTS

INTRODUCTION

Seneca, full name Lucius Annaeus Seneca, was a Roman Stoic philosopher, statesman, dramatist, and advisor to Emperor Nero. Born around 4 BCE in Corduba (present-day Córdoba, Spain) and dying in 65 CE, Seneca was a prominent figure in the Roman Empire.

Seneca's *Morals*, a cornerstone of Stoic philosophy, offers profound insights into ethical living, self-discipline, and the pursuit of virtue. As a Roman statesman and philosopher, Seneca wrote these moral essays and letters to impart practical wisdom to his contemporaries, blending philosophical doctrine with real-world applicability. His works, including "On the Shortness of Life," "On Anger," and "On the Happy Life," address the human condition, exploring themes of time management, emotional control, and the essence of happiness.

In *Morals*, Seneca emphasizes the Stoic belief that true contentment arises from within, independent of external circumstances. He advocates for rational thinking, self-examination, and the cultivation of inner peace as pathways to a virtuous life. Through vivid anecdotes and compelling arguments, Seneca challenges readers to confront their desires, fears, and societal pressures, urging them to live in accordance with nature and reason.

Seneca's eloquent prose and timeless advice continue to resonate, providing a guide for navigating the complexities of modern life. His teachings remind us that moral clarity and ethical integrity are achievable through thoughtful reflection and disciplined practice, making *Morals* a lasting contribution to the philosophical canon.

—Karl Wurf

BENEFITS

I

BENEFITS IN GENERAL

It is, perhaps, one of the most pernicious errors of a rash and inconsiderate life, the common ignorance of the world in the matter of exchanging *benefits*. And this arises from a mistake, partly in the person that we would oblige, and partly in the thing itself. To begin with the latter: "A benefit is a good office, done with intention and judgment;" that is to say, with a due regard to all the circumstances of *what, how, why, when, where, to whom, how much,* and the like; or otherwise: "It is a voluntary and benevolent action that delights the giver in the comfort it brings to the receiver." It will be hard to draw this subject, either into method or compass: the one, because of the infinite variety and complication of cases; the other, by reason of the large extent of it: for the whole business (almost) of mankind in society falls under this head; the duties of kings and subjects, husbands and wives, parents and children, masters and servants, natives and strangers, high and low, rich and poor, strong and weak, friends and enemies. The very meditation of it breeds good blood and generous thoughts; and instructs us in honor, humanity, friendship, piety, gratitude, prudence, and justice. In short, the art and skill of conferring benefits is, of all human duties, the most absolutely necessary to the well-being, both of reasonable nature, and of every individual; as the very cement of all communities, and the blessing of particulars. He that does good to another man does good also to himself; not only in the consequence, but in the very act of doing it; for the conscience of well-doing is an ample reward.

Of benefits in general, there are several sorts; as *necessary*, *profitable*, and *delightful*. Some things there are, without which we *cannot* live; others without which we *ought not* to live; and some, again, without which we *will not* live. In the first rank are those which deliver us from capital dangers, or apprehensions of death: and the favor is rated according to the hazard; for the greater the extremity, the greater seems the obligation. The next is a case wherein we may indeed live, but we had better die; as in the question of liberty, modesty, and a good conscience. In the third place, follow those things which custom, use, affinity, and acquaintance, have made dear to us; as husbands, wives, children, friends, etc., which an honest man will preserve at his utmost peril. Of things profitable there is a large field, as money, honor, etc., to which might be added, matters of superfluity and pleasure. But we shall open a way to the circumstances of a benefit by some previous and more general deliberations upon the thing itself.

II

SEVERAL SORTS OF BENEFITS

We shall divide *benefits* into *absolute* and *vulgar*; the one appertaining to good life, the other is only matter of commerce. The former are the more excellent, because they can never be made void; whereas all material benefits are tossed back and forward, and change their master. There are some offices that look like benefits, but are only desirable conveniences, as wealth, etc., and these a wicked man may receive from a good, or a good man from an evil. Others, again, that bear the face of injuries, which are only benefits ill taken; as cutting, lancing, burning, under the hand of a surgeon. The greatest benefits of all are those of good education, which we receive from our parents, either in the state of ignorance or perverseness; as, their care and tenderness in our infancy; their discipline in our childhood, to keep us to our duties by fear; and, if fair means will not do, their proceeding afterwards to severity and punishment, without which we should never have come to good. There are matters of great value, many times, that are but of small price; as instructions from a tutor, medicine from a physician, etc. And there are small matters again, which are of great consideration to us: the gift is small, and the consequence great; as a cup of cold water in a time of need may save a man's life. Some things are of great moment to the giver, others to the receiver: one man gives me a house; another snatches me out when it is falling upon my head; one gives me an estate; another takes me out of the fire, or casts me out a rope when I am sinking. Some good offices we do to friends, others to strangers; but those are the noblest that we do without pre-desert. There is an obligation of bounty, and an obligation of charity; this in case of necessity, and that in point of convenience. Some benefits are common, others are personal; as if a prince (out of pure grace) grant a privilege to a city, the obligation lies upon the community, and only upon every individual as a part of the whole; but if it be done particularly for my sake, then am I singly the debtor for it. The cherishing of strangers is one of the duties of hospitality, and exercises itself in the relief and protection of the distressed. There are benefits of good counsel, reputation, life, fortune, liberty, health, nay, and of superfluity and pleasure. One man obliges me out of his pocket; another gives me matter of ornament and curiosity; a third, consolation. To say nothing of negative benefits; for there are that reckon it an obligation if they do a body no hurt; and place it to account, as if they saved a man, when they do not undo him. To shut up all in one word; as benevolence is the most sociable of all virtues, so it is of the largest extent; for there is not any man, either so great or so little, but he is yet capable of giving and of receiving benefits.

III

A SON MAY OBLIGE HIS FATHER,
AND A SERVANT HIS MASTER

The question is (in the first place) whether it may not be possible for a father to owe more to a son, in other respects, than the son owes to his father for his being? That many sons are both greater and better than their fathers, there is no question; as there are many other things that derive their beings from others, which yet are far greater than their original. Is not the tree larger than the seed? the river than the fountain? The foundation of all things lies hid, and the superstructure obscures it. If I owe all to my father, because he gives me life, I may owe as much to a physician that saved his life; for if my father had not been cured, I had never been begotten: or, if I stand indebted for all that I am to my beginning, my acknowledgment must run back to the very original of all human beings. My father gave me the benefit of life: which he had never done, if his father had not first given it to him. He gave me life, not knowing to whom; and when I was in a condition neither to feel death nor to fear it. That is the great benefit, to give life to one that knows how to use it, and that is capable of the apprehension of death. It is true, that without a father I could never have had a being; and so, without a nurse, that being had never been improved: but I do not therefore owe my virtue either to my nativity or to her that gave me suck. The generation of me was the last part of the benefit: for to live is common with brutes; but to live well is the main business; and that virtue is all my own, saving what I drew from my education. It does not follow that the *first* benefit must be the *greatest*, because without the first the greatest could never have been. The father gives life to the son but once; but if the son save the father's life often, though he do but his duty, it is yet a greater benefit. And again, the benefit that a man receives is the greater, the more he needs it; but the living has more need of life than he that is not yet born; so that the father receives a greater benefit in the continuance of his life than the son in the beginning of it. What if a son deliver his father from the rack; or, which is more, lay himself down in his place? The giving of him a being was but the office of a father; a simple act, a benefit given at a venture: beside that, he had a participant in it, and a regard to his family. He gave only a single life, and he received a happy one. My mother brought me into the world naked, exposed, and void of reason; but my reputation and my fortune are advanced by my virtue. Scipio (as yet in his minority) rescued his father in a battle with Hannibal, and afterward from the practices and persecution of a powerful faction; covering him with consulary honors, and the spoils of public enemies. He made himself as eminent for his moderation as for his piety and military knowledge: he was the defender and the establisher of his country: he left the empire without a competitor, and made himself as well the ornament of Rome as the security of it: and did not Scipio, in all this, more than requite his father barely for begetting of him? Whether did Anchises more for Aeneas, in dandling the child in his arms; or Aeneas for his father, when he carried him upon his back through the flames of Troy, and made his name famous to future ages among the founders of the Roman Empire? T. Manlius was the son of a sour and imperious father, who banished him his house as a blockhead, and a scandal to the family. This Manlius, hearing that his father's life was in question, and a day set for his trial, went to the tribune that was concerned in his cause, and discoursed with him about it: the tribune told him the appointed time, and withal (as an obligation upon the young man) that his cruelty to his son would be part of his accusation. Manlius, upon this, takes the tribune aside, and presenting a poniard to his breast, "Swear," says he, "that you will let this cause fall, or you shall have this dagger in the heart of you; and now it is at your choice which way you will deliver my father." The tribune swore and kept his word, and made a fair report of the whole matter to the council. He that makes himself famous by his eloquence, justice, or arms, illustrates his extraction, let it be never so mean; and gives inestimable reputation to his parents. We should never have heard of Sophroniscus, but for his son Socrates; nor for Aristo and Gryllus, if it had not been for Xenophon and Plato.

This is not to discountenance the veneration we owe to parents; nor to make children the worse, but the better; and to stir up generous emulations: for, in contests of good offices, both parties are happy; as well the vanquished as those that overcome. It is the only honorable dispute that can arise betwixt a father and son, which of the two shall have the better of the other in the point of benefits.

In the question betwixt a master and a servant, we must distinguish betwixt benefits, duties, and actions ministerial. By *benefits*, we understand those good offices that we receive from strangers, which are voluntary, and may be forborne without blame. *Duties* are the parts of a son and wife, and incumbent upon kindred and relations. *Offices ministerial* belong to the part of a servant. Now, since it is the *mind*, and not the *condition* of a person, that prints the value upon the benefit, a servant may oblige his master, and so may a subject his sovereign, or a common soldier his general, by doing more than he is expressly bound to do. Some things there are, which the law neither commands nor forbids; and here the servant is free. It would be very hard for a servant to be chastised for doing less than his duty, and not thanked for it when he does more. His body, it is true, is his master's, but his mind is his own: and there are many commands which a servant ought no more to obey than a master to impose. There is no man so great, but he may both need the help and service, and stand in fear of the power and unkindness, even of the meanest of mortals. One servant kills his master; another saves him, nay, preserves his master's life, perhaps, with the loss of his own: he exposes himself to torment and death; he stands firm against all threats and batteries: which is not only a benefit in a servant, but much the greater for his being so.

When Domitius was besieged in Corfinium, and the place brought to great extremity, he pressed his servant so earnestly to poison him, that at last he was prevailed upon to give him a potion; which, it seems, was an innocent opiate, and Domitius outlived it: Caesar took the town, and gave Domitius his life, but it was his servant that gave it him first.

There was another town besieged, and when it was upon the last pinch, two servants made their escape, and went over to the enemy: upon the Romans entering the town, and in the heat of the soldiers' fury, these two fellows ran directly home, took their mistress out of her house, and drove her before them, telling every body how barbarously she had used them formerly, and that they would now have their revenge; when they had her without the gates, they kept her close till the danger was over; by which means they gave their mistress her life, and she gave them their freedom. This was not the action of a servile mind, to do so glorious a thing, under an appearance of so great a villainy; for if they had not passed for deserters and parricides, they could not have gained their end.

With one instance more (and that a very brave one) I shall conclude this chapter.

In the civil wars of Rome, a party coming to search for a person of quality that was proscribed, a servant put on his master's clothes, and delivered himself up to the soldiers as the master of the house; he was taken into custody, and put to death, without discovering the mistake. What could be more glorious, than for a servant to die for his master, in that age, when there were not many servants that would not betray their masters? So generous a tenderness in a public cruelty; so invincible a faith in a general corruption; what could be more glorious, I say, than so exalted a virtue, as rather to choose death for the reward of his fidelity, than the greatest advantages he might otherwise have had for the violation of it?

IV

IT IS THE INTENTION, NOT THE MATTER, THAT MAKES THE BENEFIT

The *good-will* of the benefactor is the fountain of all benefits; nay it is the benefit itself, or, at least, the stamp that makes it valuable and current. Some there are, I know, that take the matter for the benefit, and tax the obligation by weight and measure. When anything is given them, they presently cast it up; "What may such a house be worth? such an office? such an estate?" as if that were the benefit which is only the sign and mark of it: for the obligation rests in the mind, not in the matter; and all those advantages which we see, handle, or hold in actual possession by the courtesy of another, are but several modes or ways of explaining and putting the good-will in execution. There needs no great subtlety to prove, that both benefits and injuries receive their value from the intention, when even brutes themselves are able to decide this question. Tread upon a dog by chance, or put him to pain upon the dressing of a wound; the one he passes by as an accident; and the other, in his fashion, he acknowledges as a kindness: but, offer to strike at him, though you do him no hurt at all, he flies yet in the face of you, even for the mischief that you barely meant him.

It is further to be observed, that all benefits are good; and (like the distributions of Providence) made up of wisdom and bounty; whereas the gift itself is neither good nor bad, but may indifferently be applied, either to the one or to the other. The benefit is immortal, the gift perishable: for the benefit itself continues when we have no longer either the use or the matter of it. He that is dead was alive; he that has lost his eyes, did see; and, whatsoever is done, cannot be rendered undone. My friend (for instance) is taken by pirates; I redeem him; and after that he falls into other pirates' hands; his obligation to me is the same still as if he had preserved his freedom. And so, if I save a man from any misfortune, and he falls into another; if I give him a sum of money, which is afterwards taken away by thieves; it comes to the same case. Fortune may deprive us of the matter of a benefit, but the benefit itself remains inviolable. If the benefit resided in the matter, that which is good for one man would be so for another; whereas many times the very same thing, given to several persons, work contrary effects, even to the difference of life or death; and that which is one body's cure proves another body's poison. Beside that, the timing of it alters the value; and a crust of bread, upon a pinch, is a greater present than an imperial crown. What is more familiar than in a battle to shoot at an enemy and kill a friend? or, instead of a friend, to save an enemy? But yet this disappointment, in the event, does not at all operate upon the intention. What if a man cures me of a wen with a stroke that was designed to cut off my head? or, with a malicious blow upon my stomach, breaks an imposthume? or, what if he saves my life with a draught that was prepared to poison me? The providence of the issue does not at all discharge the obliquity of the intent. And the same reason holds good even in religion itself. It is not the incense, or the offering, that is acceptable to God, but the purity and devotion of the worshipper: neither is the bare will, without action, sufficient, that is, where we have the means of acting; for, in that case, it signifies as little to *wish* well, without *well-doing*, as to *do* good without *willing* it. There must be effect as well as intention, to make me owe a benefit; but, to will against it, does wholly discharge it. In fine, the conscience alone is the judge, both of benefits and injuries.

It does not follow now, because the benefit rests in the good-will, that therefore the good-will should be always a benefit; for if it be not accompanied with government and discretion, those offices, which we call *benefits*, are but the works of passion, or of chance; and many times, the greatest of all injuries. One man does me good by mistake; another ignorantly; a third upon force: but none of these cases do I take to be an obligation; for they were neither directed to me, nor was there any kindness of intention; we do not thank the seas for the advantages we receive by navigation; or the rivers with supplying us with fish and flowing of our grounds; we do not thank the trees either for their fruits or shades, or the winds for a fair gale; and what is the difference betwixt a reasonable creature that does not know and an inanimate that cannot? A good *horse* saves one man's life; a good suit of *arms* another's; and a *man*, perhaps, that never intended it, saves a third. Where is the difference now betwixt the obligation of one and of the other? A man falls into a river, and the fright cures him of the ague; we may call this a kind of lucky mischance, but not a remedy. And so it is with the good we receive, either without, or beside, or contrary to intention. It is the mind, and not the event, that distinguishes a benefit from an injury.

V

THERE MUST BE JUDGMENT IN A BENEFIT, AS WELL AS MATTER AND INTENTION; AND ESPECIALLY IN THE CHOICE OF THE PERSON

As it is the *will* that designs the benefit, and the *matter* that conveys it, so it is the *judgment* that perfects it; which depends upon so many critical niceties, that the least error, either in the person, the matter, the manner, the quality, the quantity, the time, or the place, spoils all.

The consideration of the *person* is a main point: for we are to give by choice, and not by hazard. My inclination bids me oblige one man; I am bound in duty and justice to serve another; here it is a charity, there it is pity; and elsewhere, perhaps, encouragement. There are some that want, to whom I would not give; because, if I did, they would want still. To one man I would barely offer a benefit; but I would press it upon another. To say the truth, we do not employ any more profit than that which we bestow; and it is not to our friends, our acquaintances or countrymen, nor to this or that condition of men, that we are to restrain our bounties; but wheresoever there is a man, there is a place and occasion for a benefit. We give to some that are good already; to others, in hope to make them so: but we must do all with discretion; for we are as well answerable for what we give as for what we receive; nay, the misplacing of a benefit is worse than the not receiving of it; for the one is another man's fault; but the other is mine. The error of the giver does oft-times excuse the ingratitude of the receiver: for a favor ill-placed is rather a profusion than a benefit. It is the most shameful of losses, an inconsiderate bounty. I will choose a man of integrity, sincere, considerate, grateful, temperate, well-natured, neither covetous nor sordid: and when I have obliged such a man, though not worth a groat in the world, I have gained my end. If we give only to receive, we lose the fairest objects of our charity: the absent, the sick, the captive, and the needy. When we oblige those that can never pay us again in kind, as a stranger upon his last farewell, or a necessitous person upon his death-bed, we make Providence our debtor, and rejoice in the conscience even of a fruitless benefit. So long as we are affected with passions, and distracted with hopes and fears, and (the most unmanly of vices) with our pleasures, we are incompetent judges where to place our bounties: but when death presents itself, and that we come to our last will and testament, we leave our fortunes to the most worthy. He that gives nothing, but in hopes of receiving, must die intestate. It is the honesty of another man's mind that moves the kindness of mine; and I would sooner oblige a grateful man than an ungrateful: but this shall not hinder me from doing good also to a person that is known to be ungrateful: only with this difference, that I will serve the one in all extremities with my life and fortune, and the other no farther than stands with my convenience. But what shall I do, you will say, to know whether a man will be grateful or not? I will follow probability, and hope the best. He that sows is not sure to reap; nor the seaman to reach his port; nor the soldier to win the field: he that weds is not sure his wife shall be honest, or his children dutiful: but shall we therefore neither sow, sail, bear arms, nor marry? Nay, if I knew a man to be incurably thankless, I would yet be so kind as to put him in his way, or let him light a candle at mine, or draw water at my well; which may stand him perhaps in great stead, and yet not be reckoned as a benefit from me; for I do it carelessly, and not for his sake, but my own; as an office of humanity, without any choice or kindness.

VI

THE MATTER OF OBLIGATIONS, WITH ITS CIRCUMSTANCES

Next to the choice of the *person* follows that of the *matter*; wherein a regard must be had to time, place, proportion, quality; and to the very nicks of opportunity and humor. One man values his peace above his honor, another his honor above his safety; and not a few there are that (provided they may save their bodies) never care what becomes of their souls. So that good offices depend much upon construction. Some take themselves to be obliged, when they are not; others will not believe it, when they are; and some again take obligations and injuries, the one for the other.

For our better direction, let it be noted, "That a benefit is a common tie betwixt the giver and receiver, with respect to both:" wherefore it must be accommodated to the rules of discretion; for all things have their bounds and measures, and so must liberality among the rest; that it be neither too much for the one nor too little for the other; the excess being every jot as bad as the defect. Alexander bestowed a city upon one of his favorites; who modestly excusing himself, "That it was too much for him to receive." "Well, but," says Alexander, "it is not too much for me to give." A haughty certainly, and an imprudent speech; for that which was not fit for the one to take could not be fit for the other to give. It passes in the world for greatness of mind to be perpetually giving and loading of people with bounties; but it is one thing to know how to *give*, and another thing not to know how to *keep*. Give me a heart that is easy and open, but I will have no holes in it; let it be bountiful with judgment, but I will have nothing run out of it I know not how. How much greater was he that refused the city than the other that offered it? Some men throw away their money as if they were angry with it, which is the error commonly of weak minds and large fortunes. No man esteems of anything that comes to him by chance; but when it is governed by reason, it brings credit both to the giver and receiver; whereas those favors are, in some sort, scandalous, that make a man ashamed of his patron.

It is a matter of great prudence, for the benefactor to suit the benefit to the condition of the receiver: who must be either his superior, his inferior, or his equal; and that which would be the highest obligation imaginable to the one, would perhaps be as great a mockery and affront to the other; as a plate of broken meat (for the purpose) to a rich man were an indignity, which to a poor man is a charity. The benefits of princes and of great men, are honors, offices, monies, profitable commissions, countenance, and protection: the poor man has nothing to present but good-will, good advice, faith, industry, the service and hazard of his person, an early apple, peradventure, or some other cheap curiosity: equals indeed may correspond in kind;

but whatsoever the present be, or to whomsoever we offer it, this general rule must be observed, that we always design the good and satisfaction of the receiver, and never grant anything to his detriment. It is not for a man to say, I was overcome by importunity; for when the fever is off, we detest the man that was prevailed upon to our destruction. I will no more undo a man with his will, than forbear saving him against it. It is a benefit in some cases to grant, and in others to deny; so that we are rather to consider the advantage than the desire of the petitioner. For we may in a passion earnestly beg for (and take it ill to be denied too) that very thing, which, upon second thoughts, we may come to curse, as the occasion of a most pernicious bounty. Never give anything that shall turn to mischief, infamy, or shame. I will consider another man's want or safety; but so as not to forget my own; unless in the case of a very excellent person, and then I shall not much heed what becomes of myself. There is no giving of water to a man in a fever; or putting a sword into a madman's hand. He that lends a man money to carry him to a bawdy-house, or a weapon for his revenge, makes himself a partaker of his crime.

He that would make an acceptable present, will pitch upon something that is desired, sought for, and hard to be found; that which he sees nowhere else, and which few have; or at least not in that place or season; something that may be always in his eye, and mind him of his benefactor. If it be lasting and durable, so much the better; as plate, rather than money; statues than apparel; for it will serve as a monitor to mind the receiver of the obligation, which the presenter cannot so handsomely do. However, let it not be improper, as arms to a woman, books to a clown, toys to a philosopher: I will not give to any man that which he cannot receive, as if I threw a ball to a man without hands; but I will make a *return*, though he cannot receive it; for my business is not to oblige him, but to free myself: nor anything that may reproach a man of his vice or infirmity; as false dice to a cheat; spectacles to a man that is blind. Let it not be unseasonable neither; as a furred gown in summer, an umbrella in winter. It enhances the value of the present, if it was never given to him by anybody else, nor by me to any other; for that which we give to everybody is welcome to nobody.

The particularity does much, but yet the same thing may receive a different estimate from several persons; for there are ways of marking and recommending it in such a manner, that if the same *good office* be done to twenty people, every one of them shall reckon himself peculiarly obliged as a cunning whore, if she has a thousand sweethearts, will persuade every one of them she loves him best. But this is rather the artifice of conversation than the virtue of it.

The citizens of Megara send ambassadors to Alexander in the height of his glory, to offer him, as a compliment, the freedom of their city. Upon Alexander's smiling at the proposal, they told him, that it was a present which they had never made but to Hercules and himself. Whereupon Alexander treated them kindly, and accepted of it; not for the presenters' sake, but because they had joined him with Hercules; now unreasonably soever; for Hercules conquered nothing for himself, but made his business to vindicate and to protect the miserable, without any private interest or design; but this intemperate young man (whose virtue was nothing else but a successful temerity) was trained up from his youth in the trade of violence; the common enemy of mankind, as well of his friends as of his foes, and one that valued himself upon being terrible to all mortals: never considering, that the dullest creatures are as dangerous and as dreadful, as the fiercest; for the poison of a toad, or the tooth of a snake, will do a man's business, as sure as the paw of a tiger.

VII

THE MANNER OF OBLIGING

There is not any benefit so glorious in itself, but it may yet be exceedingly sweetened and improved by the *manner* of conferring it. The virtue, I know, rests in the *intent,* the profit in the judicious application of the *matter*; but the beauty and ornament of an obligation lies in the *manner* of it; and it is then perfect when the dignity of the office is accompanied with all the charms and delicacies of humanity, good-nature, and address; and with dispatch too; for he that puts a man off from time to time, was never right at heart.

In the first place, whatsoever we give, let us do it *frankly*: a kind benefactor makes a man happy as *soon* as he can, and as *much* as he can. There should be no *delay* in a benefit but the modesty of the receiver. If we cannot forsee the request, let us, however, immediately grant it, and by no means suffer the repeating of it. It is so grievous a thing to say, *I BEG*; the very word puts a man out of countenance; and it is a double kindness to do the thing, and save an honest man the confusion of a blush. It comes too late that comes for the asking: for nothing costs us so dear as that we purchase with our prayers: it is all we give, even for heaven itself; and even there too, where our petitions are at the fairest, we choose rather to present them in secret ejaculations than by word of mouth. That is the lasting and the acceptable benefit that meets the receiver half-way. The rule is, we are to *give*, as we would *receive*, *cheerfully*, *quickly*, and without *hesitation*; for there is no grace in a benefit that sticks to the fingers. Nay, if there should be occasion for delay, let us, however, not seem to deliberate; for *demurring* is next door to *denying*; and so long as we suspend, so long are we unwilling. It is a court-humor to keep people upon the tenters; their injuries are quick and sudden, but their benefits are slow. Great ministers love to rack men with attendance, and account it an ostentation of their power to hold their suitors in hand, and to have many witnesses of their interest. A benefit should be made acceptable by all possible means, even to the end that the receiver, who is never to forget it, may bear it in his mind with satisfaction. There must be no mixture of sourness, severity, contumely, or reproof, with our obligations; nay, in case there should be any occasion for so much as an admonition, let it be referred to another time. We are a great deal apter to remember injuries than benefits; and it is enough to forgive an obligation that has the nature of an offence.

There are some that spoil a good office after it is done and others, in the very instant of doing it. There be so much entreaty and importunity; nay, if we do but suspect a petitioner, we put on a sour face; look another way; pretend haste, company, business; talk of other matters, and keep him off with artificial delays, let his necessities be never so pressing; and when we are put to it at last, it comes so hard from us that it is rather extorted than obtained; and not so properly the giving of a bounty, as the quitting of a man's hold upon the tug, when another is too strong for him; so that this is but doing one kindness for me, and another for himself: he gives for his own quiet, after he has tormented me with difficulties and delays. The *manner* of *saying* or of *doing* any thing, goes a great way in the value of the thing itself. It was well said of him that called a good office, that was done harshly, and with an ill will, a *stony piece of bread*; it is necessary for him that is hungry to receive it, but it almost chokes a man in the going down. There must be no pride, arrogance of looks, or tumor of words, in the bestowing of benefits; no insolence of behavior, but a modesty of mind, and a diligent care to catch at occasions and prevent necessities. A pause, an unkind tone, word, look, or action, destroys the grace of a courtesy. It corrupts a bounty, when it is accompanied with state, haughtiness, and elation of mind, in the giving of it. Some have a trick of shifting off a suitor with a point of wit, or a cavil. As in the case of the Cynic that begged a talent of Antigonus: "That is too much," says he, "for a Cynic to ask;" and when he fell to a penny, "That is too little," says he, "for a prince to give." He might have found a way to have compounded this controversy, by giving him a *penny* as to a *Cynic* and a *talent* as from a *prince*. Whatsoever we bestow, let it be done with a frank and cheerful countenance: a man must not give with his hand, and deny with his looks. He that gives quickly, gives willingly.

We are likewise to accompany *good deeds* with *good words,* and say, (for the purpose,) "Why should you make such a matter of this? why did not you come to me sooner? why would you make use of any body else? I take it ill that you should bring me a recommendation; pray let there be no more of this, but when you have occasion hereafter, come to me upon your own account." That is the glorious bounty, when the receiver can say to himself; "What a blessed day has this been to me! never was any thing done so generously, so tenderly, with so good a grace. What is it I would not do to serve this man? A thousand times as much another way could not have given me this satisfaction." In such a case, let the benefit be never so considerable, the manner of conferring it is yet the noblest part. Where there is harshness of language, countenance, or behavior, a man had better be without it. A flat denial is infinitely before a vexatious delay: as a quick death is a mercy, compared with a lingering torment. But to be put to waitings and intercessions, after a promise is passed, is a cruelty intolerable. It is troublesome to stay long for a benefit, let it be never so great; and he that holds me needlessly in pain, loses two precious things, time, and the proof of friendship. Nay, the very hint of a man's want comes many times too late. "If I had money," said

Socrates, "I would buy me a cloak." They that knew he wanted one should have prevented the very intimation of that want. It is not the value of the present, but the benevolence of the mind, that we are to consider. "He gave me but a little, but it was generously and frankly done; it was a little out of a little: he gave it me without asking; he pressed it upon me; he watched the opportunity of doing it, and took it as an obligation upon himself." On the other side, many benefits are great in show, but little or nothing perhaps in effect, when they come hard, slow, or at unawares. That which is given with pride and ostentation, is rather an ambition than a bounty.

Some favors are to be conferred in *public*, others in *private*. In *public* the rewards of great actions; as honors, charges, or whatsoever else gives a man reputation in the world; but the good offices we do for a man in want, distress, or under reproach, these should be known only to those that have the benefit of them. Nay, not to them neither, if we can handsomely conceal it from whence the favor came; for the secrecy, in many cases, is a main part of the benefit. There was a good man that had a friend, who was both poor and sick, and ashamed to own his condition: he privately conveyed a bag of money under his pillow, that he might seem rather to find than receive it. Provided I know that I give it, no matter for his knowing from whence it comes that receives it. Many a man stands in need of help that has not the face to confess it: if the discovery may give offence, let it lie concealed; he that gives to be seen would never relieve a man in the dark. It would be too tedious to run through all the niceties that may occur upon this subject; but, in two words, he must be a wise, a friendly, and a well-bred man, that perfectly acquits himself in the art and duty of obliging: for all his actions must be squared according to the measures of *civility*, *good-nature* and *discretion*.

VIII

THE DIFFERENCE AND VALUE OF BENEFITS

We have already spoken of *benefits* in *general*; the *matter* and the *intention*, together with the *manner* of conferring them. It follows now, in course, to say something of the *value* of them; which is rated, either by the good they do us, or by the inconvenience they save us, and has no other standard than that of a judicious regard to circumstance and occasion. Suppose I save a man from drowning, the advantage of life is all one to him, from what hand soever it comes, or by what means; but yet there may be a vast difference in the obligation. I may do it with hazard, or with security, with trouble, or with ease; willingly, or by compulsion; upon intercession, or without it: I may have a prospect of vain-glory or profit: I may do it in kindness to another, or an hundred *by-ends* to myself; and every point does exceedingly vary the case. Two persons may part with the same sum of money, and yet not the same benefit: the one had it of his *own*, and it was but a *little* out of a *great deal*; the other *borrowed* it, and bestowed upon me that which he wanted for himself. Two boys were sent out to fetch a certain person to their master: the one of them hunts up and down, and comes home again weary, without finding him; the other falls to play with his companions at the wheel of Fortune, sees him by chance passing by, delivers him his errand, and brings him. He that found him by chance deserves to be punished; and he that sought for him, and missed him, to be rewarded for his good-will.

In some cases we value the *thing*, in others the *labor* and *attendance*. What can be more precious than good manners, good letters, life, and health? and yet we pay our physicians and tutors only for their service in the professions. If we buy things cheap, it matters not, so long as it is a bargain: it is no obligation from the seller, if nobody else will give him more for it. What would not a man give to be set ashore in a tempest? for a house in a wilderness? a shelter in a storm? a fire, or a bit of meat, when a man is pinched with hunger or cold? a defence against thieves, and a thousand other matters of moment, that cost but little? And yet we know that the skipper has but his freight for our passage; and the carpenters and bricklayers do their work by the day. Those are many times the greatest obligations in truth, which in vulgar opinions are the smallest: as comfort to the sick, poor captives; good counsel, keeping of people from wickedness, etc. Wherefore we should reckon ourselves to owe most for the noblest benefits. If the physician adds care and friendship to the duty of his calling, and the tutor to the common method of his business, I am to esteem them as the nearest of my relations: for to watch with me, to be troubled for me, and to put off all other patients for my sake, is a particular kindness: and so it is in my tutor, if he takes more pains with me than with the rest of my fellows. It is not enough, in this case, to pay the one his fees, and the other his salary; but I am indebted to them over and above for their friendship. The meanest of mechanics, if he does his work with industry and care, it is an usual thing to cast in something by way of reward more than the bare agreement: and shall we deal worse with the preservers of our lives, and the reformers of our manners? He that gives me himself (if he be worth taking) gives the greatest benefit: and this is the present which Aeschines, a poor disciple of Socrates, made to his master, and as a matter of great consideration: "Others may have given you much," says he, "but I am the only man that has left nothing to himself." "This gift," says Socrates, "you shall never repent of; for I will take care to return it better than I found it." So that a brave mind can never want matter for liberality in the meanest condition; for Nature has been so kind to us, that where we have nothing of Fortune's, we may bestow something of our own.

It falls out often, that a benefit is followed with an injury; let which will be foremost, it is with the latter as with one writing upon another; it does in a great measure hide the former, and keep it from appearing, but it does not quite take it away. We may in some cases divide them, and both requite the one, and revenge the other; or otherwise compare them, to know whether I am creditor or debtor. You have obliged me in my servant, but wounded me in my brother; you have saved my son, but have destroyed my father; in this instance, I will allow as much as piety, and justice, and good nature, will bear; but I am not willing to set an injury against a benefit. I would have some respect to the time; the obligation came first; and then, perhaps, the one was designed, the other against his will; under these considerations I would amplify the benefit, and lessen the injury; and extinguish the one with the other; nay, I would pardon the injury even *without* the benefit, but much more *after* it. Not that a man can be bound by one benefit to suffer all sorts of injuries; for there are some cases wherein we lie under no obligation for a benefit; because a greater injury absolves it: as, for example, a man helps me out of a law-suit, and afterwards commits a rape upon my daughter; where the following impiety cancels the antecedent obligation. A man lends me a little money, and then sets my house on fire; the debtor is here turned creditor, when the injury outweighs the benefit. Nay, if a man does but so much as repent the good office done, and grow sour and insolent upon it, and upbraid me with it; if he did it only for his own sake, or for any other reason than for mine, I am in some degree, more or less, acquitted of the obligation. I am not at all beholden to him that makes me the instrument of his own advantage. He that does me good for his own sake, I will do him good for mine.

Suppose a man makes suit for a place, and cannot obtain it, but upon the ransom of ten slaves out of the galleys. If there be ten, and *no more*, they owe him nothing for their redemption; but *they* are indebted to him for the choice, where he might have taken ten others as well as these. Put the case again, that by an act of grace so many prisoners are to be released, their names to be drawn by lot, and mine happens to come out among the rest: one part of my obligation is to him that put me in a capacity of freedom, and the other is to Providence for my being one of that number. The greatest benefits of all have no witnesses, but lie concealed in the conscience.

There is a great difference betwixt a common obligation and a particular; he that lends my country money, obliges me only as a part of the whole. Plato crossed the river, and the ferry-man would take no money of him: he reflected upon it as honor done to himself; and told him, "That Plato was in debt." But Plato, when he found it to be no more than he did for others, recalled his words, "For," says he, "Plato will owe nothing in particular for a benefit in common; what I owe with others, I will pay with others."

Some will have it that the necessity of wishing a man well is some abatement to the obligation in the doing of him a good office. But I say, on the contrary, that it is the greater; because the good-will cannot be changed. It is one thing to say, that a man could not but do me this or that civility, because he was forced to do it; and another thing, that he could not quit the good-will of doing it. In the former case, I am a debtor to him that imposeth the force, in the other to himself. The unchangeable good-will is an indispensable obligation: and, to say, that nature cannot go out of her course, does not discharge us of *what we owe to Providence*. Shall he be said to will, that may change his mind the next moment? and shall we question the will of the Almighty, whose nature admits no change? Must the stars quit their stations, and fall foul one upon another? must the sun stand still in the middle of his course, and heaven and earth drop into confusion? must a devouring fire seize upon the universe; the harmony of the creation be dissolved; and the whole frame of nature swallowed up in a dark abyss; and will nothing less than this serve to convince the world of their audacious and impertinent follies? It is not to say, that *these heavenly bodies are not made for us*; for in part they are so; and we are the better for their virtues and motions, whether we will or not; though, undoubtedly, the principal cause is the unalterable law of God. Providence is not moved by anything from without; but the Divine will is an everlasting law, an immutable decree; and the impossibility of variation proceeds from God's purpose of preserving; for he never repents of his first counsels. It is not with our heavenly as with our earthly father. God thought of us and provided for us, before he made us: (for unto him all future events are present.) Man was not the work of chance; his mind carries him above the slight of fortune, and naturally aspires to the contemplation of heaven and divine mysteries. How desperate a frenzy is it now to undervalue, nay, to contemn and to disclaim these divine blessings, without which we are utterly incapable of enjoying any other!

IX

AN HONEST MAN CANNOT BE OUTDONE IN COURTESY

It passes in the world for a generous and magnificent saying, that "it is a shame for a man to be outdone in courtesy;" and it is worth the while to examine, both the truth of it, and the mistake. First, there can be no shame in a virtuous emulation; and, secondly, there can be no victory without crossing the cudgels, and yielding the cause. One man may have the advantage of strength, of means, of fortune; and this will undoubtedly operate upon the events of good purposes, but yet without any diminution to the virtue. The good will may be the same in both, and yet one may have the heels of the other; for it is not in a good office as in a course, where he wins the plate that comes first to the post: and even there also, chance has many times a great hand in the success. Where the contest is about benefits; and that the one has not only a *good will*, but *matter* to work upon, and a power to put that good intent in execution; and the other has barely a *good-will*, without either the *means*, or the *occasion*, of a requital; if he does but affectionately wish it, and endeavor it, the latter is no more overcome in courtesy than he is in courage that dies with his sword in his hand, and his face to the enemy, and without shrinking maintains his station: for where *fortune* is *partial*, it is enough that the *good-will* is *equal*. There are two errors in this proposition: first, to imply that a good man may be overcome; and then to imagine that anything shameful can befall him. The Spartans prohibited all those exercises where the victory was declared by the confession of the contendant. The 300 Fabii were never said to be *conquered*, but *slain*; nor Regulus to be *overcome*, though he was taken *prisoner* by the Carthaginians. The mind may stand firm under the greatest malice and iniquity of fortune; and yet the giver and receiver continue upon equal terms: as we reckon it a drawn battle, when two combatants are parted, though the one has lost more blood than the other. He that knows how to owe a courtesy, and heartily wishes that he could requite it, is invincible; so that every man may be as grateful as he pleases. It is your happiness to give, it is my fortune that I can only receive. What advantage now has your chance over my virtue? But there are some men that have philosophized themselves almost out of the sense of human affections; as Diogenes, that walked naked and unconcerned through the middle of Alexander's treasures, and was, as well in other men's opinions as in his own, even above Alexander himself, who at that time had the whole world at his feet: for there was more that the one scorned to take than that the other had it in his power to give: and it is a greater generosity for a beggar to refuse money than for a prince to bestow it. This is a remarkable instance of an immovable mind, and there is hardly any contending with it; but a man is never the less valiant for being worsted by an invulnerable enemy; nor the fire one jot the weaker for not consuming an incombustible body; nor a sword ever a whit the worse for not cleaving a rock that is impenetrable; neither is a grateful mind overcome for want of an answerable fortune. No matter for the inequality of the things given and received, so long as, in point of good affection, the two parties stand upon the same level. It is no shame not to overtake a man, if we follow him as fast as we can. That tumor of a man, the vain-glorious Alexander, was used to make his boast, that never any man went beyond him in benefits; and yet he lived to see a poor fellow in a tub, to whom there was nothing that he could give, and from whom there was nothing that he could take away.

Nor is it always necessary for a poor man to fly to the sanctuary of an invincible mind to quit scores with the bounties of a plentiful fortune; but it does often fall out, that the returns which he cannot make in *kind* are more than supplied in *dignity* and *value*. Archelaus, a king of Macedon, invited Socrates to his palace: but he excused himself, as unwilling to receive greater benefits than he was able to requite. This perhaps was not *pride* in Socrates, but *craft*; for he was afraid of being forced to accept of something which might possibly have been unworthy of him; beside, that he was a man of liberty, and loath to make himself a voluntary slave. The truth of it is, that Archelaus had more need of Socrates than Socrates of Archelaus; for he wanted a man to teach him the art of life and death, and the skill of government, and to read the book of Nature to him, and show him the light at noon-day: he wanted a man that, when the sun was in an eclipse, and he had locked himself up in all the horror and despair imaginable; he wanted a man, I say, to deliver him from his apprehensions, and to expound the prodigy to him, by telling him, that there was no more in it than only that the *moon* was got betwixt the *sun* and the *earth*, and all would be well again presently. Let the world judge now, whether Archelaus' *bounty*, or Socrates' *philosophy*, would have been the greater present: he does not understand the value of wisdom and friendship that does not know a wise friend to be the noblest of presents. A rarity scarce to be found, not only in a family, but in an age; and nowhere more wanted than where there seems to be the greatest store. The greater a man is, the more need he has of him; and the more difficulty there is both of finding and of knowing him. Nor is it to be said, that "I cannot requite such a benefactor because I am poor, and have it not;" I can give good counsel; a conversation wherein he may take both delight and profit; freedom of discourse, without flattery; kind attention, where he deliberates; and faith inviolable where he trusts; I may bring him to a love and knowledge of truth; deliver him from the errors of his credulity, and teach him to distinguish betwixt friends and parasites.

X

THE QUESTION DISCUSSED, WHETHER OR NOT A MAN MAY GIVE OR RETURN A BENEFIT TO HIMSELF

There are many cases, wherein a man speaks of himself as of another. As, for example, "I may thank myself for this; I am angry at myself; I hate myself for that." And this way of speaking has raised a dispute among the Stoics, "whether or not a man may give or return a benefit to himself?" For, say they, if I may hurt myself, I may oblige myself; and that which were a benefit to another body, why is it not so to myself? And why am I not as criminal in being ungrateful to myself as if I were so to another body? And the case is the same in flattery and several other vices; as, on the other side, it is a point of great reputation for a man to command himself. Plato thanked Socrates for what he had *learned* of him; and why might not Socrates as well thank Plato for that which he had *taught* him? "That which you want," says Plato, "borrow it of yourself." And why may not I as well give to myself as lend? If I may be angry with myself, I may thank myself; and if I chide myself, I may as well commend myself, and do myself good as well as hurt; there is the same reason of contraries: it is a common thing to say, "Such a man hath done himself an injury." If an injury, why not a benefit? But I say, that no man can be a debtor to himself; for the benefit must naturally precede the acknowledgment; and a debtor can no more be without a creditor than a husband without a wife. Somebody must give, that somebody may receive; and it is neither giving nor receiving, the passing of a thing from one hand to the other. What if a man should be ungrateful in the case? there is nothing lost; for he that gives it has it: and he that gives and he that receives are one and the same person. Now, properly speaking, no man can be said to bestow any thing upon himself, for he obeys his nature, that prompts every man to do himself all the good he can. Shall I call him liberal, that gives to himself; or good-natured, that pardons himself; or pitiful, that is affected with his own misfortunes? That which were bounty, clemency, compassion, to another, to myself is nature. A benefit is a voluntary thing; but to do good to myself is a thing necessary. Was ever any man commended for getting out of a ditch, or for helping himself against thieves? Or what if I should allow, that a man might confer a benefit upon himself; yet he cannot owe it, for he returns it in the same instant that he receives it. No man gives, owes, or makes a return, but to another. How can one man do that to which two parties are requisite in so many respects? Giving and receiving must go backward and forward betwixt two persons. If a man give to himself, he may sell to himself; but to sell is to alienate a thing, and to translate the right of it to another; now, to make a man both the giver and the receiver is to unite two contraries. That is a benefit, which, when it is given, may possibly not be requited; but he that gives to himself, must necessarily receive what he gives; beside, that all benefits are given for the receiver's sake, but that which a man does for himself, is for the sake of the giver.

This is one of those subtleties, which, though hardly worth a man's while, yet it is not labor absolutely lost neither. There is more of trick and artifice in it than solidity; and yet there is matter of diversion too; enough perhaps to pass away a winter's evening, and keep a man waking that is heavy-headed.

XI

HOW FAR ONE MAN MAY BE OBLIGED FOR A BENEFIT DONE TO ANOTHER

The question now before us requires *distinction* and *caution*. For though it be both natural and generous to wish well to my friend's friend, yet a *second-hand benefit* does not bind me any further than to a *second-hand gratitude*: so that I may receive great satisfaction and advantage from a good office done to my friend, and yet lie under no obligation myself; or, if any man thinks otherwise, I must ask him, in the first place, Where it begins? and, How it extends? that it may not be boundless. Suppose a man obliges the son, does that obligation work upon the father? and why not upon the uncle too? the brother? the wife? the sister? the mother? nay, upon all that have any kindness for him? and upon all the lovers of his friends? and upon all that love them too? and so *in infinitum*. In this case we must have recourse, as is said heretofore, to the intention of the benefactor, and fix the obligation upon him unto whom the kindness was directed. If a man manures my ground, keeps my house from burning or falling, it is a benefit to me, for I am the better for it, and my house and land are insensible. But if he save the life of my son, the benefit is to my son; it is a joy and a comfort to me, but no obligation. I am as much concerned as I ought to be in the health, the felicity, and the welfare of my son, as happy in the enjoyment of him; and I should be as unhappy as is possible in his loss; but it does not follow that I must of necessity lie under an obligation for being either happier or less miserable, by another body's means. There are some benefits, which although conferred upon one man, may yet work upon others; as a sum of money may be given to a poor man for his own sake, which in the consequence proves the relief of his whole family; but still the immediate receiver is the debtor for it; for the question is not, to whom it comes afterward to be transferred, but who is the principal? and upon whom it was first bestowed? My son's life is as dear to me as my own; and in saving him you preserve me too: in this case I will acknowledge myself obliged to you, that is to say, in my son's name; for in my own, and in strictness, I am not; but I am content to make myself a voluntary debtor. What if he had borrowed money? my paying of it does not at all make it my debt. It would put me to the blush perhaps to have him taken in bed with another man's wife; but that does not make me an adulterer. It is a wonderful delight and satisfaction that I receive in his safety; but still this good is not a benefit. A man may be the better for an animal, a plant, a stone; but there must be a will, an intention, to make it an obligation. You save the son without so much as knowing the father, nay, without so much as thinking of him; and, perhaps you would have done the same thing even if you had hated him.

But without any further alteration of dialogue, the conclusion is this; if you meant him the kindness, he is answerable for it, and I may enjoy the fruit of it without being obliged by it: but if it was done for my sake, then I am accountable; or howsoever, upon any occasion, I am ready to do you all the kind offices imaginable; not as the return of a benefit, but as the earnest of a friendship; which you are not to challenge neither, but to entertain as an act of honor and of justice, rather than of gratitude. If a man find the body of my dead father in a desert, and give it a burial; if he did it as to my father, I am beholden to him: but if the body was unknown to him, and that he would have done the same thing for any other body, I am no farther concerned in it than as a piece of public humanity.

There are, moreover, some cases wherein an unworthy person may be obliged and for the sake of others: and the sottish extract of an ancient nobilty may be preferred before a better man that is but of yesterday's standing. And it is but reasonable to pay a reverence even to the memory of eminent virtues. He that is not illustrious in himself, may yet be reputed so in the right of his ancestors: and there is a gratitude to be entailed upon the offspring of famous progenitors. Was it not for the *father's* sake that Cicero the *son* was made counsel? and was it not the eminence of one Pompey that raised and dignified the rest of his family? How came Caligula to be emperor of the world? a man so cruel, that he spilt blood as greedily as if he were to drink it; the empire was not given to himself, but to his father Germanicus. A brave man deserved that for him, which he could never have challenged upon his own merit. What was it that preferred Fabius Persicus, (whose very mouth was the uncleanest part about him,) what was it but the 300 of that family that so generously opposed the enemy for the safety of the commonwealth?

Nay, Providence itself is gracious to the wicked posterity of an honorable race. The counsels of heaven are guided by wisdom, mercy, and justice. Some men are made kings of their proper virtues, without any respect to their predecessors: others for their ancestors' sakes, whose virtues, though neglected in their lives, come to be afterward rewarded in their issues. And it is but equity, that our gratitude should extend as far as the influence of their heroical actions and examples.

XII

THE BENEFACTOR MUST HAVE NO BY-ENDS

We come now to the main point of the matter in question: that is to say, whether or not it be a thing desirable in itself, the giving and receiving of benefits? There is a sect of philosophers that accounts nothing valuable but what is profitable, and so makes all virtue mercenary; an unmanly mistake to imagine, that the hope of gain, or fear of loss, should make a man either the more or less honest. As who should say, "What will I get by it, and I will be an honest man?" Whereas, on the contrary, honesty is a thing in itself to be purchased at any rate. It is not for a body to say, "It will be a charge, a hazard, I shall give offence," etc. My business is to do what I ought to do: all other considerations are foreign to the office. Whensoever my duty calls me, it is my part to attend, without scrupulizing upon forms or difficulties. Shall I see an honest man oppressed at the bar, and not assist him, for fear of a court faction? or not second him upon the highway against thieves, for fear of a broken head? and choose rather to sit still, the quiet spectator of fraud and violence? Why will men be just, temperate, generous, brave, but because it carries along with it fame and a good conscience? and for the same reason, and no other, (to apply it to the subject in hand,) let a man also be bountiful. The school of Epicurus, I am sure, will never swallow this doctrine: (that effeminate tribe of lazy and voluptuous philosophers;) they will tell you, that virtue is but the servant and vassal of pleasure. "No," says Epicurus, "I am not for pleasure neither without virtue." But, why then for pleasure, say I, *before* virtue? Not that the stress of the controversy lies upon the *order* only; for the *power* of it, as well as the *dignity*, is now under debate. It is the office of virtue to superintend, to lead, and to govern; but the parts you have assigned it, are to submit, to follow, and to be under command. But this, you will say, is nothing to the purpose, so long as both sides are agreed, that there can be no happiness without *virtue*: "Take away that," says Epicurus, "and I am as little a friend to pleasure as you." The pinch, in short, is this, whether virtue itself be the supreme good or the only cause of it? It is not the inverting of the order that will clear this point; (though it is a very preposterous error, to set that first which should be last.) It does not half so much offend me; ranging of pleasure before virtue, as the very comparing of them; and the bringing of the two opposites, and professed enemies, into any sort of competition.

The drift of this discourse is, to support the cause of benefits; and to prove, that it is a mean and dishonorable thing to give for any other end than for giving's sake. He that gives for gain, profit, or any by-end, destroys the very intent of bounty; for it falls only upon those that do not want, and perverts the charitable inclinations of princes and of great men, who cannot reasonably propound to themselves any such end. What does the sun get by travelling about the universe; by visiting and comforting all the quarters of the earth? Is the whole creation made and ordered for the good of mankind, and every particular man only for the good of himself? There passes not an hour of our lives, wherein we do not enjoy the blessings of Providence, without measure and without intermission. And what design can the Almighty have upon us, who is in himself full, safe, and inviolable? If he should give only for his own sake, what would become of poor mortals, that have nothing to return him at best but dutiful acknowledgments? It is putting out of a benefit to interest only to bestow where we may place it to advantage.

Let us be liberal then, after the example of our great Creator, and give to others with the same consideration that he gives to us. Epicurus's answer will be to this, that God gives no benefits at all, but turns his back upon the world; and without any concern for us, leaves Nature to take her course: and whether he does anything himself, or nothing, he takes no notice, however, either of the good or of the ill that is done here below. If there were not an ordering and an over-ruling Providence, how comes it (say I, on the other side) that the universality of mankind should ever have so unanimously agreed in the madness of worshipping a power that can neither hear nor help us? Some blessings are freely given us; others upon our prayers are granted us; and every day brings forth instances of great and of seasonable mercies. There never was yet any man so insensible as not to feel, see, and understand, a Deity in the ordinary methods of nature, though many have been so obstinately ungrateful as not to confess it; nor is any man so wretched as not to be a partaker in that divine bounty. Some benefits, it is true, may appear to be unequally divided; but it is no small matter yet that we possess in common: and which Nature has bestowed upon us in her very self. If God be not bountiful, whence is it that we have all that we pretend to? That which we give, and that which we deny, that which we lay up, and that which we squander away? Those innumerable delights for the entertainment of our eyes, our ears, and our understandings? nay, that copious matter even for luxury itself? For care is taken, not only for our necessities, but also for our pleasures, and for the gratifying of all our senses and appetites. So many pleasant groves; fruitful and salutary plants; so many fair rivers that serve us, both for recreation, plenty, and commerce: vicissitudes of seasons; varieties of food, by nature made ready to our hands, and the whole creation itself subjected to mankind for health, medicine and dominion. We can be thankful to a friend for a few acres, or a little money: and yet for the freedom and command of the whole earth, and for the great benefits of our being, as life, health, and reason, we look upon ourselves as under no obligation. If a man bestows upon us a house that is delicately beautified with paintings, statues, gildings, and marble, we make a mighty business of it, and yet it lies at the mercy of a puff of wind, the snuff of a candle, and a hundred other accidents, to lay it in the dust. And is it nothing now to sleep under the canopy of heaven, where we have the globe of the earth for our place of repose, and the glories of the heavens for our spectacle? How comes it that we should so much value what we have, and yet at the same time be so unthankful for it? Whence is it that we have our breath, the comforts of light and of heat, the very blood that runs in our veins? the cattle that feed us, and the fruits of the earth that feed them? Whence have we the growth of our bodies, the succession of our ages, and the faculties of our minds? so many veins of metals, quarries of marble, etc. The seed of everything is in itself, and it is the blessing of God that raises it out of the dark into act and motion. To say nothing of the charming varieties of music, beautiful objects, delicious provisions for the palate, exquisite perfumes, which are cast in, over and above, to the common necessities of our being.

All this, says Epicurus, we are to ascribe to Nature. And why not to God, I beseech ye? as if they were not both of them one and the same power, working in the whole, and in every part of it. Or, if you call him the Almighty Jupiter; the Thunderer; the Creator and Preserver of us all: it comes to the same issue; some will express him under the notion of *Fate*; which is only a connexion of causes, and himself the uppermost and original, upon which all the rest depend. The Stoics represent the several *functions* of the *Almighty Power* under several *appellations*. When they speak of him as the father and the fountain of all beings, they call him *Bacchus*: and under the name of *Hercules*, they denote him to be *indefatigable* and *invincible*; and in the contemplation of him in the *reason, order, proportion*, and *wisdom* of his proceedings, they call him *Mercury*; so that which way soever they look, and under what name soever they couch their meaning, they never fail of finding him; for he is everywhere, and fills his own work. If a man should borrow money of Seneca, and say that he owes it to Amnaeus or Lucius, he may change the name but not his creditor; for let him take which of the three names he pleases, he is still a debtor to the same person. As justice, integrity, prudence, frugality, fortitude, are all of them goods of one and the same mind, so that whichsoever of them pleases us, we cannot distinctly say that it is this or that, but the mind.

But, not to carry this digression too far; that which God himself does, we are sure is well done; and we are no less sure, that for whatsoever he gives, he neither wants, expects, nor receives, anything in return; so that the end of a benefit ought to be the advantage of the receiver; and that must be our scope without any by-regard to ourselves. It is objected to us, the singular caution we prescribe in the choice of the person: for it were a madness, we say, for a husbandman to sow the sand: which, if true, say they, you have an eye upon profit, as well in giving as in plowing and sowing. And then they say again, that if the conferring of a benefit were desirable in itself, it would have no dependence upon the choice of a man; for let us give it when, how, or wheresoever we please, it would be still a benefit. This does not at all affect our assertion; for the person, the matter, the manner, and the time, are circumstances absolutely necessary to the reason of the action: there must be a right judgment in all respects to make it a benefit. It is my duty to be true to a trust, and yet there may be a time or a place, wherein I would make little difference betwixt the renouncing of it and the delivering of it up; and the same rule holds in benefits; I will neither render the one, nor bestow the other, to the damage of the receiver. A wicked man will run all risks to do an injury, and to compass his revenge; and shall not an honest man venture as far to do a good office? All benefits must be gratuitous. A merchant sells me the corn that keeps me and my family from starving; but he sold it for his interests, as well as I bought it for mine; and so I owe him nothing for it. He that gives for profit, gives to himself; as a physician or a lawyer, gives counsel for a fee, and only makes use of me for his own ends; as a grazier fats his cattle to bring them to a better market. This is more properly the driving of a trade than the cultivating of a generous commerce. This for that, is rather a truck than a benefit; and he deserves to be cozened that gives any thing in hope of a return. And in truth, what end should a man honorably propound? not *profit*; sure that is *vulgar* and *mechanic*; and he that does not contemn it can never be grateful. And then for *glory*, it is a mighty matter indeed for a man to boast of doing his duty. We are to *give*, if it were only to avoid *not giving*; if any thing comes of it, it is clear gain; and, at worst, there is nothing lost; beside, that one benefit well placed makes amends for a thousand miscarriages. It is not that I would exclude the benefactor neither for being himself the better for a good office he does for another. Some there are that do us good only for their own sakes; others for ours; and some again for both. He that does it for me in common with himself, if he had a prospect upon both in the doing it, I am obliged to him for it; and glad with all my heart that he had a share in it. Nay, I were ungrateful and unjust if I should not rejoice, that what was beneficial to me might be so likewise to himself.

To pass now to the matter of gratitude and ingratitude. There never was any man yet so wicked as not to approve of the one, and detest the other; as the two things in the whole world, the one to be the most abominated, the other the most esteemed. The very story of an ungrateful action puts us out of all patience, and gives us a loathing for the author of it. "That inhuman villain," we cry, "to do so horrid a thing:" not, "that inconsiderate fool for omitting so profitable a virtue;" which plainly shows the sense we naturally have, both of the one and of the other, and that we are led to it by a common impulse of reason and of conscience. Epicurus fancies God to be without power, and without arms; above fear himself, and as little to be feared. He places him betwixt the orbs, solitary and idle, out of the reach of mortals, and neither hearing our prayers nor minding our concerns; and allows him only such a veneration and respect as we pay to our parents. If a man should ask him now, why any reverence at all, if we have no obligation to him, or rather, why that greater reverence to his fortuitous atoms? his answer would be, that it was for their majesty and their admirable nature, and not out of any hope or expectation from them. So that by his proper confession, a thing may be desirable for its own worth. But, says he, gratitude is a virtue that has commonly profit annexed to it. And where is the virtue, say I, that has not? but still the virtue is to be valued for itself, and not for the profit that attends it. There is no question, but gratitude for benefits received is the ready way to procure more; and in requiting one friend we encourage many: but these accessions fall in by the by; and if I were sure that the doing of good offices would be my ruin, I would yet pursue them. He that visits the sick, in hope of a legacy, let him be never so friendly in all other cases, I look upon him in this to be no better than a raven, that watches a weak sheep only to peck out the eyes of it. We never give with so much judgment or care, as when we consider the honesty of the action, without any regard to the profit of it; for our understandings are corrupted by fear, hope, and pleasure.

XIII

THERE ARE MANY CASES WHEREIN A MAN MAY BE MINDED OF A BENEFIT, BUT IT IS VERY RARELY TO BE CHALLENGED, AND NEVER TO BE UPBRAIDED

If the world were wise, and as honest as it should be, there would be no need of caution or precept how to behave ourselves in our several stations and duties; for both the giver and the receiver would do what they ought to do on their own accord: the one would be bountiful, and the other grateful, and the only way of minding a man of one good turn would be the following of it with another. But as the case stands, we must take other measures, and consult the best we can, the common ease and relief of mankind.

As there are several sorts of ungrateful men, so there must be several ways of dealing with them, either by artifice, counsel, admonition, or reproof, according to the humor of the person, and the degree of the offence: provided always, that as well in the reminding a man of a benefit, as in the bestowing of it, the good of the receiver be the principal thing intended. There is a curable ingratitude, and an incurable; there is a slothful, a neglectful, a proud, a dissembling, a disclaiming, a heedless, a forgetful, and a malicious ingratitude; and the application must be suited to the matter we have to work upon. A gentle nature may be reclaimed by authority, advice, or reprehension; a father, a husband, a friend may do good in the case. There are a sort of lazy and sluggish people, that live as if they were asleep, and must be lugged and pinched to wake them. These men are betwixt grateful and ungrateful; they will neither deny an obligation nor return it, and only want quickening. I will do all I can to hinder any man from ill-doing, but especially a friend; and yet more especially from doing ill to me. I will rub up his memory with new benefits: if that will not serve, I will proceed to good counsel, and from thence to rebuke: if all fails, I will look upon him as a desperate debtor, and even let him alone in his ingratitude, without making him my enemy: for no necessity shall ever make me spend time in wrangling with any man upon that point.

Assiduity of obligation strikes upon the conscience as well as the memory, and pursues an ungrateful man till he becomes grateful: if one good office will not do it, try a second, and then a third. No man can be so thankless, but either shame, occasion, or example, will, at some time or other, prevail upon him. The very beasts themselves, even lions and tigers, are gained by good usage: beside, that one obligation does naturally draw on another; and a man would not willingly leave his own work imperfect. "I have helped him thus far, and I will even go through with it now." So that, over and above the delight and the virtue of obliging, one good turn is a shouting-horn to another. This, of all hints, is perhaps the most effectual, as well as the most generous.

In some cases it must be carried more home: as in that of Julius Caesar, who, as he was hearing a cause, the defendant finding himself pinched; "Sir," says he, "do not you remember a strain you got in your ankle when you commanded in Spain; and that a soldier lent you his cloak for a cushion, upon the top of a craggy rock, under the shade of a little tree, in the heat of the day?" "I remember it perfectly well," says Caesar, "and that when I was ready to choke with thirst, an honest fellow fetched me a draught of water in his helmet." "But that man, and that helmet," says the soldier, "does Caesar think that he could not know them again, if he saw them?" "The man, perchance, I might," says Caesar, somewhat offended, "but not the helmet. But what is the story to my business? you are none of the man." "Pardon me, Sir," says the soldier, "I am that very man; but Caesar may well forget me: for I have been trepanned since, and lost an eye at the battle of Munda, where that helmet too had the honor to be cleft with a Spanish blade." Caesar took it as it was intended: and it was an honorable and a prudent way of refreshing his memory.

But this would not have gone down so well with Tiberius: for when an old acquaintance of his began his address to him with, "You remember, Caesar." "No," says Caesar, (cutting him short,) "I do not remember what I WAS." Now, with him, it was better to be forgotten than remembered; for an *old friend* was as bad as an *informer*. It is a common thing for men to hate the authors of their preferment, as the witnesses of their mean original.

There are some people well enough disposed to be grateful, but they cannot hit upon it without a prompter; they are a little like school-boys that have treacherous memories; it is but helping them here and there with a word, when they stick, and they will go through with their lesson; they must be taught to be thankful, and it is a fair step, if we can but bring them to be willing, and only offer at it. Some benefits we have neglected; some we are not willing to remember. He is ungrateful that disowns an obligation, and so is he that dissembles it, or to his power does not requite it; but the worst of all is he that forgets it. Conscience, or occasion, may revive the rest; but here the very memory of it is lost. Those eyes that cannot endure the light are weak, but those are stark blind that cannot see it. I do not love to hear people say, "Alas! poor man, he has forgotten it," as if that were the excuse of ingratitude, which is the very cause of it: for if he were not ungrateful, he would not be forgetful, and lay that out of the way which should be always uppermost and in sight. He that thinks as he ought to do, of requiting a benefit, is in no danger of forgetting it. There are, indeed, some benefits so great that they can never slip the memory; but those which are less in value, and more in number, do commonly escape us. We are apt enough to acknowledge that "such a man has been the making of us;" so long as we are in possession of the advantage he has brought us; but new appetites deface old kindnesses, and we carry our prospect forward to something more, without considering what we have obtained already. All that is past we give for lost; so that we are only intent upon the future. When a benefit is once out of sight, or out of use, it is buried.

It is the freak of many people, they cannot do a good office but they are presently boasting of it, drunk or sober: and about it goes into all companies what wonderful things they have done for this man, and what for the other. A foolish and a dangerous vanity, of a doubtful friend to make a certain enemy. For these reproaches and contempts will set everybody's tongue a walking; and people will conclude that these things would never be, if there were not something very extraordinary in the bottom of it. When it comes to that once, there is not any calumny but fastens more or less, nor any falsehood so incredible, but in some part or other of it, shall pass for a truth. Our great mistake is this, we are still inclined to make the most of what we give, and the least of what we receive; whereas we should do the clean contrary. "It might have been more, but he had a great many to oblige. It was as much as he could well spare; but he will make it up some other time," etc. Nay, we should be so far from making publication of our bounties, as not to hear them so much as mentioned without sweetening the matter: as, "Alas, I owe him a great deal more than that comes to. If it were in my power to serve him, I should be very glad of it." And this, too, not with the figure of a compliment, but with all humanity and truth. There was a man of quality, that in the triumviral proscription, was saved by one of Caesar's friends, who would be still twitting him with it; who it was that preserved him, and telling him over and over, "you had gone to pot, friend, but for me." "Prythee," says the proscribed, "let me hear no more of this, or even leave me as you found me: I am thankful enough of myself to acknowledge that I owe you my life, but it is death to have it rung in my ears perpetually as a reproach; it looks as if you had only saved me to carry me about for a spectacle. I would fain forget the misfortune that I was once a prisoner, without being led in triumph every day of my life."

Oh! the pride and folly of a great fortune, that turns benefits into injuries! that delights in excesses, and disgraces every thing it does! Who would receive any thing from it upon these terms? the higher it raises us, the more sordid it makes us. Whatsoever it gives it corrupts. What is there in it that should thus puff us up? by what magic is it that we are so transformed, that we do no longer know ourselves? Is it impossible for greatness to be liberal without insolence? The benefits that we receive from our superiors are then welcome when they come with an open hand, and a clear brow; without either contumely or state; and so as to prevent our necessities. The benefit is never the greater for the making of a bustle and a noise about it: but the benefactor is much the less for the ostentation of his good deeds; which makes that odious to us, which would otherwise be delightful.

Tiberius had gotten a trick, when any man begged money of him, to refer him to the senate, where all the petitioners were to deliver up the names of their creditors. His end perhaps was, to deter men from asking, by exposing the condition of their fortunes to an examination. But it was, however, a benefit turned unto a reprehension, and he made a reproach of a bounty.

But it is not enough yet to forbear the casting of a benefit in a man's teeth; for there are some that will not allow it to be so much as challenged. For an ill man, say they, will not make a return, though it be demanded, and a good man will do it of himself: and then the asking of it seems to turn it into a debt. It is a kind of injury to be too quick with the former: for to call upon him too soon reproaches him, as if he would not have done it otherwise. Nor would I recall a benefit from any man so as to force it, but only to receive it. If I let him quite alone, I make myself guilty of his ingratitude: and undo him for want of plain dealing. A father reclaims a disobedient son, a wife reclaims a dissolute husband; and one friend excites the languishing kindness of another. How many men are lost for want of being touched to the quick? So long as I am not pressed, I will rather desire a favor, than so much as mention a requital; but if my country, my family, or my liberty, be at stake, my zeal and indignation shall overrule my modesty, and the world shall then understand that I have done all I could, not to stand in need of an ungrateful man. And in conclusion the necessity of receiving a benefit shall overcome the shame of recalling it. Nor is it only allowable upon some exigents to put the receiver in mind of a good turn, but it is many times for the common advantage of both parties.

XIV

HOW FAR TO OBLIGE OR REQUITE A WICKED MAN

There are some benefits whereof a wicked man is wholly incapable; of which hereafter. There are others, which are bestowed upon him, not for his own sake, but for secondary reasons; and of these we have spoken in part already. There are, moreover, certain common offices of humanity, which are only allowed him as he is a man, and without any regard either to vice or virtue. To pass over the first point;

the second must be handled with care and distinction, and not without some seeming exceptions to the general rule; as first, here is no *choice* or *intention* in the case, but it is a good office done him for some *by-interest*, or by *chance*. Secondly, There is no *judgment* in it neither, for it is to a *wicked man*. But to shorten the matter: without these circumstances it is not properly a benefit; or at least not to him; for it looks another way. I rescue a friend from thieves, and the other escapes for company. I discharge a debt for a friend, and the other comes off too: for they were both in a bond. The third is of a great latitude, and varies according to the degree of generosity on the one side, and of wickedness on the other. Some benefactors will supererogate, and do more than they are bound to do; and some men are so lewd, that it is dangerous to do them any sort of good; no, not so much as by way of return or requital.

If the benefactor's bounty must extend to the bad as well as the good; put the case, that I promise a good office to an ungrateful man; we are first to distinguish (as I said before) betwixt a *common benefit* and a *personal*; betwixt what is given for *merit* and what for *company*. Secondly, Whether or not we know the person to be ungrateful, and can reasonably conclude, that this vice is *incurable*. Thirdly, A consideration must be had of the promise, how far that may oblige us. The two first points are cleared both in one: we cannot justify any particular kindness for one that we conclude to be a hopelessly wicked man: so that the force of the promise is in the single point in question. In the promise of a good office to a wicked or ungrateful man, I am to blame if I did it knowingly; and I am to blame nevertheless, if I did it otherwise: but I must yet make it good, (under due qualifications,) because I promised it; that is to say, matters continuing in the same state, for no man is answerable for accidents. I will sup at such a place though it be cold; I will rise at such an hour though I be sleepy; but if it prove tempestuous, or that I fall sick of a fever, I will neither do the one nor the other. I promise to second a friend in a quarrel, or to plead his cause; and when I come into the field, or into the court, it proves to be against my father or my brother: I promise to go a journey with him, but there is no traveling upon the road for robbing; my child is fallen sick; or my wife is in labor: these circumstances are sufficient to discharge me; for a promise against law or duty is void in its own nature.

The counsels of a wise man are certain, but events are uncertain: and yet if I have passed a rash promise, I will in some degree punish the temerity of making it with the damage of keeping it, unless it turn very much to my shame or detriment, and then I will be my own confessor in the point, and rather be once guilty of denying, than always of giving. It is not with a benefit as with a debt — it is one thing to trust an ill paymaster, and another thing to oblige an unworthy person — the one is an ill man, and the other only an ill husband.

There was a valiant fellow in the army, that Philip of Macedon took particular notice of, and he gave him several considerable marks of the kindness he had for him. This soldier put to sea and was cast away upon a coast where a charitable neighbor took him up half dead, carried him to the house, and there, at his own charge maintained and provided for him thirty days, until he was perfectly recovered, and, after all, furnished him over and above, with a viaticum at parting. The soldier told him the mighty matters that he would do for him in return, so soon as he should have the honor once again to see his master. To court he goes, tells Philip of the wreck, but not a syllable of his preserver, and begs the estate of this very man that kept him alive. It was with Philip as it was with many other princes, they give they know not what, especially in a time of war. He granted the soldier his request, contemplating at the same time, the impossibility of satisfying so many ravenous appetites as he had to please. When the good man came to be turned out of all, he was not so mealy-mouthed as to thank his majesty for not giving away his person too as well as his fortune; but in a bold, frank letter to Philip, made a just report of the whole story. The king was so incensed at the abuse, that he immediately commanded the right owner to be restored to his estate, and the unthankful guest and soldier to be stigmatized for an example to others.

Should Philip now have kept this promise? First, he owed the soldier nothing. Secondly, it would have been injurious and impious; and, lastly, a precedent of dangerous consequence to human society; for it would have been little less than an interdiction of fire and water to the miserable, to have inflicted such a penalty upon relieving them; so that there must be always some tacit exception or reserve: *if I can, if I may*; or, *if matters continue as they were.*

If it should be my fortune to receive a benefit from one that afterwards betrays his country, I should still reckon myself obliged to him for such a requital as might stand with my public duty; I would not furnish him with arms, nor with money or credit, or levy or pay soldiers; but I should not stick to gratify him at my own expense with such curiosities as might please him one way without doing mischief another. I would not do any thing that might contribute to the support or advantage of his party. But what should I do now in the case of a benefactor, that should afterwards become not only mine and my country's enemy, but the common enemy of mankind! I would here distinguish betwixt the wickedness of a man and the cruelty of a beast — betwixt a limited or a particular passion and a sanguinary rage that extends to the hazard and destruction of human society. In the former case I would quit scores, that I might have no more to do with him; but if he comes once to delight in blood, and to act outrages with greediness — to study and invent torments, and to take pleasure in them — the law of reasonable nature has discharged me of such a debt. But this is an impiety so rare that it might pass for a portent, and be reckoned among comets and monsters. Let us therefore restrain our discourse to such men as we detest without horror; such men as we see every day in courts, camps, and upon the seats of justice; to such wicked men I will return what I have received, without making any advantage of their unrighteousness.

It does not divert the Almighty from being still gracious, though we proceed daily in the abuse of his bounties. How many there are that enjoy the comfort of the light that do not deserve it; that wish they had never been born! and yet Nature goes quietly on with her work, and allows them a being, even in despite of their unthankfulness. Such a knave, we cry, was better used than I: and the same complaint we extend to Providence itself. How many wicked men have good crops, when better than themselves have their fruits blasted! Such a man, we say, has treated me very ill. Why, what should we do, but that very thing which is done by God himself? that is to say, give to the ignorant, and persevere to the wicked. All our ingratitude, we see, does not turn Providence from pouring down of benefits, even upon those that question whence they come. The wisdom of Heaven does all things with a regard to the good of the universe, and the blessings of nature are granted in common, to the worst as well as to the best of men; for they live promiscuously together; and it is God's will, that the wicked shall rather fare the better for the good, than that the good shall fare the worse for the wicked. It is true that a wise prince will confer peculiar honors only upon the worthy; but in the dealing of a public dole, there is no respect had to the manners of the man; but a thief or traitor shall put in for a share as well as an honest man. If a good man and a wicked man sail both in the same bottom, it is impossible that the same wind which favors the one should cross the other. The common benefits of laws, privileges, communities, letters, and medicines, are permitted to the bad as well as to the good; and no man ever yet suppressed a sovereign remedy for fear a wicked man might be cured with it. Cities are built for both sorts, and the same remedy works upon both alike. In these cases, we are to set an estimate upon the persons: there is a great difference betwixt the choosing of a man and the not excluding him: the law is open to the rebellious as well as to the obedient: there are some benefits which, if they were not allowed to all, could not be enjoyed by any. The sun was never made for me, but for the comfort of the world, and for the providential order of the seasons; and yet I am not without my private obligation also. To conclude, he that will oblige the wicked and the ungrateful, must resolve to oblige nobody; for in some sort or another we are all of us wicked, we are all of us ungrateful, every man of us.

We have been discoursing all this while how far a wicked man may be obliged, and the Stoics tell us at last, that he cannot be obliged at all. For they make him incapable of any good, and consequently of any benefit. But he has this advantage, that if he cannot be obliged, he cannot be ungrateful: for if he cannot receive, he is not bound to return. On the other side, a good man and an ungrateful, are a contradiction: so that at this rate there is no such thing as ingratitude in nature. They compare a wicked man's mind to a vitiated stomach; he corrupts whatever he receives, and the best nourishment turns to the disease. But taking this for granted, a wicked man may yet so far be obliged as to pass for ungrateful, if he does not requite what he receives: for though it be not a perfect benefit, yet he receives something like it. There are goods of the mind, the body, and of fortune. Of the first sort, fools and wicked men are wholly incapable; to the rest they may be admitted. But why should I call any man ungrateful, you will say, for not restoring that which I deny to be a benefit? I answer, that if the receiver take it for a benefit, and fails of a return, it is ingratitude in him: for that which goes for an obligation among wicked men, is an obligation upon them: and they may pay one another in their own coin; the money is current, whether it be gold or leather, when it comes once to be authorized. Nay, Cleanthes carries it farther; he that is wanting, says he, to a kind office, though it be no benefit, would have done the same thing if it had been one; and is as guilty as a thief is, that has set his booty, and is already armed and mounted with a purpose to seize it, though he has not yet drawn blood. Wickedness is formed in the heart; and the matter of fact is only the discovery and the execution of it. Now, though a wicked man cannot either receive or bestow a benefit, because he wants the will of doing good, and for that he is no longer wicked, when virtue has taken possession of him; yet we commonly call it one, as we call a man illiterate that is not learned, and naked that is not well clad; not but that the one can read, and the other is covered.

XV

A GENERAL VIEW OF THE PARTS AND DUTIES OF THE BENEFACTOR

The three main points in the question of benefits are, first, a *judicious choice* in the *object*; secondly, in the *matter* of our benevolence; and thirdly, a grateful *felicity* in the *manner* of expressing it. But there are also incumbent upon the benefactor other considerations, which will deserve a place in this discourse.

It is not enough to do one good turn, and to do it with a good grace too, unless we follow it with more, and without either upbraiding or repining. It is a common shift, to charge that upon the ingratitude of the receiver, which, in truth, is most commonly the levity and indiscretion of the giver; for all circumstances must be duly weighed to consummate the action. Some there are that we find ungrateful; but what with our forwardness, change of humor and reproaches, there are more that we make so. And this is the business: we give with design, and most to those that are able to give most again. We give to the covetous, and to the ambitious; to those that can never be thankful, (for their desires are insatiable,) and to those that *will* not. He that is a tribune would be praetor; the praetor, a consul; never reflecting upon what he *was*, but only looking forward to what he *would* be. People are still computing, *Must I lose this or that benefit?* If it be lost, the fault lies in the ill bestowing of it; for rightly placed, it is as good as consecrated; if we be deceived in another, let us not be deceived in ourselves too. A charitable man will mend the matter: and say to himself, *Perhaps he has forgot it, perchance he could not, perhaps he will yet requite it.* A patient creditor will, of an ill paymaster, in time make a good one; an obstinate goodness overcomes an ill disposition, as a barren soil is made fruitful by care and tillage. But let a man be never so ungrateful or inhuman, he shall never destroy the satisfaction of my having done a good office.

But what if *others* will be wicked? does it follow that we must be so too? If *others* will be ungrateful, must *we* therefore be inhuman? To give and to lose, is nothing; but to lose and to give still, is the part of a great mind. And the others in effect is the greater loss; for the one does but lose his benefit, and the other loses himself. The light shines upon the profane and sacrilegious as well as upon the righteous. How many disappointments do we meet with in our wives and children, and yet we couple still? He that has lost one battle hazards another. The mariner puts to sea again after a wreck. An illustrious mind does not propose the profit of a good office, but the duty. If the world be wicked, we should yet persevere in well-doing, even among evil men. I had rather never receive a kindness than never bestow one: not to return a benefit is the *greater* sin, but not to *confer* it is the *earlier*. We cannot propose to ourselves a more glorious example than that of the Almighty, who neither needs nor expects anything from us; and yet he is continually showering down and distributing his mercies and his grace among us, not only for our necessities, but also for our delights; as fruits and seasons, rain and sunshine, veins of water and of metal; and all this to the wicked as well as to the good, and without any other end than the common benefit of the receivers. With what face then can we be mercenary one to another, that have received all things from Divine Providence *gratis?* It is a common saying, "I gave such or such a man so much money: I would I had thrown it into the sea;" and yet the merchant trades again after a piracy, and the banker ventures afresh after a bad security. He that will do no good offices after a disappointment, must stand still, and do just nothing at all. The plow goes on after a barren year: and while the ashes are yet warm, we raise a new house upon the ruins of a former. What obligations can be greater than those which children receive from their parents? and yet should we give them over in their infancy, it were all to no purpose. Benefits, like grain, must be followed from the seed to the harvest. I will not so much as leave any place for ingratitude. I will pursue, and I will encompass the receiver with benefits; so that let him look which way he will, his benefactor shall be still in his eye, even when he would avoid his own memory: and then I will remit to one man because he calls for it; to another, because he does not; to a third, because he is wicked; and to a fourth, because he is the contrary. I will cast away a good turn upon a bad man, and I will requite a good one; the one because it is my duty, and the other that I may not be in debt.

I do not love to hear any man complain that he has met with a thankless man. If he has met but with one, he has either been very fortunate or very careful. And yet care is not sufficient: for there is no way to escape the hazard of losing a benefit but the not bestowing of it, and to neglect a duty to myself for fear another should abuse it. It is *another's* fault if he be ungrateful, but it is *mine* if I do not give. To find one thankful man, I will oblige a great many that are not so. The business of mankind would be at a stand, if we should do nothing for fear of miscarriages in matters of certain event. I will try and believe all things, before I give any man over, and do all that is possible that I may not lose a good office and a friend together. What do I know but *he may misunderstand the obligation? business may have put it out of his head, or taken him off from it: he may have slipt his opportunity*. I will say, in excuse of human weakness, that one man's memory is not sufficient for all things; it is but a limited capacity, so as to hold only so much, and no more: and when it is once full, it must let out part of what it had to take in anything beside; and the last benefit ever sits closest to us. In our youth we forget the obligations of our infancy, and when we are men we forget those of our youth. If nothing will prevail, let him keep what he has and welcome; but let him have a care of returning evil for good, and making it dangerous for a man to do his duty. I would no more give a benefit for such a man, than I would lend money to a beggarly spendthrift; or deposit any in the hands of a known *knight of the post*. However the case stands, an ungrateful person is never the better for a reproach; if he be already hardened in his wickedness, he gives no heed to it; and if he be not, it turns a doubtful modesty into an incorrigible impudence: beside that, he watches for all ill words to pick a quarrel with them.

As the benefactor is not to upbraid a benefit, so neither to delay it: the one is tiresome, and the other odious. We must not hold men in hand, as physicians and surgeons do their patients, and keep them longer in fear and pain than needs, only to magnify the cure. A generous man gives easily, and receives as he gives, but never exacts. He rejoices in the return, and judges favorably of it whatever it be, and contents himself with bare thanks for a requital. It is a harder matter with some to get the benefit after it is promised than the first promise of it, there must be so many friends made in the case. One must be desired to solicit another; and he must be entreated to move a third; and a fourth must be at last besought to receive it; so that the author, upon the upshot, has the least share in the obligation. It is then welcome when it comes free, and without deduction; and no man either to intercept or hinder, or to detain it. And let it be of such a quality too, that it be not only delightful in the receiving, but after it is received; which it will certainly be, if we do but observe this rule, never to do any thing for another which we would not honestly desire for ourselves.

XVI

HOW THE RECEIVER OUGHT TO BEHAVE HIMSELF

There are certain rules in common betwixt the giver and the receiver. We must do both cheerfully, that the giver may receive the fruit of his benefit in the very act of bestowing it. It is a just ground of satisfaction to *see* a friend pleased; but it is much more to *make* him so. The intention of the one is to be suited to the intention of the other; and there must be an emulation betwixt them, whether shall oblige most. Let the one say, that he has received a benefit, and let the other persuade himself that he has not returned it. Let the one say, *I am paid*, and the other, *I am yet in your debt*; let the benefactor acquit the receiver, and the receiver bind himself. The frankness of the discharge heightens the obligation. It is in *conversation* as in a *tennis-court*; benefits are to be tossed like balls; the longer the rest, the better are the gamesters. The giver, in some respect, has the odds, because (as in a race) he starts first, and the other must use great diligence to overtake him. The return must be larger than the first obligation to come up to it; and it is a kind of ingratitude not to render it with interest. In a matter of money, it is a common thing to pay a debt out of course, and before it be due; but we account ourselves to owe nothing for a good office; whereas the benefit increases by delay. So insensible are we of the most important affair of human life! That man were doubtless in a miserable condition, that could neither see, nor hear, nor taste, nor feel, nor smell; but how much more unhappy is he then that, wanting a sense of benefits, loses the greatest comfort in nature in the bliss of giving and receiving them? He that takes a benefit as it is meant is in the right; for the benefactor has then his end, and his only end, when the receiver is grateful.

The more glorious part, in appearance, is that of the giver; but the receiver has undoubtedly the harder game to play in many regards. There are some from whom I would not accept of a benefit; that is to say, from those upon whom I would not bestow one. For why should I not scorn to receive a benefit where I am ashamed to own it? and I would yet be more tender too, where I receive, than where I give; for it is no torment to be in debt where a man has no mind to pay; as it is the greatest delight imaginable to be engaged by a friend, whom I should yet have a kindness for; if I were never so much disobliged. It is a pain to an honest and a generous mind to lie under a duty of affection against inclination. I do not speak here of wise men, that love to do what they ought to do; that have their passions at command; that prescribe laws to themselves, and keep them when they have done; but of men in a state of imperfection, that may have a good will perhaps to be honest, and yet be overborne by the contumacy of their affections. We must therefore have a care to whom we become obliged; and I would be much stricter yet in the choice of a creditor for benefits than for money. In the one case, it is but paying what I had, and the debt is discharged; in the other, I do not only owe more, but when I have paid that, I am still in arrear: and this law is the very foundation of friendship. I will suppose myself a prisoner; and a notorious villain offers to lay down a good sum of money for my redemption. *First*, Shall I make use of this money or not? *Secondly*, If I do, what return shall I make him for it? To the first point, I will take it; but only as a debt; not as a benefit, that shall ever tie me to a friendship with him; and, secondly, my acknowledgment shall be only correspondent to such an obligation. It is a school question, whether or not Brutus, that thought Caesar not fit to live, (and put himself at the head of a conspiracy against him,) could honestly have received his life from Caesar, if he had fallen into Caesar's power, without examining what reason moved him to that action? How great a man soever he was in other cases, without dispute he was extremely out in this, and below the dignity of his profession. For a Stoic to fear the name of a king, when yet monarchy is the best state of government; or there to hope for liberty, where so great rewards are propounded, both for tyrants and their slaves; for him to imagine ever to bring the laws to their former state, where so many thousand lives had been lost in the contest, not so much whether they should serve or not, but who should be their master: he was strangely mistaken, in the nature and reason of things, to fancy, that when Julius was gone, somebody else would not start up in his place, when there was yet a Tarquin found, after so many kings that were destroyed, either by sword or thunder: and yet the resolution is, that he might have received it, but not as a benefit; for at that rate I owe my life to every man that does not take it away.

Graecinus Julius (whom Caligula put to death out of a pure malice to his virtue) had a considerable sum of money sent him from Fabius Persicus (a man of great and infamous example) as a contribution towards the expense of plays and other public entertainments; but Julius would not receive it; and some of his friends that had an eye more upon the present than the presenter, asked him, with some freedom, what he meant by refusing it? "Why," says he, "do you think that I will take money where I would not take so much as a glass of wine?" After this Rebilus (a man of the same stamp) sent him a greater sum upon the same score. "You must excuse me," says he to the messenger, "for I would not take any thing of Persicus neither."

To match this scruple of receiving money with another of keeping it; and the sum not above three pence, or a groat at most. There was a certain Pythagorean that contracted with a cobbler for a pair of shoes, and some three or four days after, going to pay him his money, the shop was shut up; and when he had knocked a great while at the door, "Friend," says a fellow, "you may hammer your heart out there, for the man that you look for is dead. And when our friends are dead, we hear no more news of them; but yours, that are to live again, will shift well enough," (alluding to Pythagora's transmigration). Upon this the philosopher went away, with his money chinking in his hand, and well enough content to save it: at last, his conscience took check at it; and, upon reflection, "Though the man be dead," says he, "to others, he is alive to thee; pay him what thou owest him:" and so he went back presently, and thrust it into his shop through the chink of the door. Whatever we owe, it is our part to find where to pay it, and to do it without asking too; for whether the creditor be good or bad, the debt is still the same.

If a benefit be forced upon me, as from a tyrant, or a superior, where it may be dangerous to refuse, this is rather obeying than receiving, where the necessity destroys the choice. The way to know what I have a mind to do, is to leave me at liberty whether I will do it or not; but it is yet a benefit, if a man does me good in spite of my teeth; as it is none, if I do any man good against my will. A man may both hate and yet receive a benefit at the same time; the money is never the worse, because a fool that is not read in coins refuses to take it. If the thing be good for the receiver, and so intended, no matter how ill it is taken. Nay, the receiver may be obliged, and not know it; but there can be no benefit which is unknown to the giver. Neither will I, upon any terms, receive a benefit from a worthy person that may do him a mischief: it is the part of an enemy to save himself by doing another man harm.

But whatever we do, let us be sure always to keep a grateful mind. It is not enough to say, what requital shall a poor man offer to a prince; or a slave to his patron; when it is the glory of gratitude that it depends only upon the good will? Suppose a man defends my fame; delivers me from beggary; saves my life; or gives me liberty, that is more than life; how shall I be grateful to that man? I will receive, cherish, and rejoice in the benefit. Take it kindly, and it is requited: not that the debt itself is discharged, but it is nevertheless a discharge of the conscience. I will yet distinguish betwixt the debtor that becomes insolvent by expenses upon whores and dice, and another that is undone by fire or thieves; nor do I take this gratitude for a payment, but there is no danger, I presume, of being arrested for such a debt.

In the return of benefits let us be ready and cheerful but not pressing. There is as much greatness of mind in the owing of a good turn as in doing of it; and we must no more force a requital out of season than be wanting in it. He that precipitates a return, does as good as say, "I am weary of being in this man's debt:" not but that the hastening of a requital, as a good office, is a commendable disposition, but it is another thing to do it as a discharge; for it looks like casting off a heavy and a troublesome burden. It is for the benefactor to say *when* he will receive it; no matter for the opinion of the world, so long as I gratify my own conscience; for I cannot be mistaken in myself, but another may. He that is over solicitous to return a benefit, thinks the other so likewise to receive it. If he had rather we should keep it, why should we refuse, and presume to dispose of his treasure, who may call it in, or let it lie out, at his choice? It is as much a fault to receive what I ought not, as not to give what I ought; for the giver has the privilege of choosing his own time of receiving.

Some are too proud in the conferring of benefits; others, in the receiving of them; which is, to say the truth, intolerable. The same rule serves both sides, as in the case of a father and a son; a husband and a wife; one friend or acquaintance and another, where the duties are known and common. There are some that will not receive a benefit but in private, nor thank you for it but in your ear, or in a corner; there must be nothing under hand and seal, no brokers, notaries, or witnesses, in the case: that is not so much a scruple of modesty as a kind of denying the obligation, and only a less hardened ingratitude. Some receive benefits so coldly and indifferently, that a man would think the obligation lay on the other side: as who should say, "Well, since you will needs have it so, I am content to take it." Some again so carelessly, as if they hardly knew of any such thing, whereas we should rather aggravate the matter: "You cannot imagine how many you have obliged in this act: there never was so great, so kind, so seasonable a courtesy." Furnius never gained so much upon Augustus as by a speech, upon the getting of his father's pardon for siding with Antony: "This grace," says he, "is the only injury that ever Caesar did me: for it has put me upon a necessity of living and dying ungrateful." It is safer to affront some people than to oblige them; for the better a man deserves, the worse they will speak of him: as if the possessing of open hatred to their benefactors were an argument that they lie under no obligation. Some people are so sour and ill-natured, that they take it for an affront to have an obligation or a return offered them, to the discouragement both of bounty and gratitude together. The not doing, and the not receiving, of benefits, are equally a mistake. He that refuses a new one, seems to be offended at an old one: and yet sometimes I would neither return a benefit, no, nor so much as receive it, if I might.

XVII

GRATITUDE

He that preaches gratitude, pleads the cause both of God and man; for without it we can neither be sociable nor religious. There is a strange delight in the very purpose and contemplation of it, as well as in the action; when I can say to myself, "I love my benefactor; what is there in this world that I would not do to oblige and serve him?" Where I have not the *means* of a requital, the very *meditation* of it is sufficient. A man is nevertheless an artist for not having his tools about him; or a musician, because he wants his fiddle: nor is he the less brave because his hands are bound; or the worse pilot for being upon dry ground. If I have only *will* to be grateful, I *am* so. Let me be upon the wheel, or under the hand of the executioner; let me be burnt limb by limb, and my whole body dropping in the flames, a good conscience supports me in all extremes; nay, it is comfortable even in death itself; for when we come to approach that point, what care do we take to summon and call to mind all our benefactors, and the good offices they have done us, that we leave the world fair, and set our minds in order? Without gratitude, we can neither have security, peace, nor reputation: and it is not therefore the less desirable, because it draws many adventitious benefits along with it. Suppose the sun, the moon, and the stars, had no other business than only to pass over our heads, without any effect upon our minds or bodies; without any regard to our health, fruits, or seasons; a man could hardly lift up his eyes towards the heavens without wonder and veneration, to see so many millions of radiant lights, and to observe their courses and revolutions, even without any respect to the common good of the universe. But when we come to consider that Providence and Nature are still at work when we sleep, with the admirable force and operation of their influences and motions, we cannot then but acknowledge their ornament to be the least part of their value; and that they are more to be esteemed for their virtues than for their splendor. Their main end and use is matter of life and necessity, though they may seem to us more considerable for their majesty and beauty. And so it is with gratitude; we love it rather for secondary ends, than for itself.

No man can be grateful without contemning those things that put the common people out of their wits. We must go into banishment; lay down our lives; beggar and expose ourselves to reproaches; nay, it is often seen, that loyalty suffers the punishment due to rebellion, and that treason receives the rewards of fidelity. As the benefits of it are many and great, so are the hazards; which is the case more or less of all other virtues: and it were hard, if this, above the rest, should be both painful and fruitless: so that though we may go currently on with it in a smooth way, we must yet prepare and resolve (if need be) to force our passage to it, even if the way were covered with thorns and serpents; and *fall back, fall edge*, we must be grateful still: grateful for the virtue's sake, and grateful over and above upon the point of interest; for it preserves old friends, and gains new ones. It is not our business to fish for one benefit with another; and by bestowing a little to get more; or to oblige for any sort of expedience, but because I ought to do it, and because I love it, and that to such a degree, that if I could not be grateful without appearing the contrary, if I could not return a benefit without being suspected of doing an injury; in despite of infamy itself, I would yet be grateful. No man is greater in my esteem than he that ventures the fame to preserve the conscience of an honest man; the one is but imaginary, the other solid and inestimable. I cannot call him grateful, who in the instant of returning one benefit has his eye upon another. He that is grateful for profit or fear, is like a woman that is honest only upon the score of reputation.

As gratitude is a necessary and a glorious, so it is also an obvious, a cheap, and an easy virtue; so obvious, that wheresoever there is a life there is a place for it — so cheap that the covetous man may be grateful without expense — and so easy that the sluggard may be so, likewise, without labor. And yet it is not without its niceties too; for there may be a time, a place or occasion wherein I ought not to return a benefit; nay, wherein I may better disown it than deliver it.

Let it be understood, by the way, that it is one thing to be grateful for a good office, and another thing to return it — the good will is enough in one case, being as much as the one side demands and the other promises; but the effect is requisite in the other. The physician that has done his best is acquitted though the patient dies, and so is the advocate, though the client may lose his cause. The general of an army, though the battle be lost, is yet worthy of commendation, if he has discharged all the parts of a prudent commander; in this case, the one acquits himself, though the other be never the better for it. He is a grateful man that is always willing and ready: and he that seeks for all means and occasions of requiting a benefit, though without attaining his end, does a great deal more than the man that, without any trouble, makes an immediate return. Suppose my friend a prisoner, and that I have sold my estate for his ransom; I put to sea in foul weather, and upon a coast that is pestered with pirates; my friend happens to be redeemed before I come to the place; my gratitude is as much to be esteemed as if he had been a prisoner; and if I had been taken and robbed myself, it would still have been the same case. Nay, there is a gratitude in the very countenance; for an honest man bears his conscience in his face, and propounds the requital of a good turn in the very moment of receiving it; he is cheerful and confident; and, in the possession of a true friendship, delivered from all anxiety. There is this difference betwixt a thankful man and an unthankful, the one is *always* pleased in the good he has *done*, and the other only *once* in what he has *received*. There must be a benignity in the estimation even of the smallest offices; and such a modesty as appears to be obliged in whatsoever it gives. As it is indeed a very great benefit, the opportunity of doing a good office to a worthy man. He that attends to the present, and remembers what is past, shall never be ungrateful. But who shall judge in the case? for a man may be grateful without making a return, and ungrateful with it. Our best way is to help every thing by a fair interpretation; and wheresoever there is a doubt, to allow it the most favorable construction; for he that is exceptious at words, or looks, has a mind to pick a quarrel. For my own part, when I come to cast up my account, and know what I owe, and to whom, though I make my return sooner to some, and later to others, as occasion or fortune will give me leave, yet I will be just to all: I will be grateful to God, to man, to those that have obliged me: nay, even to those that have obliged my friends. I am bound in honor and in conscience to be thankful for what I have received; and if it be not yet full, it is some pleasure still that I may hope for more. For the requital of a favor there must be virtue, occasion, means, and fortune.

It is a common thing to screw up justice to the pitch of an injury. A man may be *over-righteous*; and why not *over-grateful* too? There is a mischievous excess, that borders so close upon ingratitude, that it is no easy matter to distinguish the one from the other: but, in regard that there is good-will in the bottom of it, (however distempered, for it is effectually but kindness out of the wits,) we shall discourse it under the title of *Gratitude mistaken*.

XVIII

GRATITUDE MISTAKEN

To refuse a good office, not so much because we do not need it, as because we would not be indebted for it, is a kind of fantastical ingratitude, and somewhat akin to that nicety of humor, on the other side, of being over-grateful; only it lies another way, and seems to be the more pardonable ingratitude of the two. Some people take it for a great instance of their good-will to be wishing their benefactors such or such a mischief; only, forsooth, that they themselves may be the happy instruments of their release.

These men do like extravagant lovers, that take it for a great proof of their affection to wish one another banished, beggared, or diseased, that they might have the opportunity of interposing to their relief. What difference is there betwixt such wishing and cursing? such an affection and a mortal hatred? The intent is good, you will say, but this is a misapplication of it. Let such a one fall into my power, or into the hands of his enemies, his creditors, or the common people, and no mortal be able to rescue him but myself: let his life, his liberty, and his reputation, lie all at stake, and no creature but myself in condition to succor him; and why all this, but because he has obliged me, and I would requite him? If this be gratitude to propound jails, shackles, slavery, war, beggary, to the man that you would requite, what would you do where you are ungrateful? This way of proceeding, over and above that it is impious in itself, is likewise over-hasty and unseasonable: for he that goes too fast is as much to blame as he that does not move at all, (to say nothing of the injustice,) for if I had never been obliged, I should never have wished it.

There are seasons wherein a benefit is neither to be received nor requited. To press a return upon me when I do not desire it, is unmannerly; but it is worse to force me to desire it. How rigorous would he be to exact a requital; who is thus eager to return it! To wish a man in distress that I may relieve him, is first to wish him miserable: to wish that he may stand in need of anybody, is *against him*; and to wish that he may stand in need of me, is *for myself*: so that my business is not so much a charity to my friend as the cancelling of a bond; nay, it is half-way the wish of an enemy. It is barbarous to wish a man in chains, slavery, or want, only to bring him out again: let me rather wish him powerful and happy, and myself indebted to him! By nature we are prone to mercy, humanity compassion; may we be excited to be more so by the number of the grateful! may their number increase, and may we have no need of trying them!

It is not for an honest man to make way to a good office by a crime: as if a pilot should pray for a tempest, that he might prove his skill: or a general wish his army routed, that he may show himself a great commander in recovering the day. It is throwing a man into a river to take him out again. It is an obligation, I confess, to cure a wound or a disease; but to *make* that wound or disease on purpose to *cure* it, is a most perverse ingratitude. It is barbarous even to an enemy, much more to a friend; for it is not so much to do him a kindness, as to put him in need of it. Of the two, let me rather be a scar than a wound; and yet it would be better to have it neither. Rome had been little beholden to Scipio if he had prolonged the Punic war that he might have the finishing of it at last, or to the Decii for dying for their country, if they had first brought it to the last extremity of needing their devotion. It may be a good contemplation, but it is a lewd wish. Aeneas had never been surnamed *the Pious*, if he had wished the ruin of his country, only that he might have the honor of taking his father out of the fire. It is the scandal of a physician to make work, and irritate a disease, and to torment his patient, for the reputation of his cure. If a man should openly imprecate poverty, captivity, fear, or danger, upon a person that he has been obliged to, would not the whole world condemn him for it? And what is the difference, but the one is only a private wish, and the other a public declaration? Rutilius was told in his exile, that, for his comfort, there would be ere-long a civil war, that would bring all the banished men home again. "God forbid," says he, "for I had rather my country should blush for my banishment than mourn for my return." How much more honorable it is to owe cheerfully, than to pay dishonestly? It is the wish of an enemy to take a town that he may preserve it, and to be victorious that he may forgive; but the mercy comes after the cruelty; beside that it is an injury both to God and man; for the man must be first afflicted by *Heaven* to be relieved by *me*. So that we impose the cruelty upon God, and take the compassion to ourselves; and at the best, it is but a curse that makes way for a blessing; the bare wish is an injury; and if it does not take effect, it is because Heaven has not heard our prayers; or if they should succeed, the fear itself is a torment; and it is much more desirable to have a firm and unshaken security. It is friendly to wish it in your power to oblige me, if ever I chance to need it; but it is unkind to wish me miserable that I may need it. How much more pious is it, and humane, to wish that I may never want the occasion of obliging, nor the means of doing it; nor ever have reason to repent of what I have done?

XIX

INGRATITUDE

Ingratitude is of all the crimes, that which we are to account the most venial in others, and the most unpardonable in ourselves. It is impious to the highest degree; for it makes us fight against our children and our altars. There are, there ever were, and there ever will be criminals of all sorts, as murderers, tyrants, thieves, adulterers, traitors, robbers and sacrilegious persons; but there is hardly any notorious crime without a mixture of ingratitude. It disunites mankind, and breaks the very pillars of society; and yet so far is this prodigious wickedness from being any wonder to us, that even thankfulness it-self were much the greater of the two; for men are deterred from it by labor, expense, laziness, business; or else diverted from it by lust, envy, ambition, pride, levity, rashness, fear; nay, by the very shame of confessing what they have received. And the unthankful man has nothing to say for himself all this while, for there needs neither pains or fortune for the discharge of his duty, beside the inward anxiety and torment when a man's conscience makes him afraid of his own thoughts.

To speak against the ungrateful is to rail against mankind, for even those that complain are guilty: nor do I speak only of those that do not live up to the strict rule of virtue; but mankind itself is degenerated and lost. We live unthankfully in this world, and we go struggling and murmuring out of it, dissatisfied with our lot, whereas we should be grateful for the blessings we have enjoyed, and account that sufficient which Providence has provided for us; a little more time may make our lives longer but not happier, and whensoever it is the pleasure of God to call us, we must obey; and yet all this while we go on quarreling at the world for what we find in ourselves, and we are yet more unthankful to Heaven than we are to one another. What benefit can be great now to that man that despises the bounties of his Maker? We would be as strong as elephants, as swift as bucks, as light as birds — and we complain that we have not the sagacity of dogs, the sight of eagles, the long life of ravens — nay, that we are not immortal, and endued with the knowledge of things to come: nay, we take it ill that we are not gods upon earth, never considering the advantages of our condition, or the benignity of Providence in the comforts that we enjoy. We subdue the strongest of creatures and overtake the fleetest — we reclaim the fiercest and outwit the craftiest. We are within one degree of heaven itself, and yet we are not satisfied.

Since there is not any one creature which we had rather be, we take it ill that we cannot draw the united excellencies of all other creatures into ourselves. Why are we not rather thankful to that goodness which has subjected the whole creation to our use and service?

The principal causes of ingratitude are pride and self-conceit, avarice, envy, etc. It is a familiar exclamation, "It is true he did this or that for me, but it came so late, and it was so little, I had even as good have been without it — if he had not given it to me, he must have given it to somebody else — it was nothing out of his pocket." Nay, we are so ungrateful, that he that gives us all we have, if he leaves any thing to himself, we reckon that he does us an injury.

It cost Julius Caesar his life by the disappointment of his insatiable companions; and yet he reserved nothing of all that he got to himself but the liberty of disposing of it. There is no benefit so large but malignity will still lessen it; none so narrow, which a good interpretation will not enlarge. No man shall ever be grateful that views a benefit on the wrong side, or takes a good office by the wrong handle. The avaricious man is naturally ungrateful, for he never thinks he has enough, but, without considering what he has, only minds what he covets. Some pretend want of power to make a competent return, and you shall find in others a kind of graceless modesty, that makes a man ashamed of requiting an obligation, because it is a confession that he has received one.

Not to return one good office for another is inhuman; but to return evil for good is diabolical. There are too many even of this sort, who, the more they owe, the more they hate. There is nothing more dangerous than to oblige those people; for when they are conscious of not paying the debt, they wish the creditor out of the way. It is a mortal hatred, that which arises from the shame of an abused benefit. When we are on the asking side, what a deal of cringing there is, and profession! "Well, I shall never forget this favor, it will be an eternal obligation to me." But within a while the note is changed, and we hear no more words of it, until, by little and little, it is all quite forgotten. So long as we stand in need of a benefit, there is nothing dearer to us; nor anything cheaper, when we have received it. And yet a man may as well refuse to deliver up a sum of money that is left him in trust without a suit, as not to return a good office without asking; and when we have no value any farther for the benefit, we do commonly care as little for the author. People follow their interest: one man is grateful for his convenience, and another man is ungrateful for the same reason.

Some are ungrateful to their own country, and their country no less ungrateful to others; so that the complaint of ingratitude reaches all men. Doth not the son wish for the death of his father, the husband for that of his wife, etc. But who can look for gratitude in an age of so many gaping and craving appetites, where all people take, and none give? In an age of license to all sorts of vanity and wickedness, as lust, gluttony, avarice, envy, ambition, sloth, insolence, levity, contumacy, fear, rashness, private discords and public evils, extravagant and groundless wishes, vain confidences, sickly affections, shameless impieties, rapine authorized, and the violation of all things, sacred and profane: obligations are pursued with sword and poison; benefits are turned into crimes, and that blood most seditiously spilt for which every honest man should expose his own. Those that should be the preservers of their country are the destroyers of it; and it is a matter of dignity to trample upon the government: the sword gives the law, and mercenaries take up arms against their masters. Among these turbulent and unruly motions, what hope is there of finding honesty or good faith, which is the quietest of all virtues? There is no more lively image of human life than that of a conquered city; there is neither mercy, modesty, nor religion; and if we forget our lives, we may well forget our benefits. The world abounds with examples of ungrateful persons, and no less with those of ungrateful governments. Was not Catiline ungrateful? whose malice aimed, not only at the mastering of his country, but at the total destruction of it, by calling in an inveterate and vindictive enemy from beyond the Alps, to wreak their long-thirsted-for revenge, and to sacrifice the lives of as many noble Romans as might serve to answer and appease the ghosts of the slaughtered Gauls? Was not Marius ungrateful, that, from a common soldier, being raised up to a consul, not only gave the world for civil bloodshed and massacres, but was himself the sign of the execution; and every man he met in the streets, to whom he did not stretch out his right hand, was murdered? And was not Sylla ungrateful too? that when he had waded up to the gates in human blood, carried the outrage into the city, and there most barbarously cut two entire legions to pieces in a corner, not only after the victory, but most perfidiously after quarter given them? Good God! that ever any man should not only escape with impunity, but receive a reward for so horrid a villainy! Was not Pompey ungrateful too? who, after three consulships, three triumphs, and so many honors, usurped before his time, split the commonwealth into three parts, and brought it to such a pass, that there was no hope of safety but by slavery only;

forsooth, to abate the envy of his power, he took other partners with him into the government, as if that which was not lawful for any one might have been allowable for more; dividing and distributing the provinces, and breaking all into a *triumvirate*, reserving still two parts of the three in his own family. And was not Caesar ungrateful also, though to give him his due, he was a man of his word; merciful in his victories, and never killed any man but with his sword in his hand? Let us therefore forgive one another. Only one word more now for the shame of ungrateful Governments. Was not Camillus banished? Scipio dismissed? and Cicero exiled and plundered? But, what is all this to those who are so mad, and to dispute even the goodness of Heaven, which gives us all, and expects nothing again, but continues giving to the most unthankful and complaining?

XX

THERE CAN BE NO LAW AGAINST INGRATITUDE

Ingratitude is so dangerous to itself, and so detestable to other people, that nature, one would think, had sufficiently provided against it, without need of any other law. For every ungrateful man is his own enemy, and it seems superfluous to compel a man to be kind to himself, and to follow in his own inclinations. This, of all wickedness imaginable, is certainly the vice which does the most divide and distract human nature. Without the exercise and the commerce of mutual offices, we can be neither happy nor safe for it is only society that secures us: take us one by one, and we are a prey even to brutes as well as to one another.

Nature has brought us into the world naked and unarmed; we have not the teeth or the paws of lions or bears to make ourselves terrible; but by the two blessings of reason and union, we secure and defend ourselves against violence and fortune. This it is that makes man the master of all other creatures, who otherwise were scarce a match for the weakest of them. This it is that comforts us in sickness, in age, in misery, in pains, and in the worst of calamities. Take away this combination, and mankind is dissociated, and falls to pieces. It is true, that there is no law established against this abominable vice; but we cannot say yet that it escapes unpunished, for a public hatred is certainly the greatest of all penalties; over and above that we lose the most valuable blessings of life, in the not bestowing and receiving of benefits. If ingratitude were to be punished by a law, it would discredit the obligation; for a benefit to be given, not lent: and if we have no return at all, there is no just cause of complaint: for gratitude were no virtue, if there were any danger in being ungrateful. There are halters, I know, hooks and gibbets, provided for homicide poison, sacrilege, and rebellion; but ingratitude (here upon earth) is only punished in the schools; all farther pains and inflictions being wholly remitted to divine justice. And, if a man may judge of the conscience by the countenance the ungrateful man is never without a canker at his heart; his mind an aspect is sad and solicitous; whereas the other is always cheerful and serene.

As there are no laws extant against ingratitude, so is it utterly impossible to contrive any, that in all circumstances shall reach it. If it were actionable, there would not be courts enough in the whole world to try the causes in. There can be no setting a day for the requiting of benefits as for the payment of money, nor any estimate upon the benefits themselves; but the whole matter rests in the conscience of both parties: and then there are so many degrees of it, that the same rule will never serve all. Beside that, to proportion it as the benefit is greater or less, will be both impracticable and without reason. One good turn saves my life; another, my freedom, or peradventure my very soul. How shall any law now suit a punishment to an ingratitude under these differing degrees? It must not be said in benefits as in bonds, *Pay what you owe.* How shall a man pay life, health, credit, security, in *kind*? There can be no set rule to bound that infinite variety of cases, which are more properly the subject of humanity and religion than of law and public justice. There would be disputes also about the benefit itself, which must totally depend upon the courtesy of the judge; for no law imaginable can set it forth. One man *gives* me an estate; another only *lends* me a sword, and that sword preserves my life. Nay, the very same thing, several ways done, changes the quality of the obligation. A word, a tone, a look, makes a great alteration in the case. How shall we judge then, and determine a matter which does not depend upon the fact itself, but upon the force and intention of it? Some things are reputed benefits, not for their value, but because we desire them: and there are offices of as much greater value, that we do not reckon upon at all. If ingratitude were liable to a law, we must never give but before witnesses, which would overthrow the dignity of the benefit: and then the punishment must either be equal where the crimes are unequal, or else it must be unrighteous, so that blood must answer for blood. He that is ungrateful for my saving his life must forfeit his own. And what can be more inhuman than that benefits should conclude in sanguinary events? A man saves my life, and I am ungrateful for it. Shall I be punished in my purse? that is too little; if it be less than the benefit, it is unjust, and it must be capital to be made equal to it. There are, moreover, certain privileges granted to parents, that can never be reduced to a common rule. Their injuries may be cognizable, but not their benefits. The diversity of cases is too large and intricate to be brought within the prospect of a law: so that it is much more equitable to punish none than to punish all alike. What if a man follows a good office with an injury; whether or no shall this quit scores? or who shall compare them, and weigh the one against the other? There is another thing yet which perhaps we do not dream of: not one man upon the face of the earth would escape, and yet every man would expect to be his judge. Once again, we are all of us ungrateful; and the number does not only take away the shame, but gives authority and protection to the wickedness.

It is thought reasonable by some, that there should be a law against ingratitude; for, say they, it is common for one city to upbraid another, and to claim that of posterity which was bestowed upon their ancestors; but this is only clamor without reason. It is objected by others, as a discouragement to good offices, if men shall not be made answerable for them; but I say, on the other side, that no man would accept of a benefit upon those terms. He that gives is prompted to it by a goodness of mind, and the generosity of the action is lessened by the caution: for it is his desire that the receiver should please himself, and owe no more than he thinks fit. But what if this might occasion fewer benefits, so long as they would be franker? nor is there any hurt in putting a check upon rashness and profusion. In answer to this; men will be careful enough when they oblige without a law: nor is it possible for a judge ever to set us right in it; or indeed, anything else, but the faith of the receiver. The honor of a benefit is this way preserved, which is otherwise profaned, when it comes to the mercenary, and made matter of contention. We are even forward enough of ourselves to wrangle, without necessary provocations. It would be well, I think, if moneys might pass upon the same conditions with other benefits, and the payment remitted to the conscience, without formalizing upon bills and securities: but human wisdom has rather advised with convenience than virtue; and chosen rather to *force* honesty than *expect* it. For every paltry sum of money there must be bonds, witnesses, counterparts, powers, etc., which is no other than a shameful confession of fraud and wickedness, when more credit is given to our seals than to our minds; and caution taken lest he that has received the money should deny it. Were it not better now to be deceived by some than to suspect all? what is the difference, at this rate, betwixt the benefactor and the usurer, save only that in the benefactor's case there is nobody stands bound?

A HAPPY LIFE

I

A HAPPY LIFE, AND WHEREIN IT CONSISTS

There is not any thing in this world, perhaps, that is more talked of, and less understood, than the business of a *happy life*. It is every man's wish and design; and yet not one of a thousand that knows wherein that happiness consists. We live, however, in a blind and eager pursuit of it; and the more haste we make in a wrong way, the further we are from our journey's end. Let us therefore, *first*, consider "what it is we should be at;" and, *secondly*, "which is the readiest way to compass it." If we be right, we shall find every day how much we improve; but if we either follow the cry, or the track, of people that are out of the way, we must expect to be misled, and to continue our days in wandering in error. Wherefore, it highly concerns us to take along with us a skilful guide; for it is not in this, as in other voyages, where the highway brings us to our place of repose; or if a man should happen to be out, where the inhabitants might set him right again: but on the contrary, the beaten road is here the most dangerous, and the people, instead of helping us, misguide us. Let us not therefore follow, like beasts, but rather govern ourselves by *reason*, than by *example*. It fares with us in human life as in a routed army; one stumbles first, and then another falls upon him, and so they follow, one upon the neck of another, until the whole field comes to be but one heap of miscarriages. And the mischief is, "that the number of the multitude carries it against truth and justice;" so that we must leave the crowd, if we would be happy: for the question of a *happy life* is not to be decided by vote: nay, so far from it, that plurality of voices is still an argument of the wrong; the common people find it easier to believe than to judge, and content themselves with what is usual, never examining whether it be good or not. By the *common people* is intended *the man of title* as well as the *clouted shoe*: for I do not distinguish them by the eye, but by the mind, which is the proper judge of the man. Worldly felicity, I know, makes the head giddy; but if ever a man comes to himself again, he will confess, that "whatsoever he has done, he wishes undone;" and that "the things he feared were better than those he prayed for."

The true felicity of life is to be free from perturbations, to understand our duties towards God and man: to enjoy the present without any anxious dependence upon the future. Not to amuse ourselves with either hopes or fears, but to rest satisfied with what we have, which is abundantly sufficient; for he that is so, wants nothing. The great blessings of mankind are within us, and within our reach; but we shut our eyes, and, like people in the dark, we fall foul upon the very thing which we search for without finding it. "Tranquillity is a certain equality of mind, which no condition of fortune can either exalt or depress." Nothing can make it less: for it is the state of human perfection: it raises us as high as we can go; and makes every man his own supporter; whereas he that is borne up by any thing else may fall. He that judges aright, and perseveres in it, enjoys a perpetual calm: he takes a true prospect of things; he observes an order, measure, a decorum in all his actions; he has a benevolence in his nature; he squares his life according to reason; and draws to himself love and admiration. Without a certain and an unchangeable judgment, all the rest is but fluctuation: but "he that always wills and nills the same thing, is undoubtedly in the right." Liberty and serenity of mind must necessarily ensue upon the mastering of those things which either allure or affright us; when instead of those flashy pleasures, (which even at the best are both vain and hurtful together,) we shall find ourselves possessed of joy transporting and everlasting. It must be a *sound mind* that makes a *happy man*; there must be a constancy in all conditions, a care for the things of this world, but without trouble; and such an indifferency for the bounties of fortune, that either with them, or without them, we may live contentedly. There must be neither lamentation, nor quarrelling, nor sloth, nor fear; for it makes a discord in a man's life. "He that fears, serves." The joy of a wise man stands firm without interruption; in all places, at all times, and in all conditions, his thoughts are cheerful and quiet. As it never *came in* to him from *without*, so it will never leave him; but it is born within him, and inseparable from him. It is a solicitous life that is egged on with the hope of any thing, though never so open and easy, nay, though a man should never suffer any sort of disappointment. I do not speak this either as a bar to the fair enjoyment of lawful pleasures, or to the gentle flatteries of reasonable expectations: but, on the contrary, I would have men to be always in good humor, provided that it arises from their own souls, and be cherished in their own breasts. Other delights are trivial; they may smooth the brow, but they do not fill and affect the heart. "True joy is a serene and sober motion;" and they are miserably out that take *laughing* for *rejoicing*. The seat of it is within, and there is no cheerfulness like the resolution of a brave mind, that has fortune under his feet. He that can look death in the face, and bid it welcome; open his door to poverty, and bridle his appetites; this is the man whom Providence has established in the possession of inviolable delights. The pleasures of the vulgar are ungrounded, thin, and superficial; but the others are solid and *eternal*. As the *body* itself is rather a *necessary thing*, than a *great*; so the comforts of it are but temporary and vain; beside that, without extraordinary moderation, their end is only pain and repentance; whereas a peaceful conscience, honest thoughts, virtuous actions, and an indifference for casual events, are blessings without end, satiety, or measure. This consummated state of felicity is only a submission to the dictate of right nature; "The foundation of it is wisdom and virtue; the knowledge of what we ought to do, and the conformity of the will to that knowledge."

II

HUMAN HAPPINESS IS FOUNDED UPON
WISDOM AND VIRTUE; AND FIRST, OF WISDOM

Taking for granted that *human happiness* is founded upon *wisdom* and *virtue* we shall treat of these two points in order as they lie: and, *first*, of *wisdom*; not in the latitude of its various operations but as it has only a regard to good life, and the happiness of mankind.

Wisdom is a right understanding, a faculty of discerning good from evil; what is to be chosen, and what rejected; a judgment grounded upon the value of things, and not the common opinion of them; an equality of force, and a strength of resolution. It sets a watch over our words and deeds, it takes us up with the contemplation of the works of nature, and makes us invincible by either good or evil fortune. It is large and spacious, and requires a great deal of room to work in; it ransacks heaven and earth; it has for its object things past and to come, transitory and eternal. It examines all the circumstances of time; "what it is, when it began, and how long it will continue: and so for the mind; whence it came; what it is; when it begins; how long it lasts; whether or not it passes from one form to another, or serves only one and wanders when it leaves us; whether it abides in a state of separation, and what the action of it; what use it makes of its liberty; whether or not it retains the memory of things past, and comes to the knowledge of itself." It is the habit of a perfect mind, and the perfection of humanity, raised as high as Nature can carry it. It differs from *philosophy*, as avarice and money; the one desires, and the other is desired; the one is the effect and the reward of the other. To be wise is the use of wisdom, as seeing is the use of eyes, and well-speaking the use of eloquence. He that is perfectly wise is perfectly happy; nay, the very beginning of wisdom makes life easy to us. Neither is it enough to know this, unless we print it in our minds by daily meditation, and so bring a *good-will* to a good habit. And we must practice what we preach: for *philosophy* is not a subject for popular ostentation; nor does it rest in words, but in things. It is not an entertainment taken up for delight, or to give a taste to our leisure; but it fashions the mind, governs our actions, tells us what we are to do, and what not. It sits at the helm, and guides us through all hazards; nay, we cannot be safe without it, for every hour gives us occasion to make use of it. It informs us in all duties of life, piety to our parents, faith to our friends, charity to the miserable, judgment in counsel; it gives us *peace* by *fearing* nothing, and *riches* by *coveting nothing*.

There is no condition of life that excludes a wise man from discharging his duty. If his fortune be good, he *tempers* it; if bad, he *masters* it; if he has an estate, he will exercise his virtue in plenty; if none, in poverty: if he cannot do it in his country, he will do it in banishment; if he has no command, he will do the office of a common soldier. Some people have the skill of reclaiming the fiercest of beasts; they will make a lion embrace his keeper, a tiger kiss him, and an elephant kneel to him. This is the case of a wise man in the extremest difficulties; let them be never so terrible in themselves, when they come to him once, they are perfectly tame. They that ascribe the invention of tillage, architecture, navigation, etc., to wise men, may perchance be in the right, that they were invented by wise men, as *wise men*; for wisdom does not teach our fingers, but our minds: fiddling and dancing, arms and fortifications, were the works of luxury and discord; but wisdom instructs us in the way of nature, and in the arts of unity and concord, not in the instruments, but in the government of life; not to make us live only, but to live happily. She teaches us what things are good, what evil, and what only appear so; and to distinguish betwixt true greatness and tumor. She clears our minds of dross and vanity; she raises up our thoughts to heaven, and carries them down to hell: she discourses of the nature of the soul, the powers and faculties of it; the first principles of things; the order of Providence: she exalts us from things corporeal to things incorporeal, and retrieves the truth of all: she searches nature, gives laws to life; and tells us, "That it is not enough to God, unless we obey him:" she looks upon all accidents as acts of Providence: sets a true value upon things; delivers us from false opinions, and condemns all pleasures that are attended with repentance. She allows nothing to be good that will not be so forever; no man to be happy but that needs no other happiness than what he has within himself. This is the felicity of human life; a felicity that can neither be corrupted nor extinguished: it inquires into the nature of the heavens, the influence of the stars; how far they operate upon our minds and bodies: which thoughts, though they do not form our manners, they do yet raise and dispose us for glorious things.

It is agreed upon all hands that "right reason is the perfection of human nature," and wisdom only the dictate of it. The greatness that arises from it is solid and unmovable, the resolutions of wisdom being free, absolute and constant; whereas folly is never long pleased with the same thing, but still shifting of counsels and sick of itself. There can be no happiness without constancy and prudence, for a wise man is to write without a blot, and what he likes once he approves for ever. He admits of nothing that is either evil or slippery, but marches without staggering or stumbling, and is never surprised; he lives always true and steady to himself, and whatsoever befalls him, this great artificer of both fortunes turns to advantage; he that demurs and hesitates is not yet composed; but wheresoever virtue interposes upon the main, there must be concord and consent in the parts; for all virtues are in agreement, as well as all vices are at variance. A wise man, in what condition soever he is will be still happy, for he subjects all things to himself, because he submits himself to reason, and governs his actions by council, not by passion.

He is not moved with the utmost violence of fortune, nor with the extremities of fire and sword; whereas a fool is afraid of his own shadow, and surprised at ill accidents, as if they were all levelled at him. He does nothing unwillingly, for whatever he finds necessary, he makes it his choice. He propounds to himself the certain scope and end of human life: he follows that which conduces to it, and avoids that which hinders it. He is content with his lot whatever it be, without wishing what he has not, though, of the two, he had rather abound than want. The great business of his life like that of nature, is performed without tumult or noise. He neither fears danger or provokes it, but it is his caution, not any want of courage — for captivity, wounds and chains, he only looks upon as false and lymphatic terrors. He does not pretend to go through with whatever he undertakes, but to do that well which he does. Arts are but the servants — wisdom commands — and where the matter fails it is none of the workman's fault. He is cautelous in doubtful cases, in prosperity temperate, and resolute in adversity, still making the best of every condition and improving all occasions to make them serviceable to his fate. Some accidents there are, which I confess may affect him, but not overthrow him, as bodily pains, loss of children and friends, the ruin and desolation of a man's country. One must be made of stone or iron, not to be sensible of these calamities; and, beside, it were no virtue to *bear* them, if a body did not *feel* them.

There are *three degrees of proficients* in the school of wisdom. The *first* are those that come within sight of it, but not up to it — they have learned what they ought to do, but they have not put their knowledge in practice — they are past the hazard of a relapse, but they have still the grudges of a disease, though they are out of the danger of it. By a disease I do understand an obstinacy in evil, or an ill habit, that makes us over eager upon things which are either not much to be desired, or not at all. A *second* sort are those that have subjected their appetites for a season, but are yet in fear of falling back. A *third* sort are those that are clear of many vices but not of all. They are not covetous, but perhaps they are choleric — nor lustful, but perchance ambitious; they are firm enough in some cases but weak enough in others: there are many that despise death and yet shrink at pain. There are diversities in wise men, but no inequalities — one is more affable, another more ready, a third a better speaker; but the felicity of them all is equal. It is in this as in heavenly bodies, there is a *certain state* in greatness.

In civil and domestic affairs, a wise man may stand in need of counsel, as of a physician, an advocate, a solicitor; but in greater matters, the blessing of wise men rests in the joy they take in the communication of their virtues. If there were nothing else in it, a man would apply himself to wisdom, because it settles him in a perfect tranquillity of mind.

III

THERE CAN BE NO HAPPINESS WITHOUT VIRTUE

Virtue is that perfect good which is the complement of a *happy life*; the only immortal thing that belongs to mortality — it is the knowledge both of others and itself — it is an invincible greatness of mind, not to be elevated or dejected with good or ill fortune. It is sociable and gentle, free, steady, and fearless, content within itself, full of inexhaustible delights, and it is valued for itself. One may be a good physician, a good governor, a good grammarian, without being a good man, so that all things from without are only accessories, for the seat of it is a pure and holy mind. It consists in a congruity of actions which we can never expect so long as we are distracted by our passions: not but that a man may be allowed to change color and countenance, and suffer such impressions as are properly a kind of natural force upon the body, and not under the dominion of the mind; but all this while I will have his judgment firm, and he shall act steadily and boldly, without wavering betwixt the motions of his body and those of his mind.

It is not a thing indifferent, I know, whether a man lies at ease upon a bed, or in torment upon a wheel — and yet the former may be the worse of the two if he suffer the latter with honor, and enjoy the other with infamy. It is not the *matter*, but the *virtue*, that makes the action *good or ill*; and he that is led in triumph may be yet greater than his conqueror.

When we come once to value our flesh above our honesty we are lost: and yet I would not press upon dangers, no, not so much as upon inconveniences, unless where the man and the brute come in competition; and in such a case, rather than make a forfeiture of my credit, my reason, or my faith, I would run all extremities.

They are great blessings to have tender parents, dutiful children, and to live under a just and well-ordered government. Now, would it not trouble even a virtuous man to see his children butchered before his eyes, his father made a slave, and his country overrun by a barbarous enemy? There is a great difference betwixt the simple loss of a blessing and the succeeding of a great mischief in the place of it, over and above. The loss of health is followed with sickness, and the loss of sight with blindness; but this does not hold in the loss of friends and children, where there is rather something to the contrary to supply that loss: that is to say, *virtue*, which fills the mind, and takes away the desire of what we have not. What matters it whether the water be stopped or not, so long as the fountain is safe? Is a man ever the wiser for a multitude of friends, or the more foolish for the loss of them? so neither is he the happier, nor the more miserable. Short life, grief and pain are accessions that have no effect at all upon virtue. It consists in the action and not in the things we do — in the choice itself, and not in the subject-matter of it. It is not a despicable body or condition, nor poverty, infamy or scandal, that can obscure the glories of virtue; but a man may see her through all oppositions: and he that looks diligently into the state of a wicked man will see the canker at his heart, through all the false and dazzling splendors of greatness and fortune. We shall then discover our *childishness*, in setting our hearts upon things trivial and contemptible, and in the selling of our very country and parents for a *rattle*. And what is the difference (in effect) betwixt *old men* and *children*, but that the *one* deals in *paintings* and *statues*, and the *other* in *babies*, so that we ourselves are only the more expensive fools.

If one could but see the mind of a good man, as it is illustrated with virtue; the beauty and the majesty of it, which is a dignity not so much as to be thought of without love and veneration — would not a man bless himself at the sight of such an object as at the encounter of some supernatural power — a power so miraculous that it is a kind of charm upon the souls of those that are truly affected with it. There is so wonderful a grace and authority in it that even the worst of men approve it, and set up for the reputation of being accounted virtuous themselves. They covet the fruit indeed, and the profit of wickedness; but they hate and are ashamed of the imputation of it. It is by an impression of Nature that all men have a reverence for virtue — they know it and they have a respect for it though they do not practice it — nay, for the countenance of their very *wickedness*, they miscall it *virtue*. Their injuries they call *benefits*, and expect a man should thank them for doing him a mischief — they cover their most notorious iniquities with a pretext of justice.

He that robs upon the highway had rather find his booty than force it; ask any of them that live upon rapine, fraud, oppression, if they had not rather enjoy a fortune honestly gotten, and their consciences will not suffer them to deny it. Men are vicious only for the proof of villainy; for at the same time that they commit it they condemn it; nay, so powerful is virtue, and so gracious is Providence, that every man has a light set up within him for a guide, which we do, all of us, both see and acknowledge, though we do not pursue it. This it is that makes the prisoner upon the torture happier than the executioner, and sickness better than health, if we bear it without yielding or repining — this it is that overcomes ill-fortune and moderates good — for it marches betwixt the one and the other, with an equal contempt for both. It turns (like fire) all things into itself, our actions and our friendships are tinctured with it, and whatever it touches becomes amiable.

That which is frail and mortal rises and falls, grows, wastes, and varies from itself; but the state of things divine is always the same; and so is virtue, let the matter be what it will. It is never the worse for the difficulty of the action, nor the better for the easiness of it. It is the same in a rich man as in a poor; in a sickly man as in a sound; in a strong as in a weak; the virtue of the besieged is as great as that of the besiegers. There are some virtues, I confess, which a good man cannot be without, and yet he had rather have no occasion to employ them. If there were any difference, I should prefer the virtues of patience before those of pleasure; for it is braver to break through difficulties than to temper our delights. But though the subject of virtue may possibly be against nature, as to be burnt or wounded, yet the virtue itself of *an invincible patience* is according to nature. We may seem, perhaps, to promise more than human nature is able to perform; but we speak with a respect to the mind, and not to the body.

If a man does not live up to his own rules, it is something yet to have virtuous meditations and good purposes, even without acting; it is generous, the very adventure of being good, and the bare proposal of an eminent course of life, though beyond the force of human frailty to accomplish. There is something of honor yet in the miscarriage; nay, in the naked contemplation of it. I would receive my own death with as little trouble as I would hear of another man's; I would bear the same mind whether I be rich or poor, whether I get or lose in the world; what I have, I will neither sordidly spare, or prodigally squander away, and I will reckon upon benefits well-placed as the fairest part of my possession: not valuing them by number or weight, but by the profit and esteem of the receiver; accounting myself never the poorer for that which I give to a worthy person. What I do shall be done for conscience, not ostentation. I will eat and drink, not to gratify my palate, or only to fill and empty, but to satisfy nature: I will be cheerful to my friends, mild and placable to my enemies: I will prevent an honest request if I can foresee it, and I will grant it without asking: I will look upon the whole world as my country, and upon the gods, both as the witnesses and the judges of my words and deeds. I will live and die with this testimony, that I loved good studies, and a good conscience; that I never invaded another man's liberty; and that I preserved my own. I will govern my life and my thoughts as if the whole world were to see the one, and to read the other; for "what does it signify to make anything a secret to my neighbor, when to God (who is the searcher of our hearts) all our privacies are open?"

Virtue is divided into two parts, *contemplation* and *action*. The one is delivered by institution, the other by admonition: one part of virtue consists in discipline, the other in exercise: for we must first learn, and then practice. The sooner we begin to apply ourselves to it, and the more haste we make, the longer shall we enjoy the comforts of a rectified mind; nay, we have the fruition of it in the very act of forming it: but it is another sort of delight, I must confess, that arises from a contemplation of a soul which is advanced into the possession of wisdom and virtue. If it was so great a comfort to us to pass from the subjection of our childhood into a state of liberty and business, how much greater will it be when we come to cast off the boyish levity of our minds, and range ourselves among the philosophers? We are past our minority, it is true, but not our indiscretions; and, which is yet worse, we have the authority of seniors, and the weaknesses of children, (I might have said of infants, for every little thing frights the one, and every trivial fancy the other.) Whoever studies this point well will find that many things are the less to be feared the more terrible they appear. To think anything good that is not honest, were to reproach Providence; for good men suffer many inconveniences; but virtue, like the sun, goes on still with her work, let the air be never so cloudy, and finishes her course, extinguishing likewise all other splendors and oppositions; insomuch that calamity is no more to a virtuous mind, than a shower into the sea. That which is right, is not to be valued by *quantity*, *number*, or *time*; a life of a day may be as honest as a life of a hundred years: but yet virtue in one man may have a larger field to show itself in than in another. One man, perhaps, may be in a station to administer unto cities and kingdoms; to contrive good laws, create friendships, and do beneficial offices to mankind.

For virtue is open to all; as well to servants and exiles, as to princes: it is profitable to the world and to itself, at all distances and in all conditions; and there is no difficulty can excuse a man from the exercise of it; and it is only to be found in a wise man, though there may be some faint resemblances of it in the common people. The Stoics hold all virtues to be equal; but yet there is great variety in the matter they have to work upon, according as it is larger or narrower, illustrious or less noble, of more or less extent; as all good men are equal, that is to say, as they are good; but yet one may be young, another old; one may be rich, another poor; one eminent and powerful, another unknown and obscure. There are many things which have little or no grace in themselves, and are yet glorious and remarkable by virtue. Nothing can be good which gives neither greatness nor security to the mind; but, on the contrary, infects it with insolence, arrogance, and tumor: nor does virtue dwell upon the tip of the tongue, but in the temple of a purified heart. He that depends upon any other good becomes covetous of life, and what belongs to it; which exposes a man to appetites that are vast, unlimited, and intolerable. Virtue is free and indefatigable, and accompanied with concord and gracefulness; whereas pleasure is mean, servile, transitory, tiresome, and sickly and scarce outlives the tasting of it: it is the good of the belly, and not of the man; and only the felicity of brutes. Who does not know that fools enjoy their pleasures, and that there is great variety in the entertainments of wickedness? Nay, the mind itself has its variety of perverse pleasures as well as the body: as insolence, self-conceit, pride, garrulity, laziness, and the abusive wit of turning everything into *ridicule*, whereas virtue weighs all this, and corrects it. It is the knowledge both of others and of itself; it is to be learned from itself; and the very will itself may be taught; which will cannot be right, unless the whole habit of the mind be right from whence the will comes. It is by the impulse of virtue that we love virtue, so that the very way to virtue, lies by virtue, which takes in also, at a view, the laws of human life.

Neither are we to value ourselves upon a day, or an hour, or any one action, but upon the whole habit of the mind. Some men do one thing bravely, but not another; they will shrink at infamy, and bear up against poverty: in this case, we commend the fact, and despise the man. The soul is never in the right place until it be delivered from the cares of human affairs; we must labor and climb the hill, if we will arrive at virtue, whose seat is upon the top of it. He that masters avarice, and is truly good, stands firm against ambition; he looks upon his last hour not as a punishment, but as the equity of a common fate; he that subdues his carnal lusts shall easily keep himself untainted with any other: so that reason does not encounter this or that vice by itself, but beats down all at a blow. What does he care for ignominy that only values himself upon conscience, and not opinion? Socrates looked a scandalous death in the face with the same constancy that he had before practiced towards the thirty tyrants: his virtue consecrated the very dungeon: as Cato's repulse was Cato's honor, and the reproach of the government. He that is wise will take delight even in an ill opinion that is well gotten; it is ostentation, not virtue, when a man will have his good deeds published; and it is not enough to be just where there is honor to be gotten, but to continue so, in defiance of infamy and danger.

But virtue cannot lie hid, for the time will come that shall raise it again (even after it is buried) and deliver it from the malignity of the age that oppressed it: immortal glory is the shadow of it, and keeps it company whether we will or not; but sometimes the shadow goes before the substance, and other whiles it follows it; and the later it comes, the larger it is, when even envy itself shall have given way to it. It was a long time that Democritus was taken for a madman, and before Socrates had any esteem in the world. How long was it before Cato could be understood? Nay, he was affronted, contemned, and rejected; and the people never knew the value of him until they had lost him: the integrity and courage of mad Rutilius had been forgotten but for his sufferings. I speak of those that fortune has made famous for their persecutions: and there are others also that the world never took notice of until they were dead; as Epicurus and Metrodorus, that were almost wholly unknown, even in the place where they lived. Now, as the body is to be kept in upon the down-hill, and forced upwards, so there are some virtues that require the rein and others the spur. In *liberality, temperance, gentleness* of nature, we are to check ourselves for fear of falling; but in *patience, resolutions*, and *perseverance*, where we are to mount the hill, we stand in need of encouragement. Upon this division of the matter, I had rather steer the smoother course than pass through the experiments of sweat and blood: I know it is my duty to be content in all conditions; but yet, if it were at my election, I would choose the fairest. When a man comes once to stand in need of fortune, his life is anxious, suspicious, timorous, dependent upon every moment, and in fear of all accidents. How can that man resign himself to God, or bear his lot, whatever it be, without murmuring, and cheerfully submit to Providence, that shrinks at every motion of pleasure or pain? It is virtue alone that raises us above griefs, hopes, fears and chances; and makes us not only patient, but willing, as knowing that whatever we suffer is according to the decree of Heaven. He that is overcome with pleasure, (so contemptible and weak an enemy) what will become of him when he comes to grapple with dangers, necessities, torments, death, and the dissolution of nature itself? Wealth, honor, and favor, may come upon a man by chance; nay, they may be cast upon him without so much as looking after them: but virtue is the work of industry and labor; and certainly it is worth the while to purchase that good which brings all others along with it. A good man is happy within himself, and independent upon fortune: kind to his friend, temperate to his enemy, religiously just, indefatigably laborious; and he discharges all duties with a constancy and congruity of actions.

IV

PHILOSOPHY IS THE GUIDE OF LIFE

If it be true, that the *understanding* and the *will* are the *two eminent faculties of the reasonable soul*, it follows necessarily, that *wisdom* and *virtue*, (which are the best improvements of these two faculties,) must be the perfection also of our *reasonable being*; and consequently, *the undeniable foundation of a happy life*. There is not any duty to which Providence has not annexed a blessing; nor any institution of Heaven which, even in this life, we may not be the better for; not any temptation, either of fortune or of appetite, that is not subject to our reason; nor any passion or affliction for which virtue has not provided a remedy. So that it is our own fault if we either fear or hope for anything; which two affections are the root of all our miseries. From this general prospect of the *foundation* of our *tranquillity*, we shall pass by degrees to a particular consideration of the *means* by which it may be *procured*, and of the *impediments* that *obstruct* it; beginning with that *philosophy* which principally regards our manners, and instructs us in the measures of a virtuous and quiet life.

Philosophy is divided into *moral, natural,* and *rational*: the *first* concerns our *manners*; the *second* searches the works of *Nature*; and the *third* furnishes us with propriety of *words* and *arguments*, and the faculty of *distinguishing*, that we may not be imposed upon with tricks and fallacies. The *causes* of things fall under *natural philosophy, arguments* under *rational*, and *actions* under *moral*. *Moral philosophy* is again divided into matter of *justice*, which arises from the estimation of things and of men; and into *affections* and *actions*; and a failing in any one of these, disorders all the rest: for what does it profit us to know the true value of things, if we be transported by our passion? or to master our appetites without understanding the *when*, the *what*, the *how*, and other circumstances of our proceedings? For it is one thing to know the rate and dignity of things, and another to know the little nicks and springs of acting. *Natural philosophy* is conversant about things *corporeal* and *incorporeal*; the disquisition of *causes* and *effects*, and the contemplation of the *cause of causes*. *Rational philosophy* is divided into *logic* and *rhetoric*; the one looks after *words*, *sense*, and *order*; the other treats barely of *words*, and the *significations* of them. Socrates places all *philosophy* in *morals*; and *wisdom* in the distinguishing of *good* and *evil*. It is the art and law of life, and it teaches us what to do in all cases, and, like good marksmen, to hit the white at any distance. The force of it is incredible; for it gives us in the weakness of a man the security of a *spirit*: in sickness it is as good as a remedy to us; for whatsoever eases the mind is profitable also to the body. The *physician* may prescribe diet and exercise, and accommodate his rule and medicine to the disease, but it is *philosophy* that must bring us to a contempt of death, which is the remedy of all diseases. In poverty it gives us riches, or such a state of mind as makes them superfluous to us. It arms us against all difficulties: one man is pressed with death, another with poverty; some with envy, others are offended at Providence, and unsatisfied with the condition of mankind: but *philosophy* prompts us to relieve the prisoner, the infirm, the necessitous, the condemned; to show the ignorant their errors, and rectify their affections. It makes us inspect and govern our manners; it rouses us where we are faint and drowsy: it binds up what is loose, and humbles in us that which is contumacious: it delivers the mind from the bondage of the body, and raises it up to the contemplation of its divine original. Honors, monuments, and all the works of vanity and ambition are demolished and destroyed by time; but the reputation of wisdom is venerable to posterity, and those that were envied or neglected in their lives are adored in their memories, and exempted from the very laws of created nature, which has set bounds to all other things. The very shadow of *glory* carries a man of *honor* upon all dangers, to the contempt of fire and sword; and it were a shame if *right reason* should not inspire as generous resolutions into a man of *virtue*.

Neither is *philosophy* only profitable to the public, but one wise man helps another, even in the exercise of the virtues; and the one has need of the other, both for conversation and counsel; for they kindle a mutual emulation in good offices. We are not so perfect yet, but that many new things remain still to be found out, which will give us the reciprocal advantages of instructing one another: for as one wicked man is contagious to another, and the more vices are mingled, the worse it is, so is it on the contrary with good men and their virtues. As men of letters are the most useful and excellent of friends, so are they the best of subjects; as being better judges of the blessings they enjoy under a well-ordered government, and of what they owe to the magistrate for their freedom and protection. They are men of sobriety and learning, and free from boasting and insolence; they reprove the vice without reproaching the person; for they have learned to be without either pomp or envy. That which we see in high mountains, we find in *philosophers*; they seem taller near at hand than at a distance. They are raised above other men, but their greatness is substantial. Nor do they stand upon tiptoe, that they may seem higher than they are, but, content with their own stature, they reckon themselves tall enough when fortune cannot reach them. Their laws are short, and yet comprehensive too, for they bind all.

It is the bounty of *nature* that we *live*; but of *philosophy* that we *live well*, which is in truth a greater benefit than life itself. Not but that *philosophy* is also the gift of Heaven, so far as to the faculty, but not to the science; for that must be the business of industry. No man is born wise; but wisdom and virtue require a tutor, though we can easily learn to be vicious without a master. It is *philosophy* that gives us a veneration for God, a charity for our neighbor, that teaches us our duty to Heaven, and exhorts us to an agreement one with another; it unmasks things that are terrible to us, assuages our lusts, refutes our errors, restrains our luxury, reproves our avarice, and works strangely upon tender natures. I could never hear Attalus (says Seneca) upon the vices of the age and the errors of life, without a compassion for mankind; and in his discourses upon poverty, there was something methought that was more than human. "More than we use," says he, "is more than we need, and only a burden to the bearer." That saying of his put me out of countenance at the superfluities of my own fortune. And so in his invectives against vain pleasures, he did at such a rate advance the felicities of a sober table, a pure mind, and a chaste body that a man could not hear him without a love for continence and moderation. Upon these lectures of his, I denied myself, for a while after, certain delicacies that I had formerly used: but in a short time I fell to them again, though so sparingly, that the proportion came little short of a total abstinence.

Now, to show you (says our author) how much earnester my entrance upon philosophy was than my progress, my tutor Sotion gave me a wonderful kindness for Pythagoras, and after him for Sextius: the former forbore shedding of blood upon his *metempsychosis:* and put men in fear of it, lest they should offer violence to the souls of some of their departed friends or relations. "Whether," says he, "there be a transmigration or not; if it be true, there is no hurt; if false, there is frugality: and nothing is gotten by cruelty neither, but the cozening a wolf, perhaps, or a vulture, of a supper."

Now, Sextius abstained upon another account, which was, that he would not have men inured to hardness of heart by the laceration and tormenting of living creatures; beside, "that Nature had sufficiently provided for the sustenance of mankind without blood." This wrought upon me so far that I gave over eating of flesh, and in one year I made it not only easy to me but pleasant; my mind methought was more at liberty, (and I am still of the same opinion,) but I gave it over nevertheless; and the reason was this: it was imputed as a superstition to the Jews, the forbearance of some sorts of flesh, and my father brought me back again to my old custom, that I might not be thought tainted with their superstition. Nay, and I had much ado to prevail upon myself to suffer it too. I make use of this instance to show the aptness of youth to take good impressions, if there be a friend at hand to press them. Philosophers are the tutors of mankind; if they have found out remedies for the mind, it must be our part to employ them. I cannot think of Cato, Lelius, Socrates, Plato, without veneration: their very names are sacred to me. Philosophy is the health of the mind; let us look to that health first, and in the second place to that of the body, which may be had upon easier terms; for a strong arm, a robust constitution, or the skill of procuring this, is not a philosopher's business. He does some things as a *wise man,* and other things as he is a *man*; and he may have strength of body as well as of mind; but if he runs, or casts the sledge, it were injurious to ascribe that to his wisdom which is common to the greatest of fools. He studies rather to fill his mind than his coffers; and he knows that gold and silver were mingled with dirt, until avarice or ambition parted them. His life is ordinate, fearless, equal, secure; he stands firm in all extremities, and bears the lot of his humanity with a divine temper. There is a great difference betwixt the splendor of philosophy and of fortune; the one shines with an original light, the other with a borrowed one; beside that it makes us happy and immortal: for learning shall outlive palaces and monuments. The house of a wise man is safe, though narrow; there is neither noise nor furniture in it, no porter at the door, nor anything that is either vendible or mercenary, nor any business of fortune, for she has nothing to do where she has nothing to look after. This is the way to Heaven which Nature has chalked out, and it is both secure and pleasant; there needs no train of servants, no pomp or equipage, to make good our passage; no money or letters of credit, for expenses upon the voyage; but the graces of an honest mind will serve us upon the way, and make us happy at our journey's end.

To tell you my opinion now of the *liberal sciences*; I have no great esteem for any thing that terminates in profit or money; and yet I shall allow them to be so far beneficial, as they only *prepare* the understanding without *detaining* it. They are but the rudiments of wisdom, and only then to be learned when the mind is capable of nothing better, and the knowledge of them is better worth the keeping than the acquiring. They do not so much as pretend to the making of us virtuous, but only to give us an aptitude of disposition to be so. The *grammarian's* business lies in a *syntax* of speech; or if he proceed to *history*, or the measuring of a *verse*, he is at the end of his line; but what signifies a congruity of periods, the computing of syllables, or the modifying of numbers, to the taming of our passions, or the repressing of our lusts? The *philosopher* proves the body of the sun to be large, but for the true dimensions of it we must ask the *mathematician*: *geometry* and *music*, if they do not teach us to master our hopes and fears, all the rest is to little purpose. What does it concern us which was the elder of the two, Homer or Hesiod? or which was the taller, Helen or Hecuba? We take a great deal of pains to trace Ulysses in his wanderings, but were it not time as well spent to look to ourselves that we may not wander at all? Are not we ourselves tossed with tempestuous passions? and both *assaulted* by terrible *monsters* on the one hand, and *tempted* by *syrens* on the other? Teach me my duty to my country, to my father, to my wife, to mankind. What is it to me whether Penelope was *honest* or not? teach me to know how to be so myself, and to live according to that knowledge. What am I the better for putting so many parts together in *music*, and raising a harmony out of so many different tones? teach me to tune my affections, and to hold constant to myself. *Geometry* teaches me the art of *measuring acres*; teach me to *measure my appetites*, and to know when I have enough; teach me to divide with my brother, and to rejoice in the prosperity of my neighbor. You teach me how I may hold my own, and keep my estate; but I would rather learn how I may lose it all, and yet be contented. "It is hard," you will say, "for a man to be forced from the fortune of his family." This estate, it is true, was my *father's*; but whose was it in the time of my *grandfather*? I do not only say, what *man's* was it? but what *nation's*? The *astrologer* tells me of Saturn and Mars in *opposition*; but I say, let them be as they will, their courses and their positions are ordered them by an unchangeable decree of fate. Either they produce and point out the effects of all things, or else they signify them; if the former, what are we the better for the knowledge of that which must of necessity come to pass? If the latter, what does it avail us to foresee what we cannot avoid? So that whether we know or not know, the event will still be the same.

He that designs the institution of human life should not be over-curious of his words; it does not stand with his dignity to be solicitous about sounds and syllables, and to debase the mind of man with trivial things; placing wisdom in matters that are rather difficult than great. If it be *eloquent*, it is his *good fortune*, not his *business*. Subtle disputations are only the sport of wits, that play upon the catch, and are fitter to be contemned than resolved. Were not I a madman to sit wrangling about words, and putting of nice and impertinent questions, when the enemy has already made the breach, the town fired over my head, and the mine ready to play that shall blow me up into the air? were this a time for fooleries? Let me rather fortify myself against death and inevitable necessities; let me understand that the good of life does not consist in the length or space, but in the use of it. When I go to *sleep*, who knows whether I shall ever *wake* again? and when I *wake*, whether ever I shall *sleep* again? When I go *abroad*, whether ever I shall come *home* again? and when I *return*, whether ever I shall go *abroad* again? It is not at sea only that life and death are within a few inches one of another; but they are as near everywhere else too, only we do not take so much notice of it. What have we to do with frivolous and captious questions, and impertinent niceties? Let us rather study how to deliver ourselves from sadness, fear, and the burden of all our secret lusts: let us pass over all our most solemn levities, and make haste to a good life, which is a thing that presses us. Shall a man that goes for a midwife, stand gaping upon a post to see *what play to-day*? or, when his house is on fire, stay the curling of a periwig before he calls for help? Our houses are on fire, our country invaded, our goods taken away, our children in danger; and, I might add to these, the calamities of earthquakes, shipwrecks, and whatever else is most terrible. Is this a time for us now to be playing fast and loose with idle questions, which are in effect so many unprofitable riddles? Our duty is the cure of the mind rather than the delight of it; but we have only the words of wisdom without the works; and turn philosophy into a pleasure that was given for a remedy. What can be more ridiculous than for a man to *neglect* his *manners* and *compose* his *style*? We are sick and ulcerous, and must be lanced and scarified, and every man has as much business within himself as a physician in a common pestilence. "Misfortunes," in fine, "cannot be avoided; but they may be sweetened, if not overcome; and our lives may be made happy by philosophy."

V

THE FORCE OF PRECEPTS

There seems to be so near an affinity betwixt *wisdom, philosophy*, and *good counsels*, that it is rather matter of curiosity than of profit to divide them; *philosophy*, being only a *limited wisdom*; and *good counsels a communication of that wisdom*, for the good of *others*, as well as of *ourselves*; and to *posterity*, as well as to the *present*. The *wisdom* of the *ancients*, as to the government of life, was no more than certain precepts, what to do and what not: and men were much better in that simplicity; for as they came to be more *learned*, they grew less careful of being *good*. That *plain* and *open virtue* is now turned into a *dark* and *intricate science*; and we are taught to *dispute* rather than to *live*. So long as wickedness was simple, simple remedies also were sufficient against it; but now it has taken root, and spread, we must make use of stronger.

There are some dispositions that embrace good things as soon as they hear them; but they will still need quickening by admonition and precept. We are rash and forward in some cases, and dull in others; and there is no repressing of the one humor, or raising of the other, but by removing the causes of them; which are (in one word) *false admiration* and *false fear*.

Every man knows his duty to his country, to his friends, to his guests; and yet when he is called upon to draw his sword for the one, or to labor for the other, he finds himself distracted betwixt his apprehensions and his delights: he knows well enough the injury he does his wife in the keeping of a wench, and yet his lust overrules him: so that it is not enough to give good advice, unless we can take away that which hinders the benefit of it. If a man does what he ought to do, he will never do it constantly or equally, without knowing why he does it: and if it be only chance or custom, he that does well by chance, may do ill so too. And farther, a precept may direct us what we *ought* to do, and yet fall short in the manner of doing it: an expensive entertainment may, in one case be extravagance or gluttony, and yet a point of honor and discretion in another. Tiberius Caesar had a huge *mullet* presented him, which he sent to the market to be sold: "and now," says he, "my masters," to some company with him, "you shall see that either Apicius or Octavius will be the chapman for this fish." Octavius beat the price, and gave about thirty pounds sterling[1] for it. Now, there was a great difference between Octavius, that bought it for his luxury, and the *other* that purchased it for a *compliment* to Tiberius. Precepts are idle, if we be not first taught what opinion we are to have of the matter in question; whether it be *poverty*, *riches*, *disgrace*, *sickness*, *banishment*, etc. Let us therefore examine them one by one; not what they are *called*, but what in truth they *are*. And so for the *virtues*; it is to no purpose to set a high esteem upon prudence, *fortitude*, *temperance*, *justice*, if we do not first know *what virtue is*; whether *one* or *more*; or if he that has *one*, has *all*; or *how they differ*.

Precepts are of great weight; and a few useful ones at hand do more toward a happy life than whole volumes or cautions, that

---

1   A comparison of the value of money then and now is completely meaningless. Because, even if we are able to calculate this 'value', they could not buy the goods of this time with their money and we cannot buy the goods of that time with our money.

we know not where to find. These salutary precepts should be our daily meditation, for they are the rules by which we ought to square our lives. When they are contracted into *sentences*, they strike the *affections*: whereas *admonition* is only *blowing* of the *coal*; it moves the vigor of the mind, and excites virtue: we have the thing already, but we know not where it lies. It is by precept that the understanding is nourished and augmented: the offices of prudence and justice are guided by them, and they lead us to the execution of our duties. A *precept* delivered in *verse* has a much greater effect than in *prose*: and those very people that never think they have enough, let them but hear a sharp sentence against *avarice*, how will they clap and admire it, and bid open defiance to money? So soon as we find the affections struck, we must follow the blow; not with *syllogisms* or quirks of *wit*; but with *plain* and *weighty reason* and we must do it with *kindness* too, and *respect* for "there goes a blessing along with counsels and discourses that are bent wholly upon the good of the hearer:" and those are still the most efficacious that take reason along with them; and tell us as well why we are to do this or that, as *what* we are to do: for some understandings are weak, and need an instructor to expound to them what is good and what is evil. It is a great virtue to *love*, to *give*, and to *follow good counsel*; if it does not *lead* us to honesty, it does at least *prompt* us to it. As several parts make up but one harmony, and the most agreeable music arises from discords; so should a wise man gather many acts, many precepts, and the examples of many arts, to inform his own life. Our forefathers have left us in charge to avoid three things; *hatred*, *envy*, and *contempt*; now, it is hard to avoid envy and not incur *contempt*; for in taking too much care not to usurp upon others, we become many times liable to be trampled upon ourselves. Some people are afraid of others, because it is possible that others may be afraid of them: but let us secure ourselves upon all hands; for *flattery* is as dangerous as *contempt*. It is not to say, in case of admonition, I knew this before, for we know many things, but we do not think of them; so that it is the part of a *monitor*, not so much to *teach* as to *mind* us of our duties. Sometimes a man oversees that which lies just under his nose; otherwhile he is careless, or *pretends* not to see it: we do all know that friendship is sacred, and yet we violate it; and the greatest libertine expects that his own wife should be honest.

Good counsel is the most needful service that we can do to mankind; and if we give it to *many*, it will be sure to profit *some*: for of many trials, some or other will undoubtedly succeed. He that places a man in the possession of himself does a great thing; for wisdom does not show itself so much in precept as in life; in a firmness of mind and a mastery of appetite: it teaches us to *do* as well as to *talk*: and to make our words and actions all of a color. If that fruit be pleasantest which we gather from a tree of our own planting, how much greater delight shall we take in the growth and increase of good manners of our own forming! It is an eminent mark of wisdom for a man to be always like himself. You shall have some that keep a thrifty table, and lavish out upon building; profuse upon themselves, and forbid to others; niggardly at home, and lavish abroad. This diversity is vicious, and the effect of a dissatisfied and uneasy mind; whereas every wise man lives by rule. This disagreement of purposes arises from hence, either that we do not propound to ourselves what we would be at; or if we do, that we do not pursue it, but pass from one thing to another; and we do not only *change* neither but return to the very thing which we had both quitted and condemned.

In all our undertakings, let us first examine our own strength; the enterprise next; and, thirdly, the persons with whom we have to do. The first point is most important; for we are apt to overvalue ourselves, and reckon that we can do more than indeed we can. One man sets up for a speaker, and is out as soon as he opens his mouth; another overcharges his estate, perhaps, or his body: a bashful man is not fit for public business: some again are too stiff and peremptory for the court: many people are apt to fly out in their anger, nay, and in a frolic too; if any sharp thing fall in their way, they will rather venture a neck than lose a jest. These people had better be quiet in the world than busy. Let him that is naturally choleric and impatient avoid all provocations, and those affairs also that multiply and draw on more; and those also from which there is no retreat. When we may come off at pleasure, and fairly hope to bring our matters to a period, it is well enough. If it so happen that a man be tied up to business, which he can neither loosen nor break off, let him imagine those shackles upon his mind to be irons upon his legs: they are troublesome at first; but when there is no remedy but patience, custom makes them easy to us, and necessity gives us courage. We are all slaves to fortune: some only in loose and golden chains, others in strait ones, and coarser: nay, and *they that bind us are slaves too themselves*; some to honor, others to wealth; some to offices, and others to contempt; some to their superiors, others to themselves: nay, life itself is a servitude: let us make the best of it then, and with our philosophy mend our fortune. Difficulties may be softened, and heavy burdens disposed of to our ease. Let us covet nothing out of our reach, but content ourselves with things hopeful and at hand; and without envying the advantages of others; for greatness stands upon a craggy precipice, and it is much safer and quieter living upon a level. How many great men are forced to keep their station upon mere necessity; because they find there is no coming down from it but headlong? These men should do well to fortify themselves against ill consequences by such virtues and meditations as may make them less solicitous for the future. The surest expedient in this case is to bound our desires, and to leave nothing to fortune which we may keep in our own power. Neither will this course wholly compose us, but it shows us at worst the end of our troubles.

It is but a main point to take care that we propose nothing but what is hopeful and honest. For it will be equally troublesome to us, either not to succeed, or to be ashamed of the success. Wherefore let us be sure not to admit any ill design into our heart; that we may lift up pure hands to heaven and ask nothing which another shall be a loser by. Let us pray for a good mind, which is a wish to no man's injury. I will remember always that I am a man, and then consider, that if I am *happy*, it will not last *always*; if *unhappy*, I may be *other* if I please. I will carry my life in my hand, and deliver it up readily when it shall be called for. I will have a care of being a slave to myself; for it is a perpetual, a shameful, and the heaviest of all servitudes: and this may be done by moderate desires. I will say to myself, "What is it that I labor, sweat, and solicit for, when it is but very little that I want, and it will not be long that I will need any thing?" He that would make a trial of the firmness of his mind, let him set certain days apart for the practice of his virtues. Let him mortify himself with fasting, coarse clothes, and hard lodging; and then say to himself, "Is this the thing now that I was afraid of?" In a state of security, a man may thus prepare himself against hazards, and in plenty fortify himself against want. If you will have a man resolute when he comes to the push, train him up to it beforehand. The soldier does duty in peace, that he may be in breath when he comes to battle. How many great and wise men have made experiment of their moderation by a practice of abstinence, to the highest degree of hunger and thirst; and convinced themselves that a man may fill his belly without being beholden to fortune; which never denies any of us wherewith to satisfy our necessities, though she be never so angry! It is as easy to *suffer* it *always* as to *try* it *once*; and it is no more than thousands of servants and poor people do every day in their lives. He that would live happily, must neither trust to good fortune nor submit to bad: he must stand upon his guard against all assaults; he must stick to himself, without any dependence upon other people. Where the mind is tinctured with philosophy, there is no place for grief, anxiety, or superfluous vexations. It is prepossessed with virtue to the neglect of fortune, which brings us to a degree of security not to be disturbed. It is easier to give counsel than to take it; and a common thing for one choleric man to condemn another. We may be sometimes earnest in advising, but not violent or tedious. Few words, with gentleness and efficacy, are best: the misery is, that the wise do not need counsel, and fools will not take it. A good man, it is true, delights in it; and it is a mark of folly and ill-nature to hate reproof.

To a friend I would be always frank and plain; and rather fail in the success than be wanting in the matter of faith and trust. There are some precepts that serve in common both to the rich and poor, but they are too general; as "Cure your avarice, and the work is done." It is one thing not to desire money, and another thing not to understand how to use it. In the choice of the persons we have to do withal, we should see that they be worth our while; in the choice of our business, we are to consult nature, and follow our inclinations. He that gives sober advice to a witty droll must look to have every thing turned into ridicule. "As if you philosophers," says Marcellinus, "did not love your whores and your guts as well as other people:" and then he tells you of such and such that were taken in the manner. We are all sick, I must confess, and it is not for sick men to play the physicians; but it is yet lawful for a man in an hospital to discourse of the common condition and distempers of the place. He that should pretend to teach a madman how to speak, walk, and behave himself, were not he the most mad man of the two? He that directs the pilot, makes him move the helm, order the sails so or so, and makes the best of a scant wind, after this or that manner. And so should we do in our counsels.

Do not tell me what a man should do in health or poverty, but show me the way to be either sound or rich. Teach me to master my vices: for it is to no purpose, so long as I am under their government, to tell me what I must do when I am clear of it. In case of an avarice a little eased, a luxury moderated, a temerity restrained, a sluggish humor quickened; precepts will then help us forward, and tutor us how to behave ourselves. It is the first and the main tie of a soldier his military oath, which is an engagement upon him both of religion and honor. In like manner, he that pretends to a happy life must first lay a foundation of virtue, as a bond upon him, to live and die true to that cause. We do not find felicity in the veins of the earth where we dig for gold, nor in the bottom of the sea where we fish for pearls, but in a pure and untainted mind, which, if it were not holy, were not fit to entertain the Deity. "He that would be truly happy, must think his own lot best, and so live with men, as considering that God sees him, and so speak to God as if men heard him."

VI

NO FELICITY LIKE PEACE OF CONSCIENCE

"A good conscience is the testimony of a good life, and the reward of it." This is it that fortifies the mind against fortune, when a man has gotten the mastery of his passions; placed his treasure and security within himself; learned to be content with his condition; and that death is no evil in itself, but only the end of man. He that has dedicated his mind to virtue, and to the good of human society, whereof he is a member, has consummated all that is either profitable or necessary for him to know or to do toward the establishment of his peace. Every man has a judge and a witness within himself of all the good and ill that he does, which inspires us with great thoughts, and administers to us wholesome counsels. We have a veneration for all the works of Nature, the heads of rivers, and the springs of medicinal waters; the horrors of groves and of caves strike us with an impression of religion and worship. To see a man fearless in dangers, untainted with lusts, happy in adversity, composed in a tumult, and laughing at all those things which are generally either coveted or feared; all men must acknowledge that this can be nothing else but a beam of divinity that influences a mortal body. And this is it that carries us to the disquisition of things divine and human; what the state of the world was before the distribution of the first matter into parts; what power it was that drew order out of that confusion, and gave laws both to the whole, and to every particle thereof; what that space is beyond the world; and whence proceed the several operations of Nature.

Shall any man see the glory and order of the universe; so many scattered parts and qualities wrought into one mass; such a medley of things, which are yet distinguished: the world enlightened, and the disorders of it so wonderfully regulated; and shall he not consider the Author and Disposer of all this; and whither we ourselves shall go, when our souls shall be delivered from the slavery of our flesh? The whole creation we see conforms to the dictates of Providence, and follows God both as a governor and as a guide. A great, a good, and a right mind, is a kind of divinity lodged in flesh, and may be the blessing of a slave as well as of a prince; it came from heaven, and to heaven it must return; and it is a kind of heavenly felicity, which a pure and virtuous mind enjoys, in some degree, even upon earth: whereas temples of honor are but empty names, which, probably, owe their beginning either to ambition or to violence.

I am strangely transported with the thoughts of eternity; nay, with the belief of it; for I have a profound veneration for the opinions of great men, especially when they promise things so much to my satisfaction: for they do promise them, though they do not prove them. In the question of the immortality of the soul, it goes very far with me, a general consent to the opinion of a future reward and punishment; which meditation raises me to the contempt of this life, in hopes of a better. But still, though we know that we have a soul; yet what the soul is, how, and from whence, we are utterly ignorant: this only we understand, that all the good and ill we do is under the dominion of the mind; that a clear conscience states us in an inviolable peace; and that the greatest blessing in Nature is that which every honest man may bestow upon himself. The body is but the clog and prisoner of the mind; tossed up and down, and persecuted with punishments, violences, and diseases; but the mind itself is sacred and eternal, and exempt from the danger of all actual impression.

Provided that we look to our consciences, no matter for opinion: let me deserve well, though I hear ill. The common people take stomach and audacity for the marks of magnanimity and honor; and if a man be soft and modest, they look upon him as an easy fop; but when they come once to observe the dignity of his mind in the equality and firmness of his actions; and that his external quiet is founded upon an internal peace, the very same people who have him in esteem and admiration; for there is no man but approves of virtue, though but few pursue it; we see where it is, but we dare not venture to come at it: and the reason is, we overvalue that which we must quit to obtain it.

A good conscience fears no witnesses, but a guilty conscience is solicitous even of solitude. If we do nothing but what is honest, let all the world know it; but if otherwise, what does it signify to have nobody else know it, so long as I know it myself? Miserable is he that slights that witness! Wickedness, it is true, may escape the law, but not the conscience; for a private conviction is the first and the greatest punishment to offenders; so that sin plagues itself; and the fear of vengeance pursues even those that escape the stroke of it. It were ill for good men that iniquity may so easily evade the law, the judge, and the execution, if Nature had not set up torments and gibbets in the consciences of transgressors. He that is guilty lives in perpetual terror; and while he expects to be punished, he punishes himself; and whosoever deserves it expects it. What if he be not detected? he is still in apprehension yet that he may be so. His sleeps are painful, and never secure; and he cannot speak of another man's wickedness without thinking of his own, whereas a good conscience is a continual feast.

Those are the only certain and profitable delights, which arise from the consciousness of a well-acted life; no matter for noise abroad, so long as we are quiet within: but if our passions be seditious, that is enough to keep us waking without any other tumult. It is not the posture of the body, or the composure of the bed, that will give rest to an uneasy mind: there is an impatient sloth that may be roused by action, and the vices of laziness must be cured by business. True happiness is not to be found in excesses of wine, or of women, or in the largest prodigalities of fortune; what she has given to me, she may take away, but she shall not tear it from me; and, so long as it does not grow to me, I can part with it without pain. He that would perfectly know himself, let him set aside his money, his fortune, his dignity, and examine himself naked, without being put to learn from others the knowledge of himself.

It is dangerous for a man too suddenly, or too easily, to believe himself. Wherefore let us examine, observe, and inspect our own hearts, for we ourselves are our own greatest flatterers: we should every night call ourselves to account, "What infirmity have I mastered to-day? what passion opposed? what temptation resisted? what virtue acquired?" Our vices will abate of themselves, if they be brought every day to the shrift. Oh the blessed sleep that follows such a diary! Oh the tranquillity, liberty, and greatness of that mind that is a spy upon itself, and a private censor of its own manners! It is my custom (says our author) every night, so soon as the candle is out, to run over all the words and actions of the past day; and I let nothing escape me; for why should I fear the sight of my own errors, when I can admonish and forgive myself? "I was a little too hot in such a dispute: my opinion might have been as well spared, for it gave offence, and did no good at all. The thing was true, but all truths are not to be spoken at all times; I would I had held my tongue, for there is no contending either with fools or our superiors. I have done ill, but it shall be so no more." If every man would but thus look into himself, it would be the better for us all. What can be more reasonable than this daily review of a life that we cannot warrant for a moment? Our fate is set, and the first breath we draw is only the first motion toward our last: one cause depends upon another; and the course of all things, public and private, is but a long connection of providential appointments. There is a great variety in our lives, but all tends to the same issue. Nature may use her own bodies as she pleases; but a good man has this consolation, that nothing perishes which he can call his own. It is a great comfort that we are only condemned to the same fate with the universe; the heavens themselves are mortal as well as our bodies; Nature has made us passive, and to suffer is our lot. While we are in flesh, every man has his chain and his clog, only it is looser and lighter to one man than to another; and he is more at ease that takes it up and carries it, than he that drags it. We are born, to lose and to perish, to hope and to fear, to vex ourselves and others;

and there is no antidote against a common calamity but virtue; for "the foundation of true joy is in the conscience."

VII

A GOOD MAN CAN NEVER BE MISERABLE, NOR A WICKED MAN HAPPY

There is not in the scale of nature a more inseparable connection of cause and effect, than in the case of happiness and virtue; nor anything that more naturally produces the one, or more necessarily presupposes the other. For what is it to be happy, but for a man to content himself with his lot, in a cheerful and quiet resignation to the appointments of God? All the actions of our lives ought to be governed with respect to good and evil: and it is only reason that distinguishes; by which reason we are in such manner influenced, as if a ray of the Divinity were dipt in a mortal body, and that is the perfection of mankind. It is true, we have not the eyes of eagles or the sagacity of hounds: nor if we had, could we pretend to value ourselves upon anything which we have in common with brutes. What are we the better for that which is foreign to us, and may be given and taken away? As the beams of the sun irradiate the earth, and yet remain where they were; so is it in some proportion with a holy mind that illustrates all our actions, and yet it adheres to its original. Why do we not as well commend a horse for his glorious trappings, as a man for his pompous additions? How much a braver creature is a lion, (which by nature ought to be fierce and terrible) how much braver (I say) in his natural horror than in his chains? so that everything in its pure nature pleases us best. It is not health, nobility, riches, that can justify a wicked man: nor is it the want of all these that can discredit a good one. That is the sovereign blessing, which makes the possessor of it valuable without anything else, and him that wants it contemptible, though he had all the world besides. It is not the painting, gilding, or carving, that makes a good ship; but if she be a nimble sailer, tight and strong to endure the seas; that is her excellency. It is the edge and temper of the blade that makes a good sword, not the richness of the scabbard: and so it is not money or possessions, that makes a man considerable, but his virtue.

It is every man's duty to make himself profitable to mankind — if he can, to many — if not, to fewer — if not so neither, to his neighbor — but, however, to himself. There are two republics: a great one, which is human nature; and a less, which is the place where we were born. Some serve both at a time, some only the greater, and some again only the less. The greater may be served in privacy, solitude, contemplation, and perchance that way better than any other; but it was the intent of Nature, however, that we should serve both. A good man may serve the public, his friend, and himself in any station: if he be not for the sword, let him take the gown; if the bar does not agree with him, let him try the pulpit; if he be silenced abroad, let him give counsel at home, and discharge the part of a faithful friend and a temperate companion. When he is no longer a citizen, he is yet a man; but the whole world is his country, and human nature never wants matter to work upon: but if nothing will serve a man in the *civil government* unless he be *prime minister*, or in the *field* but to *command in chief*, it is his own fault.

The common soldier where he cannot use his hands, fights with his looks, his example, his encouragement, his voice, and stands his ground even when he has lost his hands, and does service too with his very clamor, so that in any condition whatsoever, he still discharges the duty of a good patriot — nay, he that spends his time well even in a retirement, gives a great example.

We may enlarge, indeed, or contract, according to the circumstances of time, place, or abilities; but above all things we must be sure to keep ourselves in action, for he that is slothful is dead even while he lives. Was there ever any state so desperate as that of Athens under the thirty tyrants — where it was capital to be honest, and the senate-house was turned into a college of hangmen? Never was any government so wretched and so hopeless; and yet Socrates at the same time preached *temperance* to the *tyrants*, and courage to the rest, and afterwards died an eminent example of faith and resolution, and a sacrifice for the common good.

It is not for a wise man to stand shifting and fencing with fortune, but to oppose her barefaced, for he is sufficiently convinced that she can do him no hurt; she may take away his servants, possessions, dignity, assault his body, put out his eyes, cut off his hands, and strip him of all the external comforts of life. But what does all this amount to more than the recalling of a trust which he has received, with condition to deliver it up again upon demand? He looks upon himself as precarious, and only lent to himself, and yet he does not value himself ever the less because he is not his own, but takes such care as an honest man should do of a thing that is committed to him in trust. Whensoever he that lent me myself and what I have, shall call for all back again, it is not a loss but a restitution, and I must willingly deliver up what most undeservedly was bestowed upon me, and it will become me to return my mind better than I received it.

Demetrius, upon the taking of Megara, asked Stilpo, the philosopher, what he had lost. "Nothing," said he, "for I had all that I could call my own about me." And yet the enemy had then made himself master of his patrimony, his children, and his country; but these he looked upon as only adventitious goods, and under the command of fortune. Now, he that neither lost any thing nor feared any thing in a public ruin, but was safe and at peace in the middle of the flames, and in the heat of a military intemperance and fury — what violence or provocation imaginable can put such a man as this out of the possession of himself? Walls and castles may be mined and battered, but there is no art or engine that can subvert a steady mind. "I have made my way," says Stilpo, "through fire and blood — what has become of my children I know not; but these are transitory blessings, and servants that are bound to change their masters; what was my own before is my own still. Some have lost their estates, others their dear-bought mistresses, their commissions and offices: the usurers have lost their bonds and securities: but, Demetrius, for my part I have saved all, and do not imagine after all this, either that Demetrius is a conqueror, or that Stilpo is overcome — it is only thy fortune has been too hard for mine."

Alexander took Babylon, Scipio took Carthage, the capitol was burnt; but there is no fire or violence that can discompose a generous mind; and let us not take this character either for a chimera, for all ages afford some, though not many, instances of this elevated virtue.

A good man does his duty, let it be never so painful, so hazardous, or never so great a loss to him; and it is not all the money, the power, and the pleasure in the world; not any force of necessity, that can make him wicked: he considers what he is to do, not what he is to suffer, and will keep on his course, though there should be nothing but gibbets and torments in the way. And in this instance of Stilpo, who, when he had lost his country, his wife, his children, the town on fire over his head, himself escaping very hardly and naked out of the flames; "I have saved all my goods," says he, "my justice, my courage, my temperance, my prudence;" accounting nothing his own, or valuable, and showing how much easier it was to overcome a nation than one wise man. It is a certain mark of a brave mind not to be moved by any accidents: the upper region of the air admits neither clouds nor tempests; the thunder, storms, and meteors, are formed below; and this is the difference betwixt a mean and an exalted mind; the former is rude and tumultuary; the latter is modest, venerable, composed, and always quiet in its station. In brief, it is the conscience that pronounces upon the man whether he be happy or miserable. But, though sacrilege and adultery be generally condemned, how many are there still that do not so much as blush at the one, and in truth that take a glory in the other? For nothing is more common than for great thieves to ride in triumph when the little ones are punished. But let "wickedness escape as it may at the bar, it never fails of doing justice upon itself; for every guilty person is his own hangman."

VIII

THE DUE CONTEMPLATION OF DIVINE PROVIDENCE
IS THE CERTAIN CURE OF ALL MISFORTUNES

Whoever observes the world, and the order of it, will find all the motions in it to be only vicissitudes of falling and rising; nothing extinguished, and even those things which seem to us to perish are in truth but changed. The seasons go and return, day and night follow in their courses, the heavens roll, and Nature goes on with her work: all things succeed in their turns, storms and calms; the law of Nature will have it so, which we must follow and obey, accounting all things that are done to be well done; so that what we cannot mend we must suffer, and wait upon Providence without repining. It is the part of a cowardly soldier to follow his commander groaning: but a generous man delivers himself up to God without struggling; and it is only for a narrow mind to condemn the order of the world, and to propound rather the mending of Nature than of himself. No man has any cause of complaint against Providence, if that which is right pleases him. Those glories that appear fair to the eye, their lustre is but false and superficial; and they are only vanity and delusion: they are rather the goods of a dream than a substantial possession: they may cozen us at a distance, but bring them once to the touch, they are rotten and counterfeit. There are no greater wretches in the world than many of those which the people take to be happy. Those are the only true and incorruptible comforts that will abide all trials, and the more we turn and examine them, the more valuable we find them; and the greatest felicity of all is, not to stand in need of any. What is *poverty*? No man lives so poor as he was born. What is *pain*? It will either have an end itself, or make an end of us. In short, Fortune has no weapon that reaches the mind: but the bounties of Providence are certain and permanent blessings; and they are the greater and the better, the longer we consider them; that is to say, "the power of contemning things terrible, and despising what the common people covet." In the very methods of Nature we cannot but observe the regard that Providence had to the good of mankind, even in the disposition of the world, in providing so amply for our maintenance and satisfaction. It is not possible for us to comprehend what the Power is which has made all things: some few sparks of that Divinity are discovered, but infinitely the greater part of it lies hid. We are all of us, however, thus far agreed, first, in the acknowledgement and belief of that almighty Being; and, secondly, that we are to ascribe to it all majesty and goodness.

"If there be a Providence," say some, "how comes it to pass that good men labor under affliction and adversity, and wicked men enjoy themselves in ease and plenty?" My answer is, that God deals by us as a good father does by his children; he tries us, he hardens us, and fits us for himself. He keeps a strict hand over those that he loves; and by the rest he does as we do by our slaves; he lets them go on in license and boldness.

As the master gives his most hopeful scholars the hardest lessons, so does God deal with the most generous spirits; and the cross encounters of fortune we are not to look upon as a cruelty, but as a contest: the familiarity of dangers brings us to the contempt of them, and that part is strongest which is most exercised: the seaman's hand is callous, the soldier's arm is strong, and the tree that is most exposed to the wind takes the best root: there are people that live in a perpetual winter, in extremity of frost and penury, where a cave, a lock of straw, or a few leaves, is all their covering, and wild beasts their nourishment; all this by custom is not only made tolerable, but when it is once taken up upon necessity, by little and little, it becomes pleasant to them. Why should we then count that condition of life a calamity which is the lot of many nations? There is no state of life so miserable but that there are in it remissions, diversions, nay, and delights too; such is the benignity of Nature towards us, even in the severest accidents of human life. There were no living if adversity should hold on as it begins, and keep up the force of the first impression. We are apt to murmur at many things as great evils, that have nothing at all of evil in them besides the complaint, which we should more reasonably take up against ourselves. If I be sick, it is part of my fate; and for other calamities, they are usual things; they ought to be; nay, which is more, they must be, for they come by divine appointment. So that we should not only submit to God, but assent to him, and obey him out of *duty*, even if there were no *necessity*. All those terrible appearances that make us groan and tremble are but the tribute of life; we are neither to wish, nor to ask, nor to hope to escape them; for it is a kind of dishonesty to pay a tribute unwillingly. Am I troubled with the stone, or afflicted with continual losses? nay, is my body in danger? All this is no more than what I prayed for when I prayed for old age. All these things are as familiar in a long life, as dust and dirt in a long way. Life is a warfare; and what brave man would not rather choose to be in a tent than in shambles? Fortune does like a swordsman, she scorns to encounter a fearful man: there is no honor in the victory where there is no danger in the way to it; she tries Mucius by *fire*; Rutilius by *exile*; Socrates by *poison*; Cato by *death*.

It is only in adverse fortune, and in bad times, that we find great examples. Mucius thought himself happier with his hand in the flame, than if it had been in the bosom of his mistress. Fabricius took more pleasure in eating the roots of his own planting than in all the delicacies of luxury and expense. Shall we call Rutilius miserable, whom his very enemies have adored? who, upon a glorious and a public principle, chose rather to lose his country than to return from banishment? the only man that denied any thing to Sylla the dictator, who recalled him. Nor did he only refuse to come, but drew himself further off: "Let them," says he, "that think banishment a misfortune, live slaves at Rome, under the imperial cruelties of Sylla: he that sets a price upon the heads of senators; and after a law of his own institution against cut-throats, becomes the greatest himself." Is it not better for a man to live in exile abroad than to be massacred at home? In suffering for virtue, it is not the torment but the cause, that we are to consider; and the more pain, the more renown. When any hardship befalls us, we must look upon it as an act of Providence, which many times suffers particulars to be wounded for the conservation of the whole: beside that, God chastises some people under an appearance of blessing them, turning their prosperity to their ruin as a punishment for abusing his goodness. And we are further to consider, that many a good man is afflicted, only to teach others to suffer; for we are born for example; and likewise that where men are contumacious and refractory, it pleases God many times to cure greater evils by less, and to turn our miseries to our advantage.

How many casualties and difficulties are there that we dread as insupportable mischiefs, which, upon farther thoughts, we find to be mercies and benefits? as banishment, poverty, loss of relations, sickness, disgrace. Some are cured by the lance; by fire, hunger, thirst; taking out of bones, lopping off limbs, and the like: nor do we only fear things that are many times beneficial to us; but, on the other side, we hanker after and pursue things that are deadly and pernicious: we are poisoned in the very pleasure of our luxury, and betrayed to a thousand diseases by the indulging of our palate. To lose a child or a limb, is only to part with what we have received, and Nature may do what she pleases with her own. We are frail ourselves, and we have received things transitory — that which was given us may be taken away — calamity tries virtue as the fire does gold, nay, he that lives most at ease is only delayed, not dismissed, and his portion is to come. When we are visited with sickness or other afflictions we are not to murmur as if we were ill used — it is a mark of the general's esteem when he puts us upon a post of danger: we do not say "My captain uses me ill," but "he does me honor;" and so should we say that are commanded to encounter difficulties, for this is our case with God Almighty.

What was Regulus the worse, because Fortune made choice

of him for an eminent instance both of faith and patience? He was thrown into a case of wood stuck with pointed nails, so that which way soever he turned his body, it rested upon his wounds; his eyelids were cut off to keep him waking; and yet Mecaenas was not happier upon his *bed* than Regulus upon his *torments*. Nay, the world is not yet grown so wicked as not to prefer Regulus before Mecaenas: and can any man take that to be an evil of which Providence accounted this brave man worthy? "It has pleased God," says he, "to single me out for an experiment of the force of human nature." No man knows his own strength or value but by being put to the proof. The pilot is tried in a storm; the soldier in a battle; the rich man knows not how to behave himself in poverty: he that has lived in popularity and applause, knows not how he would bear infamy and reproach: nor he that never had children how he would bear the loss of them. Calamity is the occasion of virtue, and a spur to a great mind. The very apprehension of a wound startles a man when he first bears arms; but an old soldier bleeds boldly, because he knows that a man may lose blood, and yet win the day. Nay, many times a calamity turns to our advantage; and great ruins have but made way to greater glories. The crying out of *fire* has many times quieted a fray, and the interposing of a wild beast has parted the thief and the traveller; for we are not at leisure for less mischiefs while we are under the apprehensions of greater. One man's life is saved by a disease: another is arrested, and taken out of the way, just when his house was falling upon his head.

To show now that the favors or the crosses of fortune, and the accidents of sickness and of health, are neither good nor evil, God permits them indifferently both to good and evil men. "It is hard," you will say, "for a virtuous man to suffer all sorts of misery, and for a wicked man not only to go free, but to enjoy himself at pleasure." And is it not the same thing for men of prostituted impudence and wickedness to sleep in a whole skin, when men of honor and honesty bear arms; lie in the trenches, and receive wounds? or for the vestal virgins to rise in the night to their prayers, when common strumpets lie stretching themselves in their beds? We should rather say with Demetrius, "If I had known the will of Heaven before I was called to it, I would have offered myself." If it be the pleasure of God to take my children, I have brought them up to that end: if my fortune, any part of my body, or my life, I would rather present it than yield it up:

I am ready to part with all, and to suffer all; for I know that nothing comes to pass but what God appoints: our fate is decreed, and things do not so much happen, as in their due time proceed, and every man's portion of joy and sorrow is predetermined.

There is nothing falls amiss to a good man that can be charged upon Providence; for wicked actions, lewd thoughts, ambitious projects, blind lusts, and insatiable avarice — against all these he is armed by the benefit of reason: and do we expect now that God should look to our luggage too? (I mean our bodies.) Demetrius discharged himself of his treasure as the clog and burden of his mind: shall we wonder then if God suffers that to befall a good man which a good man sometimes does to himself? I lose a son, and why not, when it may sometimes so fall out that I myself may kill him? Suppose he be banished by an order of state, is it not the same thing with a man's voluntarily leaving his country never to return? Many afflictions may befall a good man, but no evil, for contraries will never incorporate — all the rivers in the world are never able to change the taste or quality of the sea. Prudence and religion are above accidents, and draw good out of every thing — affliction keeps a man in use, and makes him strong, patient, and hardy. Providence treats us like a generous father, and brings us up to labors, toils, and dangers; whereas the indulgence of a fond mother makes us weak and spiritless.

God loves us with a masculine love, and turns us loose to injuries and indignities: he takes delight to see a brave and a good man wrestling with evil fortune, and yet keeping himself upon his legs, when the whole world is in disorder about him. And are not we ourselves delighted, to see a bold fellow press with his lance upon a boar or lion? and the constancy and resolution of the action is the grace and dignity of the spectacle. No man can be happy that does not stand firm against all contingencies; and say to himself in all extremities, "I should have been content, if it might have been so or so, but since it is otherwise determined, God will provide better." The more we struggle with our necessities, we draw the knot the harder, and the worse it is with us: and the more a bird flaps and flutters in the snare, the surer she is caught: so that the best way is to submit and lie still, under this double consideration, that "the proceedings of God are unquestionable, and his decrees are not to be resisted."

IX

LEVITY OF MIND, AND OTHER
IMPEDIMENTS OF A HAPPY LIFE

Now, to sum up what is already delivered, we have showed what happiness is, and wherein it consists: that it is founded upon wisdom and virtue; for we must first know what we ought to do, and then live according to that knowledge. We have also discoursed the helps of philosophy and precept toward a *happy life*; the blessing of a good conscience; that a good man can never be miserable, nor a wicked man happy; nor any man unfortunate that cheerfully submits to Providence. We shall now examine, how it comes to pass that, when the certain way to happiness lies so fair before us, men will yet steer their course on the other side, which as manifestly leads to ruin.

There are some that live without any design at all, and only pass in the world like straws upon a river; they do not go, but they are carried. Others only deliberate upon the parts of life, and not upon the whole, which is a great error: for there is no disposing of the circumstances of it, unless we first propound the main scope. How shall any man take his aim without a mark? or what wind will serve him that is not yet resolved upon his port? We live as it were by chance, and by chance we are governed. Some there are that torment themselves afresh with the memory of what is past: "Lord! what did I endure? never was any man in my condition; everybody gave me over; my very heart was ready to break," etc. Others, again, afflict themselves with the apprehension of evils to come; and very ridiculously: for the *one* does not *now* concern us, and the *other* not *yet*: beside that, there may he remedies for mischiefs likely to happen; for they give us warning by signs and symptoms of their approach. Let him that would be quiet take heed not to provoke men that are in power, but live without giving offence; and if we cannot make all great men our friends, it will suffice to keep them from being our enemies. This is a thing we must avoid, as a mariner would do a storm.

A rash seaman never considers what wind blows, or what course he steers, but runs at a venture, as if he would brave the rocks and the eddies; whereas he that is careful and considerate, informs himself beforehand where the danger lies, and what weather it is like to be: he consults his compass, and keeps aloof from those places that are infamous for wrecks and miscarriages; so does a wise man in the common business of life; he keeps out of the way from those that may do him hurt: but it is a point of prudence not to let them take notice that he does it on purpose; for that which a man shuns he tacitly condemns. Let him have a care also of *listeners*, *newsmongers*, and *meddlers* in other people's matters; for their discourse is commonly of such things as are never profitable, and most commonly dangerous either to be spoken or heard.

Levity of mind is a great hindrance of repose, and the very change of wickedness is an addition to the wickedness itself; for it is inconstancy added to iniquity; we relinquish the thing we sought, and then we take it up again; and so divide our lives between our lust and our repentances. From one appetite we pass to another, not so much upon choice as for change; and there is a check of conscience that casts a damp upon all our unlawful pleasures, which makes us lose the day in expectation of the night, and the night itself for fear of the approaching light.

Some people are *never* at quiet, others are *always* so, and they are both to blame: for that which looks like vivacity and industry in the one is only a restlessness and agitation; and that which passes in the other for moderation and reserve is but a drowsy and unactive sloth. Let motion and rest both take their turns, according to the order of Nature, which makes both the day and the night. Some are perpetually shifting from one thing to another; others, again, make their whole life but a kind of uneasy sleep: some lie tossing and turning until very weariness brings them to rest; others, again, I cannot so properly call inconstant as lazy. There are many proprieties and diversities of vice; but it is one never-failing effect of it to live displeased. We do all of us labor under inordinate desires; we are either timorous, and dare not venture, or venturing we do not succeed; or else we cast ourselves upon uncertain hopes, where we are perpetually solicitous, and in suspense. In this distraction we are apt to propose to ourselves things dishonest and hard; and when we have taken great pains to no purpose, we come then to repent of our undertakings: we are afraid to go on, and we can neither master our appetites nor obey them: we live and die restless and irresolute; and, which is worst of all, when we grow weary of the public, and betake ourselves to solitude for relief, our minds are sick and wallowing, and the very house and walls are troublesome to us; we grow impatient and ashamed of ourselves, and suppress our inward vexation until it breaks our heart for want of vent. This is it that makes us sour and morose, envious of others, and dissatisfied with ourselves; until at last, betwixt our troubles for other people's successes and the despair of our own, we fall foul upon Fortune and the times, and get into a corner perhaps, where we sit brooding over our own disquiets. In these dispositions there is a kind of pruriginous fancy, that makes some people take delight in labor and uneasiness, like the clawing of an itch until the blood starts.

This is it that puts us upon rambling voyages; one while by land; but still disgusted with the present: the town pleases us to-day, the country to-morrow: the splendors of the court at one time, the horrors of a wilderness at another, but all this while we carry our plague about us; for it is not the place we are weary of, but ourselves. Nay, our weakness extends to everything; for we are impatient equally of toil and of pleasure. This trotting of the ring, and only treading the same steps over and over again, has made many a man lay violent hands upon himself. It must be the change of the mind, not of the climate, that will remove the heaviness of the heart; our vices go along with us, and we carry in ourselves the causes of our disquiets. There is a great weight lies upon us, and the bare shocking of it makes it the more uneasy; changing of countries, in this case, is not travelling, but wandering. We must keep on our course, if we would gain our journey's end. "He that cannot live happily anywhere, will live happily nowhere." What is a man the better for travelling? as if his cares could not find him out wherever he goes? Is there any retiring from the fear of death, or of torments? or from those difficulties which beset a man wherever he is? It is only philosophy that makes the mind invincible, and places us out of the reach of fortune, so that all her arrows fall short of us. This it is that reclaims the rage of our lusts, and sweetens the anxiety of our fears. Frequent changing of places or councils, shows an instability of mind; and we must fix the body before we can fix the soul. We can hardly stir abroad, or look about us, without encountering something or other that revives our appetites. As he that would cast off an unhappy love avoids whatsoever may put him in mind of the person, so he that would wholly deliver himself from his beloved lusts must shun all objects that may put them in his head again, and remind him of them. We travel, as children run up and down after strange sights, for novelty, not profit; we return neither the better nor the sounder; nay, and the very agitation hurts us. We learn to call towns and places by their names, and to tell stories of mountains and of rivers; but had not our time been better spent in the study of wisdom and of virtue? in the learning of what is already discovered, and in the quest of things not yet found out? If a man break his leg, or strain his ankle, he sends presently for a surgeon to set all right again, and does not take horse upon it, or put himself on ship-board; no more does the change of place work upon our disordered minds than upon our bodies. It is not the place, I hope, that makes either an orator or a physician. Will any man ask upon the road, Pray, which is the way to prudence, to justice, to temperance, to fortitude? No matter whither any man goes that carries his affections along with him. He that would make his travels delightful must make himself a temperate companion.

A great traveller was complaining that he was never the better for his travels; "That is very true," said Socrates, "because you travelled with yourself." Now, had not he better have made himself another man than to transport himself to another place? It is no matter what manners we find anywhere; so long as we carry our own. But we have all of us a natural curiosity of seeing fine sights, and of making new discoveries, turning over antiquities, learning the customs of nations, etc. We are never quiet; to-day we seek an office, to-morrow we are sick of it. We divide our lives betwixt a dislike of the present and a desire of the future: but he that lives as he should, orders himself so, as neither to fear nor to wish for to-morrow; if it comes, it is welcome; but if not, there is nothing lost; for that which is come, is but the same over again with what is past. As levity is a pernicious enemy to quiet, so pertinacity is a great one too. The one changes nothing, the other sticks to nothing; and which of the two is the worse, may be a question. It is many times seen, that we beg earnestly for those things, which, if they were offered us, we would refuse; and it is but just to punish this easiness of asking with an equal facility of granting. There are some things we would be thought to desire, which we are so far from desiring that we dread them. "I shall tire you," says one, in the middle of a tedious story. "Nay, pray be pleased to go on," we cry, though we wish his tongue out at half-way: nay, we do not deal candidly even with God himself. We should say to ourselves in these cases, "This I have drawn upon myself. I could never be quiet until I had gotten this woman, this place, this estate, this honor, and now see what is come of it."

One sovereign remedy against all misfortunes is constancy of mind: the changing of parties and countenances looks as if a man were driven with the wind. Nothing can be above him that is above fortune. It is not violence, reproach, contempt, or whatever else from without, that can make a wise man quit his ground: but he is proof against calamities, both great and small: only our error is, that what we cannot do ourselves, we think nobody else can; so that we judge of the wise by the measures of the weak. Place me among princes or among beggars, the one shall not make me proud, nor the other ashamed. I can take as sound a sleep in a barn as in a palace, and a bundle of hay makes me as good a lodging as a bed of down. Should every day succeed to my wish, it should not transport me; nor would I think myself miserable if I should not have one quiet hour in my life. I will not transport myself with either pain or pleasure; but yet for all that, I could wish that I had an easier game to play, and that I were put rather to moderate my joys than my sorrows. If I were an imperial prince, I had rather take than be taken; and yet I would bear the same mind under the chariot of my conqueror that I had in my own. It is no great matter to trample upon those things that are most coveted or feared by the common people. There are those that will laugh upon the wheel, and cast themselves upon a certain death, only upon a transport of love, perhaps anger, avarice, or revenge; how much more then upon an instinct of virtue, which is invincible and steady! If a short obstinacy of mind can do this, how much more shall a composed and deliberate virtue, whose force is equal and perpetual.

To secure ourselves in this world, first, we must aim at nothing that men count worth the wrangling for. Secondly, we must not value the possession of any thing which even a common thief would think worth the stealing. A man's body is no booty. Let the way be never so dangerous for robberies, the poor and the naked pass quietly. A plain-dealing sincerity of manners makes a man's life happy, even in despite of scorn and contempt, which is every clear man's fate. But we had better yet be contemned for simplicity than lie perpetually upon the torture of a counterfeit; provided that care be taken not to confound simplicity with negligence; and it is, moreover, an uneasy life that of a disguise; for a man to seem to be what he is not, to keep a perpetual guard upon himself, and to live in fear of a discovery. He takes every man that looks upon him for a spy, over and above the trouble of being put to play another man's part. It is a good remedy in some cases for a man to apply himself to civil affairs and public business; and yet, in this state of life too, what betwixt ambition and calumny, it is hardly safe to be honest. There are, indeed, some cases wherein a wise man will give way; but let him not yield over easily neither; if he marches off, let him have a care of his honor, and make his retreat with his sword in his hand, and his face to the enemy. Of all others, a studious life is the least tiresome: it makes us easy to ourselves and to others, and gains us both friends and reputation.

X

HE THAT SETS UP HIS REST UPON
CONTINGENCIES SHALL NEVER BE QUIET

Never pronounce any man happy that depends upon fortune for his happiness; for nothing can be more preposterous than to place the good of a reasonable creature in unreasonable things. If I have lost any thing, it was adventitious; and the less money, the less trouble; the less favor, the less envy; nay, even in those cases that put us out of their wits, it is not the loss itself, but the opinion of the loss, that troubles us. It is a common mistake to account those things necessary that are superfluous, and to depend upon fortune for the felicity of life, which arises only from virtue. There is no trusting to her smiles; the sea swells and rages in a moment, and the ships are swallowed at night, in the very place where they sported themselves in the morning. And fortune has the same power over princes that it has over empires, over nations that it has over cities, and the same power over cities that it has over private men. Where is that estate that may not be followed upon the heel with famine and beggary? that dignity which the next moment may not be laid in the dust? that kingdom that is secure from desolation and ruin? The period of all things is at hand, as well that which casts out the fortunate as the other that delivers the unhappy; and that which may fall out at any time may fall out this very day. What *shall* come to pass I know not, but what *may* come to pass I know: so that I will despair of nothing, but expect everything; and whatsoever Providence remits is clear gain. Every moment, if it spares me, deceives me; and yet in some sort it does not deceive me; for though I know that any thing may happen, yet I know likewise that everything will not. I will hope the best, and provide for the worst. Methinks we should not find so much fault with Fortune for her inconstancy when we ourselves suffer a change every moment that we live; only other changes make more noise, and this steals upon us like the shadow upon a dial, every jot as certainly, but more insensibly.

The burning of Lyons may serve to show us that we are never safe, and to arm us against all surprises. The terror of it must needs be great, for the calamity is almost without example. If it had been fired by an enemy, the flame would have left some further mischief to have been done by the soldiers; but to be wholly consumed, we have not heard of many earthquakes so pernicious: so many rarities to be destroyed in one night; and in the depth of peace to suffer an outrage beyond the extremity of war; who would believe it? but twelve hours betwixt so fair a city and none at all! It was laid in ashes in less time than it would require to tell the story.

To stand unshaken in such a calamity is hardly to be expected, and our wonder can but be equal to our grief. Let this accident teach us to provide against all possibilities that fall within the power of fortune. All external things are under her dominion: one while she calls our hands to her assistance; another while she contents herself with her own force, and destroys us with mischiefs of which we cannot find the author. No time, place, or condition, is excepted; she makes our very pleasures painful to us; she makes war upon us in the depth of peace, and turns the means of our security into an occasion of fear; she turns a friend into an enemy, and makes a foe of a companion; we suffer the effects of war without any adversary; and rather than fail, our felicity shall be the cause of our destruction. Lest we should either forget or neglect her power, every day produces something extraordinary. She persecutes the most temperate with sickness, the strongest constitutions with the phthisis; she brings the innocent to punishment, and the most retired she assaults with tumults. Those glories that have grown up with many ages, with infinite labor and expense, and under the favor of many auspicious providences, one day scatters and brings to nothing. He that pronounced a day, nay, an hour, sufficient for the destruction of the greatest empire, might have fallen to a moment.

It were some comfort yet to the frailty of mankind and of human affairs, if things might but decay as slowly as they rise; but they grow by degrees, and they fall to ruin in an instant. There is no felicity in anything either private or public; men, nations, and cities, have all their fates and periods; our very entertainments are not without terror, and our calamity rises there where we least expect it. Those kingdoms that stood the shock both of foreign wars and civil, come to destruction without the sight of an enemy. Nay, we are to dread our peace and felicity more than violence, because we are here taken unprovided; unless in a state of peace we do the duty of men in war, and say to ourselves, *Whatsoever may be, will be*. I am to-day safe and happy in the love of my country; I am to-morrow banished: to-day in pleasure, peace, health; to-morrow broken upon a wheel, led in triumph, and in the agony of sickness. Let us therefore prepare for a shipwreck in the port, and for a tempest in a calm. One violence drives me from my country, another ravishes that from me; and that very place where a man can hardly pass this day for a crowd may be to-morrow a desert. Wherefore let us set before our eyes the whole condition of human nature, and consider as well what *may* happen as what commonly *does*. The way to make future calamities easy to us in the sufferance, is to make them familiar to us in the contemplation. How many cities in Asia, Achaia, Assyria, Macedonia, have been swallowed up by earthquakes? nay, whole countries are lost, and large provinces laid under water; but time brings all things to an end; for all the works of mortals are mortal; all possessions and their possessors are uncertain and perishable; and what wonder is it to lose anything at any time, when we must one day lose all?

That which we call our own is but lent us; and what we have received *gratis* we must return without complaint. That which Fortune gives us this hour she may take away the next; and he that trusts to her favors, shall either find himself deceived, or if he be not, he will at least be troubled, because he may be so. There is no defence in walls, fortifications, and engines, against the power of fortune; we must provide ourselves within, and when we are safe there, we are invincible; we may be battered, but not taken. She throws her gifts among us, and we sweat and scuffle for them, never considering how few are the better for that which is expected by all. Some are transported with what they get; others tormented for what they miss; and many times there is a leg or an arm broken in a contest for a counter. She gives us honors, riches, favors, only to take them away again, either by violence or treachery: so that they frequently turn to the damage of the receiver. She throws out baits for us, and sets traps as we do for birds and beasts; her bounties are snares and lime-twigs to us; we think that we take, but we are taken. If they had any thing in them that was substantial, they would some time or other fill and quiet us; but they serve only to provoke our appetite without anything more than pomp and show to allay it. But the best of it is, if a man cannot mend his fortune, he may yet mend his manners, and put himself so far out of her reach, that whether she gives or takes, it shall be all one to us; for we are neither the greater for the one, nor the less for the other. We call this a dark room, or that a light one; when it is in itself neither the one nor the other, but only as the day and the night render it. And so it is in riches, strength of body, beauty, honor, command: and likewise in pain, sickness, banishment, death: which are in themselves middle and indifferent things, and only good or bad as they are influenced by virtue. To weep, lament, and groan, is to renounce our duty; and it is the same weakness on the other side to exult and rejoice. I would rather make my fortune than expect it; being neither depressed with her injuries, nor dazzled with her favors. When Zeno was told, that all his goods were drowned; "Why then," says he, "Fortune has a mind to make me a philosopher." It is a great matter for a man to advance his mind above her threats or flatteries; for he that has once gotten the better of her is safe forever.

It is some comfort yet to the unfortunate, that great men lie under the lash for company; and that death spares the palace no more than the cottage, and that whoever is above me has a power also above him. Do we not daily see funerals without trouble, princes deposed, countries depopulated, towns sacked; without so much as thinking how soon it may be our own case? whereas, if we would but prepare and arm ourselves against the iniquities of fortune, we should never be surprised.

When we see any man banished, beggared, tortured, we are to account, that though the mischief fell upon another, it was levelled at us. What wonder is it if, of so many thousands of dangers that are constantly hovering about us, one comes to hit us at last? That which befalls any man, may befall every man; and then it breaks the force of a present calamity to provide against the future. Whatsoever our lot is, we must bear it: as suppose it be contumely, cruelty, fire, sword, pains, diseases, or a prey to wild beasts; there is no struggling, nor any remedy but moderation. It is to no purpose to bewail any part of our life, when life itself is miserable throughout; and the whole flux of it only a course of transition from one misfortune to another.

A man may as well wonder that he should be cold in winter, sick at sea, or have his bones clatter together in a wagon, as at the encounter of ill accidents and crosses in the passage of human life; and it is in vain to run away from fortune, as if there were any hiding-place wherein she could not find us; or to expect any quiet from her; for she makes life a perpetual state of war, without so much as any respite or truce. This we may conclude upon, that her empire is but imaginary, and that whosoever serves her, makes himself a voluntary slave; for "the things that are often contemned by the inconsiderate, and always by the wise, are in themselves neither good nor evil:" as pleasure and pains; prosperity and adversity; which can only operate upon our outward condition, without any proper and necessary effect upon the mind.

XI

A SENSUAL LIFE IS A MISERABLE LIFE

The sensuality that we here treat of falls naturally under the head of luxury; which extends to all the excesses of gluttony, lust, effeminacy of manners; and, in short, to whatsoever concerns the overgreat care of the carcass.

To begin now with the pleasures of the palate, (which deal with us like Egyptian thieves, that strangle those they embrace), what shall we say of the luxury of Nomentanus and Apicius, that entertained their very souls in the kitchen: they have the choicest music for their ears; the most diverting spectacles for their eyes; the choicest variety of meats and drinks for their palates. What is all this, I say, but a *merry madness*? It is true, they have their delights, but not without heavy and anxious thoughts, even in their very enjoyments, beside that, they are followed with repentance, and their frolics are little more than the laughter of so many people out of their wits. Their felicities are full of disquiet, and neither sincere nor well grounded: but they have need of one pleasure to support another; and of new prayers to forgive the errors of their former. Their life must needs be wretched that get with great pains what they keep with greater.

One diversion overtakes another; hope excites hope; ambition begets ambition; so that they only change the matter of their miseries, without seeking any end of them; and shall never be without either prosperous or unhappy causes of disquiet. What if a body might have all the pleasures in the world for the asking? who would so much unman himself, as by accepting of them, to desert his soul, and become a perpetual slave to his senses? Those false and miserable palates, that judge of meats by the price and difficulty, not by the healthfulness of taste, they vomit that they may eat, and they eat that they may fetch it up again. They cross the seas for rarities, and when they have swallowed them, they will not so much as give them time to digest. Wheresoever Nature has placed men, she has provided them aliment: but we rather choose to irritate hunger by expense than to allay it at an easier rate.

What is it that we plow the seas for; or arm ourselves against men and beasts? To what end do we toil, and labor, and pile bags upon bags? We may enlarge our fortunes, but we cannot our bodies; so that it does but spill and run over, whatsoever we take more than we can hold. Our forefathers (by the force of whose virtues we are now supported in our vices) lived every jot as well as we, when they provided and dressed their own meat with their own hands; lodged upon the ground, and were not as yet come to the vanity of gold and gems; when they swore by their earthen gods, and kept their oath, though they died for it.

Did not our consuls live more happily when they cooked their own meat with those victorious hands that had conquered so many enemies and won so many laurels? Did they not live more happily, I say, than our Apicius (that corrupter of youth, and plague of the age he lived in) who, after he had spent a prodigious fortune upon his belly, poisoned himself for fear of starving, when he had yet 250,000 crowns in his coffers? which may serve to show us, that it is the mind, and not the sum, that makes any man rich; when Apicius with all his treasure counted himself in a state of beggary, and took poison to avoid that condition, which another would have prayed for. But why do we call it poison, which was the wholesomest draught of his life? His daily gluttony was poison rather, both to himself and others. His ostentation of it was intolerable; and so was the infinite pains he took to mislead others by his example, who went even fast enough of themselves without driving.

It is a shame for a man to place his felicity in those entertainments and appetites that are stronger in brutes. Do not beasts eat with a better stomach? Have they not more satisfaction in their lusts? And they have not only a quicker relish of their pleasures, but they enjoy them without either scandal or remorse. If sensuality were happiness, beasts were happier than men; but human felicity is lodged in the soul, not in the flesh. They that deliver themselves up to luxury are still either tormented with too little, or oppressed with too much; and equally miserable, by being either deserted or overwhelmed: they are like men in a dangerous sea; one while cast a-dry upon a rock, and another while swallowed up in a whirlpool; and all this from the mistake of not distinguishing good from evil. The huntsman, that with which labor and hazard takes a wild beast, runs as great a risk afterwards in the keeping of him; for many times he tears out the throat of his master; and it is the same thing with inordinate pleasures: the more in number, and the greater they are, the more general and absolute a slave is the servant of them. Let the common people pronounce him as happy as they please, he pays his liberty for his delights, and sells himself for what he buys.

Let any man take a view of our kitchens, the number of our cooks, and the variety of our meats; will he not wonder to see so much provision made for one belly? We have as many diseases as we have cooks or meats; and the service of the appetite is the study now in vogue. To say nothing of our trains of lackeys, and our troops of caterers and sewers: Good God! that ever one belly should employ so many people! How nauseous and fulsome are the surfeits that follow these excesses? Simple meats are out of fashion, and all are collected into one; so that the cook does the office of the stomach; nay, and of the teeth too; for the meat looks as if it were chewed beforehand: here is the luxury of all tastes in one dish, and liker a vomit than a soup. From these compounded dishes arise compounded diseases, which require compounded medicines. It is the same thing with our minds that it is with our tables; simple vices are curable by simple counsels, but a general dissolution of manners is hardly overcome; we are overrun with a public as well as with a private madness. The physicians of old understood little more than the virtue of some herbs to stop blood, or heal a wound; and their firm and healthful bodies needed little more before they were corrupted by luxury and pleasure; and when it came to that once, their business was not to allay hunger, but to provoke it by a thousand inventions and sauces. That which was aliment to a craving stomach is become a burden to a full one. From hence came paleness, trembling, and worse effects from crudities than famine; a weakness in the joints, the belly stretched, suffusion of choler, the torpor of the nerves, and a palpitation of the heart. To say nothing of megrims, torments of the eyes and ears, head-ache, gout, scurvy, several sorts of fevers and putrid ulcers, with other diseases that are but the punishment of luxury. So long as our bodies were hardened with labor, or tired with exercise or hunting, our food was plain and simple; many dishes have made many diseases.

It is an ill thing for a man not to know the measure of his stomach, nor to consider that men do many things in their drink that they are ashamed of sober; drunkenness being nothing else but a voluntary madness. It emboldens men to do all sorts of mischiefs; it both irritates wickedness and discovers it; it does not make men vicious, but it shows them to be so. It was in a drunken fit that Alexander killed Clytus. It makes him that is insolent prouder, him that is cruel fiercer, it takes away all shame. He that is peevish breaks out presently into ill words and blows. The lecher, without any regard to decency or scandal, turns up his whore in the market-place. A man's tongue trips, his head runs round, he staggers in his pace. To say nothing of the crudities and diseases that follow upon this distemper, consider the public mischiefs it has done. How many warlike nations and strong cities, that have stood invincible to attacks and sieges, has drunkenness overcome! Is it not a great honor to drink the company dead? a magnificent virtue to swallow more wine than the rest, and yet at last to be outdone by a hogshead? What shall we say of those men that invert the offices of day and night? as if our eyes were only given us to make use of in the dark? Is it day? "It is time to go to bed." Is it night? "It is time to rise." Is it toward morning? "Let us go to supper." When other people lie down they rise, and lie till the next night to digest the debauch of the day before. It is an argument of clownery, to do as other people do.

Luxury steals upon us by degrees; first, it shows itself in a more than ordinary care of our bodies, it slips next into the furniture of our houses; and it gets then into the fabric, curiosity, and expense of the house itself. It appears, lastly, in the fantastical excesses of our tables. We change and shuffle our meats, confound our sauces, serve that in first that used to be last, and value our dishes, not for the taste, but for the rarity. Nay, we are so delicate, that we must be told when we are to eat or drink; when we are hungry or weary; and we cherish some vices as proofs and arguments of our happiness. The most miserable mortals are they that deliver themselves up to their palates, or to their lusts: the pleasure is short and turns presently nauseous, and the end of it is either shame or repentance. It is a brutal entertainment, and unworthy of a man, to place his felicity in the service of his senses. As to the wrathful, the contentious, the ambitious, though the distemper be great, the offence has yet something in it that is manly; but the basest of prostitutes are those that dedicate themselves wholly to lust; what with their hopes and fears, anxiety of thought, and perpetual disquiets, they are never well, full nor fasting.

What a deal of business is now made about our houses and diet, which was at first both obvious and of little expense? Luxury led the way, and we have employed our wits in the aid of our vices. First we desired superfluities, our next step was to wickedness, and, in conclusion, we delivered up our minds to our bodies, and so became slaves to our appetites, which before were our servants, and are now become our masters. What was it that brought us to the extravagance of embroideries, perfumes, tire-women, etc. We passed the bounds of Nature, and launched out into superfluities; insomuch, that it is now-a-days only for beggars and clowns to content themselves with what is sufficient; our luxury makes us insolent and mad. We take upon us like princes, and fly out for every trifle, as though there were life and death in the case. What a madness is it for a man to lay out an estate upon a table or a cabinet, a patrimony upon a pain of pendants, and to inflame the price of curiosities according to the hazard either of breaking or losing of them? To wear garments that will neither defend a woman's body, nor her modesty: so thin that one could make a conscience of swearing she were naked: for she hardly shows more in the privacies of her amour than in public? How long shall we covet and oppress, enlarge our possessions, and account that too little for one man which was formerly enough for a nation? And our luxury is as insatiable as our avarice. Where is that lake, that sea, that forest, that spot of land; that is not ransacked to gratify our palate? The very earth is burdened with our buildings; not a river, not a mountain, escapes us. Oh, that there should be such boundless desires in our little bodies! Would not fewer lodgings serve us? We lie but in one, and where we are not, that is not properly ours. What with our hooks, snares, nets, dogs, etc., we are at war with all living creatures; and nothing comes amiss but that which is either too cheap, or too common; and all this is to gratify a fantastical palate. Our avarice, our ambition, our lusts, are insatiable; we enlarge our possessions, swell our families, we rifle sea and land for matter of ornament and luxury. A bull contents himself with one meadow, and one forest is enough for a thousand elephants; but the little body of a man devours more than all other living creatures. We do not eat to satisfy hunger, but ambition; we are dead while we are alive, and our houses are so much our tombs, that a man might write our *epitaphs* upon our very doors.

A voluptuous person, in fine, can neither be a good man, a good patriot, nor a good friend; for he is transported with his appetites, without considering, that the lot of man is the law of Nature. A good man (like a good soldier) will stand his ground, receive wounds, glory in his scars, and in death itself love his master for whom he falls; with that divine precept always in his mind, "Follow good:" whereas he that complains, laments, and groans, must yield nevertheless, and do his duty though in spite of his heart. Now, what a madness is it for a man to choose rather to be lugged than to follow, and vainly to contend with the calamities of human life? Whatsoever is laid upon us by necessity, we should receive generously; for it is foolish to strive with what we cannot avoid. We are born subjects, and to obey God is perfect liberty. He that does this shall be free, safe, and quiet: all his actions shall succeed to his wish: and what can any man desire more than to want nothing from without, and to have all things desirable within himself? Pleasures do but weaken our minds, and send us for our support to Fortune, who gives us money only as the wages of slavery. We must stop our eyes and our ears. Ulysses had but one rock to fear, but human life has many. Every city, nay, every man, is one; and there is no trusting even to our nearest friends. Deliver me from the superstition of taking those things which are light and vain for felicities.

XII

AVARICE AND AMBITION ARE INSATIABLE AND RESTLESS

The man that would be truly rich must not increase his fortune, but retrench his appetites: for riches are not only superfluous, but mean, and little more to the possessor than to the looker-on. What is the end of ambition and avarice, when at best we are but stewards of what we falsely call our own? All those things that we pursue with so much hazard and expense of blood, as well to keep as to get, for which we break faith and friendship, what are they but the mere *deposita* of Fortune? and not ours, but already inclining toward a new master. There is nothing our own but that which we give to ourselves, and of which we have a certain and an inexpugnable possession. Avarice is so insatiable, that it is not in the power of liberality to content it; and our desires are so boundless, that whatever we get is but in the way to getting more without end: and so long as we are solicitous for the increase of wealth, we lose the true use of it; and spend our time in putting out, calling in, and passing our accounts, without any substantial benefit, either to the world or to ourselves. What is the difference betwixt old men and children? the one cries for nuts and apples, and the other for gold and silver: the one sets up courts of justice, hears and determines, acquits and condemns, in jest; the other in earnest: the one makes houses of clay, the other of marble: so that the works of old men are nothing in the world but the progress and improvement of children's errors; and they are to be admonished and punished too like children, not in revenge for injuries received, but as a correction of injuries done, and to make them give over. There is some substance yet in gold and silver; but as to judgments and statutes, procuration and continuance-money, these are only the visions and dreams of avarice. Throw a crust of bread to a dog, he takes it open-mouthed, swallows it whole, and presently gapes for more: just so do we with the gifts of Fortune; down they go without chewing, and we are immediately ready for another chop. But what has avarice now to do with gold and silver, that is so much outdone by curiosities of a far greater value? Let us no longer complain that there was not a heavier load laid upon those precious metals, or that they were not buried deep enough, when we have found out ways by wax and parchments, and by bloody usurious contracts, to undo one another. It is remarkable, that Providence has given us all things for our advantage near at hand; but iron, gold, and silver, (being both the instrument of blood and slaughter, and the price of it) Nature has hidden in the bowels of the earth.

There is no avarice without some punishment, over and above that which it is to itself. How miserable is it in the desire! how miserable even in the attaining of our ends! For money is a greater torment in the possession than it is in the pursuit. The fear of losing it is a great trouble, the loss of it a greater, and it is made a greater yet by opinion. Nay, even in the case of no direct loss at all, the covetous man loses what he does not get. It is true, the people call the rich man a happy man, and wish themselves in his condition; but can any condition be worse than that which carries vexation and envy along with it? Neither is any man to boast of his fortune, his herds of cattle, his number of slaves, his lands and palaces; for comparing that which he has to that which he further covets, he is a beggar. No man can possess all things, but any man may contemn them; and the contempt of riches is the nearest way to the gaining of them.

Some magistrates are made for money, and those commonly are bribed with money. We are all turned merchants, and look not into the quality of things, but into the price of them; for reward we are pious, and for reward again we are impious. We are honest so long as we may thrive upon it; but if the devil himself gives better wages, we change our party. Our parents have trained us up into an admiration of gold and silver, and the love of it is grown up with us to that degree that when we would show our gratitude to Heaven, we make presents of those metals. This it is that makes poverty look like a curse and a reproach; and the poets help it forward; the chariot of the sun must be all of gold; the best of times must be the Golden Age, and thus they turn the greatest misery of mankind into the greatest blessings.

Neither does avarice make us only unhappy in ourselves, but malevolent also to mankind. The soldier wishes for war; the husbandman would have his corn dear; the lawyer prays for dissension; the physician for a sickly year; he that deals in curiosities, for luxury and excess, for he makes up his fortunes out of the corruptions of the age. High winds and public conflagrations make work for the carpenter and bricklayer, and one man lives by the loss of another; some few, perhaps, have the fortune to be detected, but they are all wicked alike. A great plague makes work for the sexton; and, in one word, whosoever gains by the dead has not much kindness for the living. Demades of Athens condemned a fellow that sold necessaries for funerals, upon proof that he wished to make himself a fortune by his trade, which could not be but by a great mortality; but perhaps he did not so much desire to have many customers, as to sell dear, and buy cheap; besides, that all of that trade might have been condemned as well as he. Whatsoever whets our appetites, flatters and depresses the mind, and, by dilating it, weakens it; first blowing it up, and then filling and deluding it with vanity.

To proceed now from the most prostitute of all vices, sensuality and avarice, to that which passes in the world for the most generous, the thirst of glory and dominion. If they that run mad after wealth and honor, could but look into the hearts of them that have already gained these points, how would it startle them to see those hideous cares and crimes that wait upon ambitious greatness: all those acquisitions that dazzle the eyes of the vulgar are but false pleasures, slippery and uncertain. They are achieved with labor, and the very guard of them is painful. Ambition puffs us up with vanity and wind: and we are equally troubled either to see any body before us, or nobody behind us; so that we lie under a double envy; for whosoever envies another is also envied himself. What matters it how far Alexander extended his conquests, if he was not yet satisfied with what he had? Every man wants as much as he covets; and it is lost labor to pour into a vessel that will never be full. He that had subdued so many princes and nations, upon the killing of Clytus (one friend) and the loss of Hyphestion (another) delivered himself up to anger and sadness; and when he was master of the world, he was yet a slave to his passions. Look into Cyrus, Cambyses, and the whole Persian line, and you shall not find so much as one man of them that died satisfied with what he had gotten. Ambition aspires from great things to greater; and propounds matters even impossible, when it has once arrived at things beyond expectation. It is a kind of dropsy; the more a man drinks, the more he covets. Let any man but observe the tumults and the crowds that attend palaces; what affronts must we endure to be admitted, and how much greater when we are in! The passage to virtue is fair, but the way to greatness is craggy and it stands not only upon a precipice, but upon ice too; and yet it is a hard matter to convince a great man that his station is slippery, or to prevail with him not to depend upon his greatness; but all superfluities are hurtful. A rank crop lays the corn; too great a burden of fruit breaks the bough; and our minds may be as well overcharged with an immoderate happiness. Nay, though we ourselves would be at rest, our fortune will not suffer it: the way that leads to honor and riches leads to troubles; and we find the source of our sorrows in the very objects of our delights.

What joy is there in feasting and luxury; in ambition and a crowd of clients; in the arms of a mistress, or in the vanity of an unprofitable knowledge? These short and false pleasures deceive us, and, like drunkenness, revenge the jolly madness of *one* hour with the nauseous and sad repentance of *many*. Ambition is like a gulf: everything is swallowed up in it and buried, beside the dangerous consequences of it; for that which one has taken from all, may be easily taken away again by all from one. It was not either virtue or reason, but the mad love of a deceitful greatness, that animated Pompey in his wars, either abroad or at home. What was it but his ambition that hurried him to Spain, Africa, and elsewhere, when he was too great already in everybody's opinion but his own? And the same motive had Julius Caesar, who could not, even then, brook a superior himself, when the commonwealth had submitted unto two already.

Nor was it any instinct of virtue that pushed on Marius, who at the head of an army was himself led on under the command of ambition: but he came at last to the deserved fate of other wicked men, and to drink himself of the same cup that he had filled to others. We impose upon our reason, when we suffer ourselves to be transported with titles; for we know that they are nothing but a more glorious sound; and so for ornaments and gildings, though there be a lustre to dazzle our eyes, our understanding tells us that it is only outside, and the matter under it is only coarse and common.

I will never envy those that the people call great and happy. A sound mind is not to be shaken with a popular and vain applause; nor is it in the power of their pride to disturb the state of our happiness. An honest man is known now-a-days by the dust he raises upon the way, and it is become a point of honor to overrun people, and keep all at a distance; though he that is put out of the way may perchance be happier than he that takes it. He that would exercise a power profitable to himself, and grievous to nobody else, let him practice it upon his passion. They that have burnt cities, otherwise invincible, driven armies before them, and bathed themselves in human blood, after they have overcome all open enemies, they have been vanquished by their lust, by their cruelty, and without any resistance.

Alexander was possessed with the madness of laying kingdoms waste. He began with Greece, where he was brought up; and there he quarried himself upon that in it which was the best; he enslaved Lacedemon, and silenced Athens: nor was he content with the destruction of those towns which his father Philip had either conquered or bought; but he made himself the enemy of human nature; and, like the worst of beasts, he worried what he could not eat.

Felicity is an unquiet thing; it torments itself, and puzzles the brain. It makes some people ambitious, others luxurious; it puffs up some, and softens others; only (as it is with wine) some heads bear it better than others; but it dissolves all. Greatness stands upon a precipice: and if prosperity carries a man never so little beyond his poise, it overbears and dashes him to pieces. It is a rare thing for a man in a great fortune to lay down his happiness gently; it being a common fate for a man to sink under the weight of those felicities that raise him. How many of the nobility did Marius bring down to herdsmen and other mean offices! Nay, in the very moment of our despising servants, we may be made so ourselves.

XIII

HOPE AND FEAR ARE THE BANE OF HUMAN LIFE

No man can be said to be perfectly happy that runs the risk of disappointment: which is the case of every man that *fears* or *hopes* for anything. For *hope* and *fear*, how distant soever they may seem to be the one from the other, they are both of them yet coupled in the same chain, as the guard and the prisoner; and the one treads upon the heels of the other. The reason of this is obvious, for they are passions that look forward, and are ever solicitous for the future; only *hope* is the more plausible weakness of the two, which in truth, upon the main, are inseparable; for the one cannot be without the other: but where the *hope* is stronger than the *fear*, or the *fear* than the *hope*, we call it the one or the other; for without *fear* it were no longer *hope*, but *certainty*; as without *hope* it were no longer *fear* but *despair*.

We may come to understand whether our disputes are vain or not, if we do but consider that we are either troubled about the *present*, the *future* or *both*. If the present, it is easy to judge, and the future is uncertain. It is a foolish thing to be miserable beforehand for fear of misery to come; for a man loses the present, which he might enjoy, in expectation of the future: nay, the fear of losing anything is as bad as the loss itself. I will be as prudent as I can, but not timorous or careless; and I will bethink myself, and forecast what inconveniences may happen before they come. It is true, a man may fear, and yet not be fearful; which is no more than to have the affection of fear without the vice of it; but yet a frequent admittance of it runs into a habit. It is a shameful and an unmanly thing to be doubtful, timorous, and uncertain; to set one step forward, and another backward; and to be irresolute. Can there be any man so fearful, that had not rather fall once than hang always in suspense?

Our miseries are endless, if we stand in fear of all possibilities; the best way, in such a case, is to drive out one nail with another, and a little to qualify fear with hope; which may serve to palliate a misfortune; though not to cure it. There is not anything that we fear, which is so certain to come, as it is certain that many things which we do fear will not come; but we are loth to oppose our credulity when it begins to move us, and so to bring our fear to the test. Well! but "what if the thing we fear should come to pass?" Perhaps it will be the better for us. Suppose it be *death* itself, why may it not prove the glory of my life? Did not poison make Socrates famous? and was not Cato's sword a great part of his honor? "Do we fear any misfortune to befall us?" We are not presently sure that it will happen. How many deliverances have come unlooked for? and how many mischiefs that we looked for have never come to pass? It is time enough to lament when it comes, and, in the *interim*, to promise ourselves the best. What do I know but something or other may delay or divert it? Some have escaped out of the fire; others, when a house has fallen over their head, have received no hurt: one man has been saved when a sword was at his throat; another has been condemned, and outlived his headsman: so that ill-fortune, we see, as well as good, has her levities; peradventure it will be, peradventure not; and until it comes to pass, we are not sure of it: we do many times take words in a worse sense than they were intended, and imagine things to be worse taken than they are. It is time enough to bear a misfortune when it comes, without anticipating it.

He that would deliver himself from all apprehensions of the future, let him first take for granted, that all fears will fall upon him; and then examine and measure the evil that he fears, which he will find to be neither great nor long. Beside, that the ills which he fears he may suffer, he suffers in the very fear of them. As in the symptoms of an approaching disease, a man shall find himself lazy and listless: a weariness in his limbs, with a yawning and shuddering all over him; so it is in the case of a weak mind, it fancies misfortunes, and makes a man wretched before his time. Why should I torment myself at present with what, perhaps, may fall out fifty years hence? This humor is a kind of voluntary disease, and an industrious contrivance of our own unhappiness, to complain of an affliction that we do not feel. Some are not only moved with grief itself, but with the mere opinion of it; as children will start at a shadow, or at the sight of a deformed person. If we stand in fear of violence from a powerful enemy, it is some comfort to us, that whosoever makes himself terrible to others is not without fear himself: the least noise makes a lion start; and the fiercest of beasts, whatsoever enrages them, makes them tremble too: a shadow, a voice, an unusual odor, rouses them.

The things most to be feared I take to be of three kinds; *want*, *sickness*, and those *violences* that may be imposed upon us by a *strong hand*. The last of these has the greatest force, because it comes attended with noise and tumult; whereas the incommodities of poverty and diseases are more natural, and steal upon us in silence, without any external circumstances of horror: but the other marches in pomp, with fire and sword, gibbets, racks, hooks; wild beasts to devour us; stakes to impale us; engines to tear us to pieces; pitched bags to burn us in, and a thousand other exquisite inventions of cruelty. No wonder then, if that be the most dreadful to us that presents itself in so many uncouth shapes; and by the very solemnity is rendered the most formidable. The more instruments of bodily pain the executioner shows us, the more frightful he makes himself: for many a man that would have encountered death in any generous form, with resolution enough, is yet overcome with the *manner* of it. As for the calamities of hunger and thirst, inward ulcers, scorching fevers, tormenting fits of the stone, I look upon these miseries to be at least as grievous as any of the rest; only they do not so much affect the fancy, because they lie out of sight. Some people talk high of danger at a distance; but (like cowards) when the executioner comes to do his duty, and show us the fire, the ax, the scaffold, and death at hand, their courage fails them upon the very pinch, when they have most need of it. Sickness, (I hope) captivity, fire, are no new things to us; the fall of houses, funerals, and conflagrations, are every day before our eyes. The man that I supped with last night is dead before morning; why should I wonder then, seeing so many fall about me, to be hit at last myself? What can be greater madness than to cry out, "Who would have dreamed of this?" And why not, I beseech you? Where is that estate that may not be reduced to beggary? that dignity which may not be followed with banishment, disgrace, and extreme contempt? that kingdom that may not suddenly fall to ruin; change its master, and be depopulated? that prince that may not pass the hand of a common hangman? That which is one man's fortune may be another's; but the foresight of calamities to come breaks the violence of them.

XIV

IT IS ACCORDING TO THE TRUE OR FALSE ESTIMATE
OF THINGS THAT WE ARE HAPPY OR MISERABLE

How many things are there that the fancy makes terrible by night, which the day turns into ridiculous! What is there in labor, or in death, that a man should be afraid of? They are much slighter in act than in contemplation; and we *may* contemn them, but we *will* not: so that it is not because they are hard that we dread them, but they are hard because we are first afraid of them. Pains, and other violences of Fortune, are the same thing to us that goblins are to children: we are more scared with them than hurt. We take up our opinions upon trust, and err for company, still judging that to be best that has most competitors. We make a false calculation of matters, because we advise with opinion, and not with Nature; and this misleads us to a higher esteem for riches, honor, and power, than they are worth: we have been used to admire and recommend them, and a private error is quickly turned into a public. The greatest and the smallest things are equally hard to be comprehended; we account many things *great*, for want of understanding what effectually is so: and we reckon other things to be *small*, which we find frequently to be of the highest value. Vain things only move vain minds. The accidents that we so much boggle at are not terrible in themselves, but they are made so by our infirmities; but we consult rather what we hear than what we feel, without examining, opposing, or discussing the things we fear; so that we either stand still and tremble, or else directly run for it, as those troops did, that, upon the raising of the dust, took a flock of sheep for the enemy. When the body and mind are corrupted, it is no wonder if all things prove intolerable; and not because they are so in truth, but because we are dissolute and foolish: for we are infatuated to such a degree, that, betwixt the common madness of men, and that which falls under the care of the physician, there is but this difference, the one labors of a disease, and the other of a false opinion.

The Stoics hold, that all those torments that commonly draw

from us groans and ejaculations, are in themselves trivial and contemptible. But these high-flown expressions apart (how true soever) let us discourse the point at the rate of ordinary men, and not make ourselves miserable before our time; for the things we apprehend to be at hand may possibly never come to pass. Some things trouble us more than they should, other things sooner; and some things again disorder us that ought not to trouble us at all; so that we either enlarge, or create, or anticipate our disquiets. For the first part, let it rest as a matter in controversy; for that which I account light, another perhaps will judge insupportable! One man laughs under the lash, and another whines for a fillip. How sad a calamity is poverty to one man, which to another appears rather desirable than inconvenient? For the poor man, who has nothing to lose, has nothing to fear: and he that would enjoy himself to the satisfaction of his soul, must be either poor indeed, or at least look as if he were so. Some people are extremely dejected with sickness and pain; whereas Epicurus blessed his fate with his last breath, in the acutest torments of the stone imaginable. And so for banishment, which to one man is so grievous, and yet to another is no more than a bare change of place: a thing that we do every day for our health, pleasure, nay, and upon the account even of common business.

How terrible is death to one man, which to another appears the greatest providence in nature, even toward all ages and conditions! It is the wish of some, the relief of many, and the end of all. It sets the slave at liberty, carries the banished man home, and places all mortals upon the same level: insomuch, that life itself were a punishment without it. When I see tyrants, tortures, violences, the prospect of death is a consolation to me, and the only remedy against the injuries of life.

Nay, so great are our mistakes in the true estimate of things, that we have hardly done any thing that we have not had reason to wish undone; and we have found the things we feared to be more desirable than those we coveted. Our very prayers have been more pernicious than the curses of our enemies; and we must pray to have our former prayers forgiven. Where is the wise man that wishes to himself the wishes of his mother, nurse, or his tutor; the worst of enemies, with the intention of the best of friends. We are undone if their prayers be heard; and it is our duty to pray that they may not; for they are no other than well-meaning execrations. They take evil for good, and one wish fights with another: give me rather the contempt of all those things whereof they wish me the greatest plenty. We are equally hurt by some that pray for us, and by others that curse us: the one imprints in us a false fear, and the other does us mischief by a mistake: so that it is no wonder if mankind be miserable, when we are brought up from the very cradle under the imprecations of our parents. We pray for trifles, without so much as thinking of the greatest blessings; and we are not ashamed many times to ask God for that which we should blush to own to our neighbor.

It is with us as with an innocent that my father had in his family; she fell blind on a sudden, and nobody could persuade her she was blind. "She could not endure the house," she cried, "it was so dark," and was still calling to go abroad. That which we laughed at in her we find to be true in ourselves, we are covetous and ambitious; but the world shall never bring us to acknowledge it, and we impute it to the place: nay, we are the worse of the two; for that blind fool called for a guide, and we wander about without one. It is a hard matter to cure those that will not believe they are sick. We are ashamed to admit a master, and we are too old to learn. Vice still goes before virtue: so that we have two works to do: we must cast off the one, and learn the other. By one evil we make way to another, and only seek things to be avoided, or those of which we are soon weary. That which seemed too much when we wished for it, proves too little when we have it; and it is not, as some imagine, that felicity is greedy, but it is little and narrow, and cannot satisfy us. That which we take to be very high at a distance, we find to be but low when we come at it. And the business is, we do not understand the true state of things: we are deceived by rumors; when we have gained the thing we aimed at, we find it to be either ill or empty; or perchance less than we expect, or otherwise perhaps great, but not good.

XV

THE BLESSINGS OF TEMPERANCE AND MODERATION

There is not anything that is necessary to us but we have it either *cheap* or *gratis*: and this is the provision that our heavenly Father has made for us, whose bounty was never wanting to our needs. It is true the belly craves and calls upon us, but then a small matter contents it: a little bread and water is sufficient, and all the rest is but superfluous. He that lives according to reason shall never be poor, and he that governs his life by opinion shall never be rich: for nature is limited, but fancy is boundless. As for meat, clothes, and lodging, a little feeds the body, and as little covers it; so that if mankind would only attend human nature, without gaping at superfluities, a cook would be found as needless as a soldier: for we may have necessaries upon very easy terms; whereas we put ourselves to great pains for excesses. When we are cold, we may cover ourselves with skins of beasts; and, against violent heats, we have natural grottoes; or with a few osiers and a little clay we may defend ourselves against all seasons. Providence has been kinder to us than to leave us to live by our wits, and to stand in need of invention and arts.

It is only pride and curiosity that involve us in difficulties: if nothing will serve a man but rich clothes and furniture, statues and plate, a numerous train of servants, and the rarities of all nations, it is not Fortune's fault, but his own, that he is not satisfied: for his desires are insatiable, and this is not a thirst, but a disease; and if he were master of the whole world, he would be still a beggar. It is the mind that makes us rich and happy, in what condition soever we are; and money signifies no more to it than it does to the gods. If the religion be sincere, no matter for the ornaments it is only luxury and avarice that make poverty grievous to us; for it is a very small matter that does our business; and when we have provided against cold, hunger, and thirst, all the rest is but vanity and excess: and there is no need of expense upon foreign delicacies, or the artifices of the kitchen. What is he the worse for poverty that despises these things? nay, is he not rather the better for it, because he is not able to go to the price of them? for he is kept sound whether he will or not: and that which a man *cannot* do, looks many times as if he *would not*.

When I look back into the moderation of past ages, it makes me ashamed to discourse, as if poverty had need of any consolation; for we are now come to that degree of intemperance, that a fair patrimony is too little for a meal. Homer had but one servant, Plato three, and Zeno (the master of the masculine sect of Stoics) had none at all. The daughters of Scipio had their portions out of the common treasury, for their father left them not a penny: how happy were the husbands that had the people of Rome for their father-in-law! Shall any man now contemn poverty after these eminent examples, which are sufficient not only to justify but to recommend it? Upon Diogenes' only servant running away from him, he was told where he was, and persuaded to fetch him back again: "What," says he, "can Manes live without Diogenes, and not Diogenes without Manes?" and so let him go.

The piety and moderation of Scipio have made his memory more venerable than his arms; and more yet after he left his country than while he defended it: for matters were come to that pass, that either Scipio must be injurious to Rome or Rome to Scipio. Coarse bread and water to a temperate man is as good as a feast; and the very herbs of the field yield a nourishment to man as well as to beasts. It was not by choice meats and perfumes that our forefathers recommended themselves, but in virtuous actions, and the sweat of honest, military, and of manly labors.

While Nature lay in common, and all her benefits were promiscuously enjoyed, what could be happier than the state of mankind, when people lived without avarice or envy? What could be richer than when there was not a poor man to be found in the world? So soon as this impartial bounty of Providence came to be restrained by covetousness, and that particulars appropriated to themselves that which was intended for all, then did poverty creep into the world, when some men, by desiring more than came to their share, lost their title to the rest; a loss never to be repaired; for though we may come yet to get much, we once had all. The fruits of the earth were in those days divided among the inhabitants of it, without either want or excess. So long as men contented themselves with their lot, there was no violence, no engrossing or hiding of those benefits for particular advantages, which were appointed for the community; but every man had as much care for his neighbor as for himself. No arms or bloodshed, no war, but with wild beasts: but under the protection of a wood or a cave, they spent their days without cares, and their nights without groans; their innocence was their security and their protection. There were as yet no beds of state, no ornaments, of pearl or embroidery, nor any of those remorses that attend them; but the heavens were their canopy, and the glories of them their spectacle. The motions of the orbs, the courses of the stars, and the wonderful order of Providence, was their contemplation. There was no fear of the house falling, or the rustling of a rat behind the arras; they had no palaces then like cities; but they had open air, and breathing room, crystal fountains, refreshing shades, the meadows dressed up in their native beauty, and such cottages as were according to nature, and wherein they lived contentedly, without fear either of losing or of falling. These people lived without either solitude or fraud; and yet I must call them rather happy than wise.

That men were generally better before they were corrupted than after, I make no doubt; and I am apt to believe that they were both stronger and hardier too but their wits were not yet come to maturity; for Nature does not give virtue; and it is a kind of art to become good. They had not as yet torn up the bowels of the earth for gold, silver, or precious stones; and so far were they from killing any man, as we do, for a spectacle, that they were not as yet come to it, either in fear or anger; nay, they spared the very fishes. But, after all this, they were innocent because they were ignorant: and there is a great difference betwixt not knowing how to offend and not being willing to do it. They had, in that rude life, certain images and resemblances of virtue, but yet they fell short of virtue itself, which comes only by institution, learning, and study, as it is perfected by practice. It is indeed the end for which we were born, but yet it did not come into the world with us; and in the best of men, before they are instructed, we find rather the matter and the seeds of virtue than the virtue itself. It is the wonderful benignity of Nature that has laid open to us all things that may do us good, and only hid those things from us that may hurt us; as if she durst not trust us with gold and silver, or with iron, which is the instrument of war and contention, for the other. It is we ourselves that have drawn out of the earth both the *causes* and the *instruments* of our dangers: and we are so vain as to set the highest esteem upon those things to which Nature has assigned the lowest place. What can be more coarse and rude in the mine than these precious metals, or more slavish and dirty than the people that dig and work them? and yet they defile our minds more than our bodies, and make the possessor fouler than the artificer of them. Rich men, in fine, are only the greater slaves; both the one and the other want a great deal.

Happy is that man that eats only for hunger, and drinks only for thirst; that stands upon his own legs, and lives by reason, not by example; and provides for use and necessity, not for ostentation and pomp! Let us curb our appetites, encourage virtue, and rather be beholden to ourselves for riches than to Fortune, who when a man draws himself into a narrow compass, has the least mark at him. Let my bed be plain and clean, and my clothes so too: my meat without much expense, or many waiters, and neither a burden to my purse nor to my body, not to go out the same way it came in. That which is too little for luxury, is abundantly enough for nature. The end of eating and drinking is satiety; now, what matters it though one eats and drinks more, and another less, so long as the one is not a-hungry, nor the other athirst? Epicurus, who limits pleasure to nature, as the Stoics do virtue, is undoubtedly in the right; and those that cite him to authorize their voluptuousness do exceedingly mistake him, and only seek a good authority for an evil cause: for their pleasures of sloth, gluttony, and lust, have no affinity at all with his precepts or meaning. It is true, that at first sight his philosophy seems effeminate; but he that looks nearer him will find him to be a very brave man only in a womanish dress.

It is a common objection, I know, that these philosophers do not live at the rate they talk; fer they can flatter their superiors, gather estates, and be as much concerned at the loss of fortune, or of friends, as other people: as sensible of reproaches, as luxurious in their eating and drinking, their furniture, their houses; as magnificent in their plate, servants, and officers; as profuse and curious in their gardens, etc. Well! and what of all this, or if it were twenty times more? It is some degree of virtue for a man to condemn himself; and if he cannot come up to the best, to be yet better than the worst; and if he cannot wholly subdue his appetites, however to check and diminish them. If I do not live as I preach, take notice that I do not speak of myself, but of virtue, nor am I so much offended with other men's vices as with my own. All this was objected to Plato, Epicurus, Zeno; nor is any virtue so sacred as to escape malevolence. The Cynic Demetrius was a great instance of severity and mortification; and one that imposed upon himself neither to possess anything, nor so much as to ask it: and yet he had this *scorn* put upon him, that his profession was *poverty*, not *virtue*. Plato is blamed for *asking* money; Aristotle for *receiving* it; Democritus for *neglecting* it; Epicurus for *consuming* it. How happy were we if we could but come to imitate these men's vices; for if we knew our own condition, we should find work enough at home. But we are like people that are making merry at a play or a tavern when their own houses are on fire, and yet they know nothing of it. Nay, Cato himself was said to be a drunkard; but *drunkenness* itself shall sooner be proved to be no crime than Cato dishonest. They that demolish temples, and overturn altars, show their good-will, though they can do the gods no hurt, and so it fares with those that invade the reputation of great men.

If the professors of virtue be as the world calls them, avaricious, libidinous, ambitious — what are they then that have a detestation for the very name of it: but malicious natures do not want wit to abuse honester men than themselves. It is the practice of the multitude to bark at eminent men as little dogs do at strangers; for they look upon other men's virtues as the upbraiding of their own wickedness. We should do well to commend those that are good, if not, let us pass them over; but, however, let us spare ourselves: for beside the blaspheming of virtue, our rage is to no purpose. But to return now to my text.

We are ready enough to limit others but loth to put bonds and restraints upon ourselves, though we know that many times a greater evil is cured by a less; and the mind that will not be brought to virtue by precepts, comes to it frequently by necessity. Let us try a little to eat upon a joint stool, to serve ourselves, to live within compass, and accommodate our clothes to the end they were made for. Occasional experiments of our moderation give us the best proof of our firmness and virtue. A well-governed appetite is a great part of liberty, and it is a blessed lot, that since no man can have all things that he would have, we may all of us forbear desiring what we have not. It is the office of temperance to overrule us in our pleasures; some she rejects, others she qualifies and keeps within bounds. Oh! the delights of rest when a man comes to be weary, and of meat when he is heartily hungry.

I have learned (says our author) by one journey how many things we have that are superfluous, and how easily they might be spared, for when we are without them upon necessity, we do not so much as feel the want of them. This is the second blessed day (says he) that my friend and I have travelled together: one wagon carries ourselves and our servants; my mattress lies upon the ground and I upon that: our diet answerable to our lodging, and never without our figs and our table-books. The muleteer without shoes, and the mules only prove themselves to be alive by their walking. In this equipage, I am not willing, I perceive, to own myself, but as often as we happen into better company, I presently fall a-blushing, which shows that I am not yet confirmed in those things which I approve and commend. I am not yet come to own my frugality, for he that is ashamed to be seen in a mean condition would be proud of a splendid one. I value myself upon what passengers think of me, and tacitly renounce my principles, whereas I should rather lift up my voice to be heard by mankind, and tell them "You are all mad — your minds are set upon superfluities and you value no man for his virtues."

I came one night weary home, and threw myself upon the bed with this consideration about me: "There is nothing ill that is well taken." My baker tells me he has no bread; but, says he, I may get some of your tenants, though I fear it is not good. No matter, said I, for I will stay until it be better — that is to say until my stomach will be glad of worse. It is discretion sometimes to practice temperance and wont ourselves to a little, for there are many difficulties both of time and place that may force us upon it.

When we come to the matter of patrimony, how strictly do we examine what every man is worth before we will trust him with a penny! "Such a man," we cry, "has a great estate, but it is shrewdly encumbered — a very fair house, but it was built with borrowed money — a numerous family, but he does not keep touch with his creditors — if his debts were paid he would not be worth a groat." Why do we not take the same course in other things, and examine what every man is worth? It is not enough to have a long train of attendants, vast possessions, or an incredible treasure in money and jewels — a man may be poor for all this. There is only this difference at best — one man borrows of the *usurer*, and the other of *fortune*. What signifies the carving or gilding of the chariot; is the master ever the better of it?

We cannot close up this chapter with a more generous instance of moderation than that of Fabricius. Pyrrhus tempted him with a sum of money to betray his country, and Pyrrhus's physician offered Fabricius, for a sum of money, to poison his *master*; but he was too brave either to be overcome by gold, or to be overcome by poison, so that he refused the money, and advised Pyrrhus to have a care of treachery: and this too in the heat of a licentious war. Fabricius valued himself upon his poverty, and was as much above the thought of riches as of poison. "Live Pyrrhus," says he "by my friendship; and turn that to thy satisfaction which was before thy trouble:" that is to say that Fabricius could not be corrupted.

XVI

CONSTANCY OF MIND GIVES A MAN
REPUTATION, AND MAKES HIM HAPPY
IN DESPITE OF ALL MISFORTUNE

The whole duty of man may be reduced to the two points of *abstinence* and *patience*; *temperance* in *prosperity*, and *courage* in *adversity*. We have already treated of the former: and the other follows now in course.

Epicurus will have it, that a wise man will *bear all injuries*; but the Stoics will not allow those things to be *injuries* which Epicurus calls so. Now, betwixt *these two*, there is the same difference that we find betwixt two *gladiators*; the one receives wounds, but yet maintains his ground, the other tells the people, when he is in blood, that *it is but a scratch*, and will not suffer anybody to part them. An *injury* cannot be received, but it must be *done*; but it may be *done* and yet not *received*; as a man may be in the water, and not swim, but if he swims, it is presumed that he is in the water. Or if a blow or a shot be levelled at us, it may so happen that a man may miss his aim, or some accident interpose that may divert the mischief. That which is hurt is passive, and inferior to that which hurts it. But you will say, that Socrates was condemned and put to death, and so received an injury; but I answer, that the tyrants *did* him an injury, and yet he *received* none. He that steals anything from me and hides it in my own house, though I have not lost it, yet he has stolen it. He that lies with his own wife, and takes her for another woman, though the woman be honest, the man is an adulterer. Suppose a man gives me a draught of poison and it proves not strong enough to kill me, his guilt is nevertheless for the disappointment. He that makes a pass at me is as much a murderer, though I put it by, as if he had struck me to the heart. It is the intention, not the effect, that makes the wickedness. He is a thief that has the will of killing and slaying, before his hand is dipt in blood; as it is sacrilege, the very intention of laying violent hands upon holy things. If a philosopher be exposed to torments, the ax over his head, his body wounded, his guts in his hands, I will allow him to groan; for virtue itself cannot divest him of the nature of a man; but if his mind stand firm, he has discharged his part. A great mind enables a man to maintain his station with honor; so that he only makes use of what he meets in his way, as a pilgrim that would fain be at his journey's end.

It is the excellency of a great mind to *ask* nothing, and to *want* nothing; and to say, "I will have nothing to do with fortune, that repulses Cato, and prefers Vatinius." He that quits his hold, and accounts anything good that is not honest, runs gaping after casualties, spends his days in anxiety and vain expectation, that man is miserable. And yet it is hard, you will say, to be banished or cast into prison: nay, what if it were to be burnt, or any other way destroyed? We have examples in all ages and cases, of great men that have triumphed over all misfortunes. Metellus suffered exile resolutely, Rutilius cheerfully; Socrates disputed in the dungeon; and though he might have made his escape, refused it; to show the world how easy a thing it was to subdue the two great terrors of mankind, *death* and a *jail*. Or what shall we say of Mucius Scevola, a man only of a military courage, and without the help either of philosophy or letters? who, when he found that he had killed the Secretary instead of Porsenna, (the prince,) burnt his right hand to ashes for the mistake; and held his arm in the flame until it was taken away by his very enemies. Porsenna did more easily pardon Mucius for his intent to kill him than Mucius forgave *himself* for missing of his aim. He might have a luckier thing, but never a braver.

Did not Cato, in the last night of his life, take Plato to bed with him, with his sword at his bed's head; the one that he might have death at his will, the other, that he might have it in his power; being resolved that no man should be able to say, either that he killed or that he saved Cato? So soon as he had composed his thoughts, he took his sword; "Fortune," says he, "I have hitherto fought for my country's liberty, and for my own, and only that I might live free among freemen; but the cause is now lost, and Cato safe." With that word he cast himself upon his sword; and after the physicians that pressed in upon him had bound up his wound, he tore it up again, and expired with the same greatness of soul that he lived. But these are the examples, you will say, of men famous in their generations.

Let us but consult history, and we shall find, even in the most effeminate of nations, and the most dissolute of times, men of all degrees, ages, and fortunes, nay, even women themselves, that have overcome the fear of death: which, in truth, is so little to be feared, that duly considered, it is one of the greatest benefits of nature. It was as great an honor for Cato, when his party was broken, that he himself stood his ground, as it would have been if he had carried the day, and settled an universal peace: for, it is an equal prudence, to make the best of a bad game, and to manage a good one. The day that he was *repulsed*, he *played*, and the night that he *killed* himself, he *read*, as valuing the loss of his life, and the missing of an office at the same rate. People, I know, are apt to pronounce upon other men's infirmities by the measure of their own, and to think it impossible that a man should be content to be burnt, wounded, killed, or shackled, though in some cases he may. It is only for a great mind to judge of great things; for otherwise, that which is our infirmity will seem to be another body's, as a straight stick in the water appears to be crooked: he that yields, draws upon his own head his own ruin; for we are sure to get the better of Fortune, if we do but struggle with her. Fencers and wrestlers, we see what blows and bruises they endure, not only for honor, but for exercise. If we turn our backs once, we are routed and pursued; that man only is happy that draws good out of evil, that stands fast in his judgment, and unmoved by any external violence; or however, so little moved, that the keenest arrow in the quiver of Fortune is but as the prick of a needle to him rather than a wound; and all her other weapons fall upon him only as hail upon the roof of a house, that crackles and skips off again, without any damage to the inhabitant.

A generous and clear-sighted young man will take it for a happiness to encounter ill fortune. It is nothing for a man to hold up his head in a calm; but to maintain his post when all others have quitted their ground, and there to stand upright where other men are beaten down, this is divine and praiseworthy. What ill is there in torments, or in those things which we commonly account grievous crosses? The great evil is the want of courage, the bowing and submitting to them, which can never happen to a wise man; for he stands upright under any weight; nothing that is to be borne displeases him; he knows his strength, and whatsoever may be any man's lot, he never complains of, if it be his own. Nature, he says, deceives nobody; she does not tell us whether our children shall be fair or foul, wise or foolish, good subjects or traitors, nor whether our fortune shall be good or bad. We must not judge of a man by his ornaments, but strip him of all the advantages and the impostures of Fortune, nay, of his very body too, and look into his mind. If he can see a naked sword at his eyes without so much as winking; if he make it a thing indifferent to him whether his life go out at his throat or at his mouth; if he can hear himself sentenced to torments or exiles, and under the very hand of the executioner, says thus to himself, "All this I am provided for, and it is no more than a man that is to suffer the fate of humanity." This is the temper of mind that speaks a man happy; and without this, all the confluences of external comforts signify no more than the personating of a king upon the stage; when the curtain is drawn, we are players again. Not that I pretend to exempt a wise man out of a number of men, as if he had no sense of pain; but I reckon him as compounded of body and soul; the body is irrational, and may be galled, burnt, tortured; but the rational part is fearless, invincible, and not to be shaken. This it is that I reckon upon as the supreme good of man; which until it be perfected, is but an unsteady agitation of thought, and in the perfection an immovable stability. It is not in our contentions with Fortune as in those of the theatre, where we may throw down our arms, and pray for quarter; but here we must die firm and resolute. There needs no encouragement to those things which we are inclined to by a natural instinct, as the preservation of ourselves with ease and pleasure; but if it comes to the trial of our faith by torments, or of our courage by wounds, these are difficulties that we must be armed against by philosophy and precept; and yet all this is no more than what we were born to, and no matter of wonder at all; so that a wise man prepares himself for it, as expecting whatsoever *may be will be*. My body is frail, and liable not only to the impressions of violence, but to afflictions also, that naturally succeed our pleasures. Full meals bring crudities; whoring and drinking make the hands to shake and the knees to tremble. It is only the surprise and newness of the thing which makes that misfortune terrible, which, by premeditation, might be made easy to us: for that which some people make light by sufferance, others do by foresight. Whatsoever is necessary, we must bear patiently. It is no new thing to die, no new thing to mourn, and no new thing to be merry again. Must I be *poor*? I shall have company: in *banishment*? I will think myself born there. If I *die*, I shall be no more sick; and it is a thing I cannot do but once.

Let us never wonder at anything we are born to; for no man has reason to complain, where we are all in the same condition. He that escapes might have suffered; and it is but equal to submit to the law of mortality. We must undergo the colds of winter, the heats of summer; the distempers of the air, and the diseases of the body. A wild beast meets us in one place, and a man that is more brutal in another; we are here assaulted by fire, there by water. Demetrius was reserved by Providence for the age he lived in, to show, that neither the times could corrupt him, nor he reform the people. He was a man of an exact judgment, steady to his purpose, and of a strong eloquence; not finical in his words, but his sense was masculine and vehement. He was so qualified in his life and discourse, that he served both for an example and a reproach. If fortune should have offered that man the government and possession of the whole world, upon condition not to lay it down again, I dare say he would have refused it: and thus have expostulated the matter with you: "Why should you tempt a freeman to put his shoulder under a burden; or an honest man to pollute himself with the dregs of mankind? Why do you offer me the spoils of princes, and of nations, and the price not only of your blood, but of your souls?"

It is the part of a great mind to be temperate in prosperity, resolute in adversity; to despise what the vulgar admire, and to prefer a mediocrity to an excess. Was not Socrates oppressed with poverty, labor, nay, the worst of wars in his own family, a fierce and turbulent woman for his wife? were not his children indocile, and like their mother? After seven-and-twenty years spent in arms, he fell under a slavery to the *thirty tyrants*, and most of them his bitter enemies: he came at last to be sentenced as "a violater of religion, a corrupter of youth, and a common enemy to God and man." After this he was imprisoned, and put to death by poison, which was all so far from working upon his mind, that it never so much as altered his countenance. We are to bear ill accidents as unkind seasons, distempers, or diseases; and why may we not reckon the actions of wicked men even among those accidents; their deliberations are not counsels but frauds, snares, and inordinate motions of the mind; and they are never without a thousand pretences and occasions of doing a man mischief. They have their informers, their knights of the post; they can make an interest with powerful men, and one may be robbed as well upon the bench as upon the highway. They lie in wait for advantages, and live in perpetual agitation betwixt hope and fear; whereas he that is truly composed will stand all shocks, either of violences, flatteries, or menaces, without perturbation. It is an inward fear that makes us curious after what we hear abroad.

It is an error to attribute either *good* or *ill* to *Fortune*; but the *matter* of it we may; and we ourselves are the occasion of it, being in effect the artificers of our own happiness or misery: for the mind is above fortune; if that be evil, it makes everything else so too; but if it be right and sincere, it corrects what is wrong, and mollifies what is hard, with modesty and courage. There is a great difference among those that the world calls wise men. Some take up private resolutions of opposing Fortune, but they cannot go through with them; for they are either dazzled with splendor on the one hand, or affrighted with terrors on the other; but there are others that will close and grapple with Fortune, and still come off victorious.

Mucius overcame the fire; Regulus, the gibbet; Socrates, poison; Rutilius, banishment; Cato, death; Fabricius, riches; Tubero, poverty; and Sextius, honors. But there are some again so delicate, that they cannot so much as bear a scandalous report; which is the same thing as if a man should quarrel for being jostled in a crowd, or dashed as he walks in the streets. He that has a great way to go must expect a slip, to stumble, and to be tired. To the luxurious man frugality is a punishment; labor and industry to the sluggard; nay, study itself is a torment to him; not that these things are hard to us by nature, but we ourselves are vain and irresolute; nay, we wonder many of us, how any man can live without wine, or endure to rise so early in a morning.

A brave man must expect to be tossed; for he is to steer his course in the teeth of Fortune, and to work against wind and weather. In the suffering of torments, though there appears but one virtue, a man exercises many. That which is most eminent is patience, (which is but a branch of fortitude.) But there is prudence also in the choice of the action, and in the bearing what we cannot avoid; and there is constancy in bearing it resolutely: and there is the same concurrence also of several virtues in other generous undertakings.

When Leonidas was to carry his 300 men into the Straits of Thermopylae, to put a stop to Xerxes's huge army: "Come, fellow-soldiers," says he, "eat your dinners here as if you were to sup in another world." And they answered his resolution. How plain and imperious was that short speech of Caeditius to his men upon a desperate action! and how glorious a mixture was there in it both of bravery and prudence! "Soldiers," says he, "it is necessary for us to go, but it is not necessary for us to return." This brief and pertinent harangue was worth ten thousand of the frivolous cavils and distinctions of the schools, which rather break the mind than fortify it; and when it is once perplexed and pricked with difficulties and scruples, there they leave it. Our passions are numerous and strong, and not to be mastered with quirks and tricks, as if a man should undertake to defend the cause of God and man with a bulrush. It was a remarkable piece of honor and policy together, that action of Caesar's upon the taking of Pompey's cabinet at the battle of Pharsalia: it is probable that the letters in it might have discovered who were his friends, and who his enemies; and yet he burnt it without so much as opening it; esteeming it the noblest way of pardoning, to keep himself ignorant both of the offender and of the offense. It was a brave presence of mind also in Alexander, who, upon advice that his physician Philip intended to poison him, took the letter of advice in one hand and the cup in the other; delivering Philip the letter to read while he himself drank the potion.

Some are of opinion that death gives a man courage to support pain, and that pain fortifies a man against death: but I say rather, that a wise man depends upon himself against both, and that he does not either suffer with patience, in hopes of death, or die willingly, because he is weary of life; but he bears the one, and waits for the other, and carries a divine mind through all the accidents of human life. He looks upon faith and honesty as the most sacred good of mankind, and neither to be forced by necessity nor corrupted by reward; kill, burn, tear him in pieces, he will be true to his trust; and the more any man labors to make him discover a secret, the deeper will he hide it. Resolution is the inexpugnable defence of human weakness, and it is a wonderful Providence that attends it.

Horatius Cocles opposed his single body to the whole army until the bridge was cut down behind him and then leaped into the river with his sword in his hand and came off safe to his party. There was a fellow questioned about a plot upon the life of a tyrant, and put to the torture to declare his confederates: he named, by one and one, all the tyrant's friends that were about him: and still as they were named, they were put to death: the tyrant asked him at last if there were any more. "Yes," says he, "yourself were in the plot; and now you have never another friend left in the world:" whereupon the tyrant cut the throats of his own guards. "He is the happy man that is the master of himself, and triumphs over the fear of death, which has overcome the conquerors of the world."

XVII

OUR HAPPINESS DEPENDS IN A GREAT
MEASURE UPON THE CHOICE OF OUR COMPANY

The comfort of life depends upon conversation. Good offices, and concord, and human society, is like the working of an arch of stone; all would fall to the ground if one piece did not support another. Above all things let us have a tenderness for blood; and it is yet too little not to hurt, unless we profit one another. We are to relieve the distressed; to put the wanderer into his way; and to divide our bread with the hungry: which is but the doing of good to ourselves; for we are only several members of one great body. Nay, we are all of a consanguinity; formed of the same materials, and designed to the same end; this obliges us to a mutual tenderness and converse; and the other, to live with a regard to equity and justice. The love of society is natural; but the choice of our company is matter of virtue and prudence. Noble examples stir us up to noble actions; and the very history of large and public souls, inspires a man with generous thoughts. It makes a man long to be in action, and doing something that the world may be the better for; as protecting the weak, delivering the oppressed, punishing the insolent. It is a great blessing the very conscience of giving a good example; beside, that it is the greatest obligation any man can lay upon the age he lives in.

He that converses with the proud shall be puffed up; a lustful acquaintance makes a man lascivious; and the way to secure a man from wickedness is to withdraw from the examples of it. It is too much to have them *near* us, but more to have them *within* us — ill examples, pleasure and ease, are, no doubt of it, great corrupters of manners.

A rocky ground hardens the horse's hoof; the mountaineer makes the best soldier; the miner makes the best pioneer, and severity of discipline fortifies the mind. In all excesses and extremities of good and of ill fortune, let us have recourse to great examples that have contemned both. "These are the best instructors that teach in their lives, and prove their words by their actions."

As an ill air may endanger a good constitution, so may a place of ill example endanger a good man, nay, there are some places that have a kind of privilege to be licentious, and where luxury and dissolution of manners seem to be lawful; for great examples give both authority and excuse to wickedness. Those places are to be avoided as dangerous to our manners. Hannibal himself was unmanned by the looseness of Campania, and though a conqueror by his arms, he was overcome by his pleasures. I would as soon live among butchers as among cooks — not but a man may be temperate in any place — but to see drunken men staggering up and down everywhere, and only the spectacle of lust, luxury and excess before our eyes, it is not safe to expose ourselves to the temptation. If the victorious Hannibal himself could not resist it, what shall become of us then that are subdued, and give ground to our lusts already? He that has to do with an enemy in his breast, has a harder task upon him than he that is to encounter one in the field; his hazard is greater if he loses ground, and his duty is perpetual, for he has no place or time for rest. If I give way to pleasure, I must also yield to grief, to poverty, to labor, ambition, anger, until I am torn to pieces by my misfortunes and lusts. But against all this philosophy propounds a liberty, that is to say, a liberty from the service of accidents and fortune. There is not anything that does more mischief to mankind than mercenary masters and philosophy, that do not live as they teach — they give a scandal to virtue. How can any man expect that a ship should steer a fortunate course, when the pilot lies wallowing in his own vomit? It is a usual thing first to learn to do ill ourselves, and then to instruct others to do so: but that man must needs be very wicked that has gathered into himself the wickedness of other people.

The best conversation is with the philosophers — that is to say, with such of them as teach us matter, not words — that preach to us things necessary and keep us to the practice of them. There can be no peace in human life without the contempt of all events. There is nothing that either puts better thoughts into a man, or sooner sets him right that is out of the way, than a good companion, for the example has the force of a precept, and touches the heart with an affection to goodness; and not only the frequent hearing and seeing of a wise man delights us, but the very encounter of him suggests profitable contemplation such as a man finds himself moved with when he goes into a holy place. I will take more care with *whom* I eat and drink than *what*, for without a friend the table is a manger.

Writing does well, but personal discourse and conversation does better; for men give great credit to their ears, and take stronger impressions from example than precept. Cleanthes had never hit Zeno so to the life if he had not been in with him at all his privacies, if he had not watched and observed him whether or not he practised as he taught. Plato got more from Socrates' *manners* than from his *words*, and it was not the *school*, but the company and *familiarity* of Epicurus that made Metrodorus, Hermachus and Polyaenus so famous.

Now, though it be by instinct that we covet society, and avoid solitude, we should yet take this along with us, that the more acquaintance the more danger: nay, there is not one man of a hundred that is to be trusted with himself. If company cannot alter us, it may interrupt us, and he that so much as stops upon the way loses a great deal of a short life, which we yet make shorter by our inconstancy. If an enemy were at our heels, what haste should we make! — but death is so, and yet we never mind it. There is no venturing of tender and easy natures among the people, for it is odds that they will go over to the major party. It would, perhaps, shake the constancy of Socrates,

Cato, Laelius, or any of us all, even when our resolutions are at the height, to stand the shock of vice that presses upon us with a kind of public authority.

It is a world of mischief that may be done by one single example of avarice or luxury. One voluptuous palate makes a great many. A wealthy neighbor stirs up envy, and a fleering companion moves ill-nature wherever he comes. What will become of those people then that expose themselves to a popular violence? which is ill both ways; either if they comply with the wicked, because they are many, or quarrel with the multitude because they are not principled alike. The best way is to retire, and associate only with those that may be the better for us, and we for them. These respects are mutual; for while we teach, we learn. To deal freely, I dare not trust myself in the hands of much company: I never go abroad that I come home again the same man I went out. Something or other that I had put in order is discomposed; some passion that I had subdued gets head again; and it is just with our minds as it is after a long indisposition with our bodies; we are grown so tender, that the least breath of air exposes us to a relapse. And it is no wonder if a numerous conversation be dangerous, where there is scarce any single man but by his discourse, example, or behavior, does either recommend to us, or imprint in us, or, by a kind of contagion, insensibly infect us with one vice or other; and the more people the greater is the peril. Especially let us have a care of public spectacles where wickedness insinuates itself with pleasure; and, above all others, let us avoid spectacles of cruelty and blood; and have nothing to do with those that are perpetually whining and complaining; there may be faith and kindness there, but no peace. People that are either sad or fearful, we do commonly, for their own sakes, set a guard upon them, for fear they should make an ill use of being alone; especially the imprudent, who are still contriving of mischief, either for others or for themselves, in cherishing their lusts, or forming their designs. So much for the choice of a *companion*; we shall now proceed to that of a *friend*.

XVIII

THE BLESSINGS OF FRIENDSHIP

Of all felicities, the most charming is that of a *firm* and *gentle friend-ship*. It sweetens all our cares, dispels our sorrows, and counsels us in all extremities. Nay, if there were no other comfort in it than the bare exercise of so generous a virtue, even for that single reason, a man would not be without it. Beside, that it is a sovereign antidote against all calamities, even against the fear of death itself.

But we are not to number our friends by the *visits* that are made us; and to confound the decencies of *ceremony* and *commerce* with the offices of *united affections*. Caius Gracchus, and after him Livius Drusus, were the men that introduced among the Romans the fashion of separating their visitants; some were taken into their *closet,* others were only admitted into the *antechamber*: and some, again, were fain to wait in the *hall* perhaps, or in the *court*. So that they had their *first*, their *second,* and their *third* rate friends; but none of them true: only they are called so in course, as we salute strangers with some title or other of respect at a venture. There is no depending upon those men that only take their compliment in their turn, and rather slip through the door than enter at it. He will find himself in a great mistake, that either seeks for a friend in a palace, or tries him at a feast.

The great difficulty rests in the choice of him; that is to say, in the first place, let him be virtuous, for vice is contagious, and there is no trusting the sound and the sick together; and he ought to be a wise man too, if a body knew where to find him; but in this case, he that is least ill is best, and the highest degree of human prudence is only the most venial folly. That friendship where men's affections are cemented by an equal and by a common love of goodness, it is not either hope or fear, or any private interest, that can ever dissolve it: but we carry it with us to our graves, and lay down our lives for it with satisfaction. Paulina's good and mine (says our author) were so wrapped up together, that in consulting her comfort I provided for my own; and when I could not prevail upon her to take less care for me, she prevailed upon me to take more care for myself.

Some people make it a question, whether is the greatest delight, the enjoying of an old friendship, or the acquiring of a new one? but it is in the preparing of a friendship, and in the possession of it, as it is with the husbandman in sowing and reaping; his delight is the hope of his labor in the one case, and the fruit of it in the other. My conversation lies among my books, but yet in the letters of a friend, methinks I have his company; and when I answer them, I do not only write, but speak: and, in effect, a friend is an eye, a heart, a tongue, a hand, at all distances. When friends see one another personally, they do not see one another as they do when they are divided, where the meditation dignifies the prospect; but they are effectually in a great measure absent even when they are present. Consider their nights apart, their private studies, their separate employments, and necessary visits; and they are almost as much together divided as present. True friends are the whole world to one another; and he that is a friend to himself is also a friend to mankind. Even in my very studies, the greatest delight I take in what I learn is the teaching of it to others; for there is no relish, methinks, in the possession of anything without a partner; nay, if wisdom itself were offered me upon condition only of keeping it to myself, I should undoubtedly refuse it.

Lucilius tells me, that he was written to by a friend, but cautions me withal not to say anything to him of the affair in question; for he himself stands upon the same guard. What is this but to affirm and to deny the same thing in the same breath, in calling a man a friend, whom we dare not trust as our own soul? For there must be no reserves in friendship: as much deliberation as you please before the league is struck, but no doubtings or jealousies after. It is a preposterous weakness to love a man before we know him, and not to care for him after. It requires time to consider of a friendship, but the resolution once taken, entitles him to my very heart. I look upon my thoughts to be as safe in his breast as in my own: I shall, without any scruple, make him the confidant of my most secret cares and counsels.

It goes a great way toward the making of a man faithful, to let him understand that you think him so: and he that does but so much as suspect that I will deceive him gives me a kind of right to cozen him. When I am with my friend, methinks I am alone, and as much at liberty to speak anything as to think it, and as our hearts are one, so must be our interest and convenience; for friendship lays all things in common, and nothing can be good to the one that is ill to the other. I do not speak of such a community as to destroy one another's propriety; but as the father and the mother have two children, not one apiece, but each of them two.

But let us have a care, above all things, that our kindness be rightfully founded; for where there is any other invitation to friendship than the friendship itself, that friendship will be bought and sold. He derogates upon the majesty of it that makes it only dependent upon good fortune. It is a narrow consideration for a man to please himself in the thought of a friend, "because," says he, "I shall have one to help me when I am sick, in prison, or in want." A brave man should rather take delight in the contemplation of doing the same offices for another. He that loves a man for his own sake is in an error. A friendship of interest cannot last any longer than the interest itself, and this is the reason that men in prosperity are so much followed, and when a man goes down the wind, nobody comes near him.

Temporary friends will never stand the test. One man is forsaken for fear of profit, another is betrayed. It is a negotiation, not a friendship, that has an eye to advantages; only, through the corruption of times, that which was formerly a friendship is now become a design upon a booty: alter your testament, and you lose your friend. But my end of friendship is to have one dearer to me than myself, and for the saving of whose life I would cheerfully lay down my own; taking this along with me, that only wise men can be friends, others are but companions; and that there is a great difference also betwixt love and friendship; the one may sometimes do us hurt, the other always does us good, for the one friend is hopeful to another in all cases, as well in prosperity as in affliction. We receive comfort, even at a distance, from those we love, but then it is light and faint; whereas, presence and conversation touch us to the quick, especially if we find the man we love to be such a person as we wish.

It is usual with princes to reproach the living by commending the dead, and to praise those people for speaking truth from whom there is no longer any danger of hearing it. This is Augustus's case: he was forced to banish his daughter Julia for her common and prostituted impudence; and still upon fresh informations, he was often heard to say, "If Agrippa or Mecenas had been now alive, this would never have been." But yet where the fault lay may be a question; for perchance it was his own, that had rather complain for the want of them than seek for others as good. The Roman losses by war and by fire, Augustus could quickly supply and repair; but for the loss of two friends he lamented his whole life after.

Xerxes, (a vain and a foolish prince) when he made war upon Greece, one told him, "It would never come to a battle";another,

"That he would find only empty cities and countries, for they would not so much as stand the very fame of his coming;" others soothed him in the opinion of his *prodigious numbers*; and they all concurred to puff him up to his destruction; only Damaratus advised him not to depend too much upon his numbers, for he would rather find them a burden to him than an advantage: and that three hundred men in the straits of the mountains would be sufficient to give a check to his whole army; and that such an accident would undoubtedly turn his vast numbers to his confusion. It fell out afterward as he foretold, and he had thanks for his fidelity. A miserable prince, that among so many thousand subjects had but one servant to tell him the truth!

XIX

HE THAT WOULD BE HAPPY MUST
TAKE AN ACCOUNT OF HIS TIME

In the distribution of human life, we find that a great part of it passes away in *evil doing*; a greater yet in doing just *nothing at all*: and effectually the whole in doing things *beside our business*. Some hours we bestow upon ceremony and servile attendances; some upon our pleasures, and the remainder runs at waste. What a deal of time is it that we spend in hopes and fears, love and revenge, in balls, treats, making of interests, suing for offices, soliciting of causes, and slavish flatteries! The shortness of life, I know, is the common complaint both of fools and philosophers; as if the time we have were not sufficient for our duties. But it is with our lives as with our estates, a good husband makes a little go a great way; whereas, let the revenue of a prince fall into the hands of a prodigal, it is gone in a moment. So that the time allotted us, if it were well employed, were abundantly enough to answer all the ends and purposes of mankind. But we squander it away in avarice, drink, sleep, luxury, ambition, fawning addresses, envy, rambling, voyages, impertinent studies, change of counsels, and the like; and when our portion is spent, we find the want of it, though we gave no heed to it in the passage: insomuch, that we have rather *made* our life short than *found* it so. You shall have some people perpetually playing with their fingers, whistling, humming, and talking to themselves; and others consume their days in the composing, hearing, or reciting of songs and lampoons. How many precious morning hours do we spend in consultation with barbers, tailors, and tire-women, patching and painting betwixt the comb and the glass! A council must be called upon every hair we cut; and one curl amiss is as much as a body's life is worth. The truth is, we are more solicitous about our dress than our manners, and about the order of our periwigs than that of the government. At this rate, let us but discount, out of a life of a hundred years, that time which has been spent upon popular negotiations, frivolous amours, domestic brawls, sauntering up and down to no purpose, diseases that we have brought upon ourselves, and this large extent of life will not amount perhaps to the minority of another man. It is a *long being*, but perchance a *short life*. And what is the reason of all this? We live as we should never die, and without any thought of human frailty, when yet the very moment we bestow upon this man or thing, may, peradventure, be our last. But the greatest loss of time is delay and expectation, which depend upon the future. We let go the present, which we have in our own power; we look forward to that which depends upon Fortune; and so quit a certainty for an uncertainty. We should do by time as we do by a torrent, make use of it while we have it, for it will not last always.

The calamities of human nature may be divided into the *fear of death*, and the *miseries and errors of life*. And it is the great work of mankind to master the one, and to rectify the other; and so live as neither to make life irksome to us, nor death terrible. It should be our care, before we are old, to live well, and when we are so, to die well; that we may expect our end without sadness: for it is the duty of life to prepare ourselves for death; and there is not an hour we live that does not mind us of our mortality.

Time runs on, and all things have their fate, though it lies in the dark. The period is certain to nature, but what am I the better for it if it be not so to me? We propound travels, arms, adventures, without ever considering that death lies in the way. Our term is set, and none of us know how near it is; but we are all of us agreed that the decree is unchangeable. Why should we wonder to have that befall us to-day which might have happened to us any minute since we were born? Let us therefore live as if every moment were to be our last, and set our accounts right every day that passes over our heads. We are not ready for death, and therefore we fear it, because we do not know what will become of us when we are gone, and that consideration strikes us with an inexplicable terror. The way to avoid this distraction is to contract our business and our thoughts — when the mind is once settled, a day or an age is all one to us; and the series of time, which is now our trouble will be then our delight; for he that is steadily resolved against all uncertainties, shall never be disturbed with the variety of them. Let us make haste, therefore, to live, since every day to a wise man is a new life — for he has done his business the day before, and so prepared himself for the next, that if it be not his last, he knows yet that it might have been so. No man enjoys the true taste of life but he that is willing and ready to quit it.

The wit of man is not able to express the blindness of human folly in taking so much more care of our fortunes, our houses, and our money, than we do of our lives — everybody breaks in upon the one *gratis*, but we betake ourselves to fire and sword if any man invades the other. There is no dividing in the case of patrimony, but people share our time with us at pleasure, so profuse are we of that only thing whereof we may be honestly covetous. It is a common practice to ask an hour or two of a friend for such or such a business, and it is as easily granted, both parties only considering the occasion, and not the thing itself. They never put time to account, which is the most valuable of all precious things; but because they do not see it they reckon upon it as nothing: and yet these easy men when they come to die would give the whole world for those hours again which they so inconsiderately cast away before; but there is no recovering of them. If they could number their days that are yet to come as they can those that are already past, how would those very people tremble at the apprehension of death, though a hundred years hence, that never so much as think of it at present, though they know not but it may take them away the next immediate minute!

It is an usual saying "I would give my life for such or such a friend," when, at the same time, we do give it without so much as thinking of it; nay, when that friend is never the better for it, and we ourselves the worse. Our time is set, and day and night we travel on. There is no baiting by the way, and it is not in the power of either prince or people to prolong it. Such is the love of life, that even those decrepit dotards that have lost the use of it will yet beg the continuance of it, and make themselves younger than they are, as if they could cozen even Fate itself! When they fall sick, what promises of amendment if they escape that bout! What exclamations against the folly of their misspent time — and yet if they recover, they relapse. No man takes care to live well, but long; when yet it is in everybody's power to do the former, and in no man's to do the latter. We consume our lives in providing the very instruments of life, and govern ourselves still with a regard to the future, so that we do not properly live, but we are about to live. How great a shame is it to be laying new foundations of life at our last gasp, and for an old man (that can only prove his age by his beard,) with one foot in the grave, to go to school again! While we are young we may learn; our minds are tractable and our bodies fit for labor and study; but when age comes on, we are seized with languor and sloth, afflicted with diseases, and at last we leave the world as ignorant as we came into it — only we *die* worse than we were *born*, which is none of Nature's fault, but ours; for our fears, suspicions, perfidy, etc., are from ourselves.

I wish with all my soul that I had thought of my end sooner, but I must make the more haste now and spur on like those that set out late upon a journey — it will be better to learn late than not at all — though it be but only to instruct me how I may leave the stage with honor.

In the division of life, there is time *present*, *past*, and *to come*. What we *do* is *short*, what we *shall do* is *doubtful*, but what we *have done* is *certain*, and out of the power of fortune. The passage of time is wonderfully quick, and a man must look backward to see it; and, in that retrospect, he has all past ages at a view; but the present gives us the slip unperceived. It is but a moment that we live, and yet we are dividing it into *childhood*, *youth*, *man's estate*, and *old age*, all which degrees we bring into that narrow compass. If we do not watch, we lose our opportunities; if we do not make haste, we are left behind; our best hours escape us, the worst are to come. The purest part of our life runs first, and leaves only the dregs at the bottom; and "that time which is good for nothing else, we dedicate to virtue;" and only propound to begin to live at an age that very few people arrive at. What greater folly can there be in the world than this loss of time, the future being so uncertain, and the damages so irreparable? If death be necessary, why should any man fear it? and if the time of it be uncertain, why should not we always expect it? We should therefore first prepare ourselves by a virtuous life against the dread of an inevitable death; and it is not for us to put off being good until such or such a business is over, for one business draws on another, and we do as good as sow it, one grain produces more. It is not enough to philosophize when we have nothing else to do, but we must attend wisdom even to the neglect of all things else; for we are so far from having time to spare, that the age of the world would be yet too narrow for our business; nor is it sufficient not to omit it, but we must not so much as intermit it.

There is nothing that we can properly call our own but our time, and yet every body fools us out of it that has a mind to it. If a man borrows a paltry sum of money, there must be bonds and securities, and every common civility is charged upon account; but he that has my time, thinks he owes me nothing for it, though it be a debt that gratitude itself can never repay. I cannot call any man poor that has enough still left, be it never so little: it is good advice yet to those that have the world before them, to play the good husbands betimes, for it is too late to spare at the bottom, when all is drawn out to the lees. He that takes away a day from me, takes away what he can never restore me. But our time is either *forced away* from us, or *stolen* from us, or *lost*; of which the last is the foulest miscarriage. It is in life as in a journey; a book or a companion brings us to our lodging before we thought we were half-way. Upon the whole matter we consume ourselves one upon another, without any regard at all to our own particular. I do not speak of such as live in notorious scandal, but even those men themselves, whom the world pronounces happy, are smothered in their felicities, servants to their professions and clients, and drowned in their lusts. We are apt to complain of the haughtiness of *great men*, when yet there is hardly any of them all so proud but that, at some time or other, a man may yet have access to him, and perhaps a good word or look into the bargain. Why do we not rather complain of *ourselves*, for being of all others, even to ourselves, the most deaf and inaccessible.

Company and business are great devourers of time, and our vices destroy our lives as well as our fortunes. The present is but a moment, and perpetually in flux; the time past, we call to mind when we please, and it will abide the examination and inspection. But the busy man has not leisure to look back, or if he has, it is an unpleasant thing to reflect upon a life to be repented of, whereas the conscience of a good life puts a man into a secure and perpetual possession of a felicity never to be disturbed or taken away: but he that has led a wicked life is afraid of his own memory; and, in the review of himself, he finds only appetite, avarice, or ambition, instead of virtue. But still he that is not at leisure many times to live, must, when his fate comes, whether he will or not, be at leisure to die. Alas! what is time to eternity? the age of a man to the age of the world? And how much of this little do we spend in fears, anxieties, tears, childhood! nay, we sleep away the one half. How great a part of it runs away in luxury and excess: the ranging of our guests, our servants, and our dishes! As if we were to eat and drink not for satiety, but ambition. The nights may well seem short that are so dear bought, and bestowed upon wine and women; the day is lost in expectation of the night, and the night in the apprehension of the morning. There is a terror in our very pleasures; and this vexatious thought in the very height of them, that *they will not last always*: which is a canker in the delights, even of the greatest and the most fortunate of men.

XX

HAPPY IS THE MAN THAT MAY
CHOOSE HIS OWN BUSINESS

Oh the blessings of privacy and leisure! The wish of the powerful and eminent, but the privilege only of inferiors; who are the only people that live to themselves: nay, the very thought and hope of it is a consolation, even in the middle of all the tumults and hazards that attend greatness. It was Augustus' prayer, that he might live to retire and deliver himself from public business: his discourses were still pointing that way, and the highest felicity which this mighty prince had in prospect, was the divesting himself of that illustrious state, which, how glorious soever in show, had at the bottom of it only anxiety and care. But it is one thing to retire for pleasure, and another thing for virtue, which must be active even in that retreat, and give proof of what it has learned: for a good and a wise man does in privacy consult the well-being of posterity. Zeno and Chrysippus did greater things in their studies than if they had led armies, borne offices, or given laws; which in truth they did, not to one city alone, but to all mankind: their *quiet* contributed more to the common benefit than the *sweat* and *labor* of other people. That retreat is not worth the while which does not afford a man greater and nobler work than business. There is no slavish attendance upon great officers, no canvassing for places, no making of parties, no disappointments in my pretension to this charge, to that regiment, or to such or such a title, no envy of any man's favor or fortune; but a calm enjoyment of the general bounties of Providence in company with a good conscience. A wise man is never so busy as in the solitary contemplation of God and the works of Nature. He withdraws himself to attend the service of future ages: and those counsels which he finds salutary to himself, he commits to writing for the good of after-times, as we do the receipts of sovereign antidotes or balsams. He that is well employed in his study, though he may seem to do nothing at all, does the greatest things yet of all others, in affairs both human and divine. To supply a friend with a sum of money, or give my voice for an office, these are only private and particular obligations: but he that lays down precepts for the governing of our lives and the moderating of our passions, obliges human nature not only in the present, but in all succeeding generations.

He that would be at quiet, let him repair to his philosophy, a study that has credit with all sorts of men. The eloquence of the bar, or whatsoever else addresses to the people, is never without enemies; but philosophy minds its own business, and even the worst have an esteem for it. There can never be such a conspiracy against virtue, the world can never be so wicked, but the very name of a *philosopher* shall still continue venerable and sacred. And yet philosophy itself must be handled modestly and with caution. But what shall we say of Cato then, for his meddling in the broil of a civil war, and interposing himself in the quarrel betwixt two enraged princes? He that, when Rome was split into *two factions* betwixt Pompey and Caesar, declared himself against *both*. I speak this of Cato's last part; for in his former time the commonwealth was made unfit for a wise man's administration. All he could do then was but bawling and beating of the air: one while he was lugged and tumbled by the rabble, spit upon and dragged out of the *forum*, and then again hurried out of the senate-house to prison. There are some things which we propound originally, and others which fall in as accessory to another proposition. If a wise man retire, it is no matter whether he does it because the commonwealth was wanting to him, or because he was wanting to it. But to what republic shall a man betake himself? Not to Athens, where Socrates was condemned, and whence Aristotle fled, for fear he should have been condemned too, and where virtue was oppressed by envy: not to Carthage, where there was nothing but tyranny, injustice, cruelty, and ingratitude. There is scarce any government to be found that will either endure a wise man, or which a wise man will endure; so that privacy is made necessary, because the only thing which is better is nowhere to be had. A man may commend navigation, and yet caution us against those seas that are troublesome and dangerous: so that he does as good as command me not to weigh anchor that commends sailing only upon these terms. He that is a slave to business is the most wretched of slaves.

"But how shall I get myself at liberty? We can run any hazards for money: take any pains for honor; and why do we not venture also something for leisure and freedom? without which we must expect to live and die in a tumult: for so long as we live in public, business breaks in upon us, as one billow drives on another; and there is no avoiding it with either modesty or quiet." It is a kind of whirlpool, that sucks a man in, and he can never disengage himself. A man of business cannot in truth be said to live, and not one of a thousand understands how to do it: for how to live, and how to die, is the lesson of every moment of our lives: all other arts have their masters.

As a busy life is always a miserable life, so it is the greatest of all miseries to be perpetually employed upon *other people's business*; for to sleep, to eat, to drink, at their hour; to walk their pace, and to love and hate as they do, is the vilest of servitudes. Now, though business must be quitted, let it not be done unseasonably; the longer we defer it, the more we endanger our liberty; and yet we must no more fly before the time than linger when the time comes: or, however, we must not love business for business' sake, nor indeed do we, but for the profit that goes along with it: for we love the reward of misery, though we hate the misery itself. Many people, I know, seek business without choosing it, and they are even weary of their lives without it for want of entertainment in their own thoughts; the hours are long and hateful to them when they are alone, and they seem as short on the other side in their debauches. When they are no longer *candidates*, they are *suffragans*; when they give over other people's business, they do their own; and pretend business, but they make it, and value themselves upon being thought men of employment.

Liberty is the thing which they are perpetually a-wishing, and never come to obtain: a thing never to be bought nor sold, but a man must ask it of himself, and give it to himself. He that has given proof of his virtue in public, should do well to make a trial of it in private also. It is not that solitude, or a country life, teaches innocence or frugality; but vice falls of itself, without witnesses and spectators, for the thing it designs is to be taken notice of. Did ever any man put on rich clothes not to be seen? or spread the pomp of his luxury where nobody was to take notice of it? If it were not for admirers and spectators there would be no temptations to excess: the very keeping of us from exposing them cures us of desiring them, for vanity and intemperance are fed with ostentation.

He that has lived at sea in a storm, let him retire and die in the haven; but let his retreat be without ostentation, and wherein he may enjoy himself with a good conscience, without the want, the fear, the hatred, or the desire, of anything, not out of malevolent detestation of mankind, but for satisfaction and repose. He that shuns both business and men, either out of envy, or any other discontent, his retreat is but to the life of a mole: nor does he live to himself, as a wise man does, but to his bed, his belly, and his lusts. Many people seem to retire out of a weariness of public affairs, and the trouble of disappointments; and yet ambition finds them out even in that recess into which fear and weariness had cast them; and so does luxury, pride, and most of the distempers of a public life.

There are many that lie close, not that they may live securely, but that they may transgress more privately: it is their conscience, not their states, that makes them keep a porter; for they live at such a rate, that to be seen before they be aware is to be detected. Crates saw a young man walking by himself; "Have a care," says he "of lewd company." Some men are busy in idleness, and make peace more laborious and troublesome than war; nay, and more wicked too, when they bestow it upon such lusts, and other vices, which even the license of a military life would not endure. We cannot call these people men of leisure that are wholly taken up with their pleasures. A troublesome life is much to be preferred before a slothful one; and it is a strange thing, methinks, that any man should fear death that has buried himself alive; as privacy without letters is but the burying of a man quick.

There are some that make a boast of their retreat, which is but a kind of lazy ambition; they retire to make people talk of them, whereas I would rather withdraw to speak to myself. And what shall that be, but that which we are apt to speak of one another? I will speak ill of myself: I will examine, accuse, and punish my infirmities. I have no design to be cried up for a great man, that has renounced the world in a contempt of the vanity and madness of human life; I blame nobody but myself, and I address only to myself. He that comes to me for help is mistaken, for I am not a physician, but a patient: and I shall be well enough content to have it said, when any man leaves me, "I took him for a happy and a learned man, and truly I find no such matter." I had rather have my retreat pardoned than envied.

There are some creatures that confound their footing about their dens, that they may not be found out, and so should a wise man in the case of his retirement. When the door is open, the thief passes it by as not worth his while; but when it is bolted and sealed, it is a temptation for people to be prying. To have it said "that such a one is never out of his study, and sees nobody," etc.; this furnishes matter for discourse. He that makes his retirement too strict and severe, does as good as call company to take notice of it.

Every man knows his own constitution; one eases his stomach by vomit — another supports it with good nourishment; he that has the gout forbears wine and bathing, and every man applies to the part that is most infirm. He that shows a gouty foot, a lame hand, or contracted nerves, shall be permitted to lie still and attend his cure; and why not so in the vices of his mind! We must discharge all impediments and make way for philosophy, as a study inconsistent with common business. To all other things we must deny ourselves openly and frankly, when we are sick refuse visits, keep ourselves close, and lay aside all public cares, and shall we not do as much when we philosophize? Business is the drudgery of the world, and only fit for slaves, but contemplation is the work of wise men. Not but that solitude and company may be allowed to take their turns: the one creates in us the love of mankind, the other that of ourselves; solitude relieves us when we are sick of company, and conversation when we are weary of being alone; so that the one cures the other. "There is no man," in fine, "so miserable as he that is at a loss how to spend his time." He is restless in his thoughts, unsteady in his counsels, dissatisfied with the present, solicitous for the future; whereas he that prudently computes his hours and his business, does not only fortify himself against the common accidents of life, but improves the most rigorous dispensations of Providence to his comfort, and stands firm under all the trials of human weakness.

XXI

THE CONTEMPT OF DEATH MAKES
ALL THE MISERIES OF LIFE EASY TO US

It is a hard task to master the natural desire of life by a philosophical contempt of death, and to convince the world that there is no hurt in it, and crush an opinion that was brought up with us from our cradles. What help? what encouragement? what shall we say to human frailty, to carry it fearless through the fury of flames, and upon the points of swords? what rhetoric shall we use to bear down the universal consent of people to so dangerous an error? The captious and superfine subtleties of the schools will never do the work: these speak many things sharp, but utterly unnecessary, and void of effect. The truth of it is, there is but one chain that holds all the world in bondage, and that is the love of life. It is not that I propound the making of death so indifferent to us, as it is, whether a man's hairs be even or odd; for what with self-love, and an implanted desire in every being of preserving itself, and a long acquaintance betwixt the soul and body, friends may be loth to part, and death may carry an appearance of evil, though in truth it is itself no evil at all. Beside, that we are to go to a strange place in the dark, and under great uncertainties of our future state; so that people die in terror, because they do not know whither they are to go, and they are apt to fancy the worst of what they do not understand: these thoughts are indeed sufficient to startle a man of great resolution without a wonderful support from above. And, moreover, our natural scruples and infirmities are assisted by the wits and fancies of all ages, in their infamous and horrid description of another world: nay, taking it for granted that there will be no reward and punishment, they are yet more afraid of an annihilation than of hell itself.

But what is it we fear? "Oh! it is a terrible thing to die." Well; and is it not better once to suffer it, than always to fear it? The earth itself suffers both *with* me, and *before* me. How many islands are swallowed up in the sea! how many towns do we sail over! nay, how many nations are wholly lost, either by inundations or earthquakes! and shall I be afraid of my little body? why should I, that am sure to die, and that all other things are mortal, be fearful of coming to my last gasp myself? It is the fear of death that makes us base, and troubles and destroys the life we would preserve; that aggravates all circumstances, and makes them formidable. We depend but upon a flying moment. Die we must; but when? what is that to us? It is the law of Nature, the tribute of mortals, and the remedy of all evils. It is only the disguise that affrights us; as children that are terrified with a vizor. Take away the instruments of death, the fire, the ax, the guards, the executioners, the whips, and the racks; take away the pomp, I say, and the circumstances that accompany it, and death is no more than what my slave yesterday contemned; the pain is nothing to a fit of the stone; if it be tolerable, it is not great; and if intolerable, it cannot last long. There is nothing that Nature has made necessary which is more easy than death: we are longer a-coming into the world than going out of it; and there is not any minute of our lives wherein we may not reasonably expect it. Nay, it is but a moment's work, the parting of the soul and body. What a shame is it then to stand in fear of anything so long that is over so soon!

Nor is it any great matter to overcome this fear; for we have examples as well of the *meanest* of men as of the greatest that have done it. There was a fellow to be exposed upon the theatre, who in disdain thrust a stick down his own throat, and choked himself; and another on the same occasion, pretended to nod upon the chariot, as if he were asleep, cast his head betwixt the spokes of the wheel, and kept his seat until his neck was broken. Caligula, upon a dispute with

Canius Julius; "Do not flatter yourself," says he, "for I have given orders to put you to death." "I thank your most gracious Majesty for it," says Canius, giving to understand, perhaps, that under his government death was a mercy: for he knew that Caligula seldom failed of being as good as his word in that case. He was at play when the officer carried him away to his execution, and beckoning to the centurion, "Pray," says he, "will you bear me witness, when I am dead and gone, that I had the better of the game?" He was a man exceedingly beloved and lamented, and, for a farewell, after he had preached moderation to his friends; "You," says he, "are here disputing about the immortality of the soul, and I am now going to learn the truth of it. If I discover any thing upon that point, you shall hear of it." Nay, the most timorous of creatures, when they see there is no escaping, they oppose themselves to all dangers; the despair gives them courage, and the necessity overcomes the fear. Socrates was thirty days in prison after his sentence, and had time enough to have starved himself, and so to have prevented the poison: but he gave the world the blessing of his life as long as he could, and took that fatal draught in the meditation and contempt of death.

Marcellinus, in a deliberation upon death, called several of his friends about him: one was fearful, and advised what he himself would have done in the case; another gave the counsel which he thought Marcellinus would like best; but a friend of his that was a Stoic, and a stout man, reasoned the matter to him after this manner; Marcellinus do not trouble yourself, as if it were such a mighty business that you have now in hand; it is nothing to *live*; all your servants do it, nay, your very beasts too; but to die honestly and resolutely, that is a great point. Consider with yourself there is nothing pleasant in life but what you have tasted already, and that which is to come is but the same over again; and how many men are there in the world that rather choose to die than to suffer the nauseous tediousness of the repetition? Upon which discourse he fasted himself to death. It was the custom of Pacuvius to solemnize, in a kind of pageantry, every day his own funeral. When he had swilled and gormandized to a luxurious and beastly excess, he was carried away from supper to bed with this song and acclamation, "He has lived, he has lived." That which he did in lewdness, will become us to do in sobriety and prudence. If it shall please God to add another day to our lives, let us thankfully receive it; but, however, it is our happiest and securest course so to compose ourselves to-night, that we may have no anxious dependence on to-morrow. "He that can say, I have lived this day, makes the next clear again."

Death is the worst that either the severity of laws or the cruelty of tyrants can impose upon us; and it is the utmost extent of the dominion of Fortune. He that is fortified against that, must, consequently, be superior to all other difficulties that are put in the way to it. Nay, and on some occasions, it requires more courage to live than to die. He that is not prepared for death shall be perpetually troubled, as well with vain apprehensions, as with real dangers. It is not death itself that is dreadful, but the fear of it that goes before it. When the mind is under a consternation, there is no state of life that can please us; for we do not so endeavor to avoid mischiefs as to run away from them, and the greatest slaughter is upon a flying enemy. Had not a man better breathe out his last once for all, than lie agonizing in pains, consuming by inches, losing of his blood by drops? and yet how many are there that are ready to betray their country, and their friends, and to prostitute their very wives and daughters, to preserve a miserable carcass! Madmen and children have no apprehension of death; and it were a shame that our reason should not do as much toward our security as their folly. But the great matter is to die considerately and cheerfully upon the foundation of virtue; for life in itself is irksome, and only eating and drinking in a circle.

How many are there that, betwixt the apprehensions of death and the miseries of life, are at their wits' end what to do with themselves? Wherefore let us fortify ourselves against those calamities from which the prince is no more exempt than the beggar. Pompey the Great had his head taken off by a boy and a eunuch, (young Ptolemy and Photinus.) Caligula commanded the tribune Daecimus to kill Lepidus; and another tribune (Chaereus) did as much for Caligula. Never was a man so great but he was as liable to suffer mischief as he was able to do it. Has not a thief, or an enemy, your throat at his mercy? nay, and the meanest of servants has the power of life and death over his master; for whosoever contemns his own life may be master of another body's. You will find in story, that the displeasure of servants has been as fatal as that of tyrants: and what matters it the power of him we fear, when the thing we fear is in every body's power? Suppose I fall into the hands of an enemy, and the conqueror condemns me to be led in triumph; it is but carrying me thither whither I should have gone without him, that is to say, toward death, whither I have been marching ever since I was born. It is the fear of our last hour that disquiets all the rest. By the justice of all constitutions, mankind is condemned to a capital punishment; now, how despicable would that man appear, who, being sentenced to death in common with the whole world, should only petition that he might be the last man brought to the block?

Some men are particularly afraid of thunder, and yet extremely careless of other and of greater dangers: as if that were all they have to fear. Will not a sword, a stone, a fever, do the work as well? Suppose the bolt should hit us, it were yet braver to die with a stroke than with the bare apprehension of it: beside the vanity of imagining that heaven and earth should be put into such a disorder only for the death of one man. A good and a brave man is not moved with lightning, tempest, or earthquakes; but perhaps he would voluntarily plunge himself into that gulf, where otherwise he should only fall. The cutting of a corn, or the swallowing of a fly, is enough to dispatch a man; and it is no matter how great that is that brings me to my death, so long as death itself is but little. Life is a small matter; but it is a matter of importance to contemn it. Nature, that begat us, expels us, and a better and a safer place is provided for us. And what is death but a ceasing to be what we were before? We are kindled and put out: to cease to be, and not to begin to be, is the same thing. We die daily, and while we are growing, our life decreases; every moment that passes takes away part of it; all that is past is lost; nay, we divide with death the very instant that we live. As the last sand in the glass does not measure the hour, but finishes it; so the last moment that we live does not make up death, but concludes. There are some that pray more earnestly for death than we do for life; but it is better to receive it cheerfully when it comes than to hasten it before the time.

"But what is it that we would live any longer for?" Not for our pleasures; for those we have tasted over and over, even to satiety: so that there is no point of luxury that is new to us. "But a man would be loth to leave his country and his friends behind him;" that is to say, he would have them go first; for that is the least part of his care. "Well;

but I would fain live to do more good, and discharge myself in the offices of life;" as if to die were not the duty of every man that lives. We are loth to leave our possessions; and no man swims well with his luggage. We are all of us equally fearful of death, and ignorant of life; but what can be more shameful than to be solicitous upon the brink of security? If death be at any time to be feared, it is always to be feared; but the way never to fear it, is to be often thinking of it. To what end is it to put off for a little while that which we cannot avoid? He that dies does but follow him that is dead. "Why are we then so long afraid of that which is so little awhile of doing?" How miserable are those people that spend their lives in the dismal apprehensions of death! for they are beset on all hands, and every minute in dread of a surprise. We must therefore look about us, as if we were in an enemy's country; and consider our last hour, not as a punishment, but as the law of Nature: the fear of it is a continual palpitation of the heart, and he that overcomes that terror shall never be troubled with any other.

Life is a navigation; we are perpetually wallowing and dashing one against another; sometimes we suffer shipwreck, but we are always in danger and in expectation of it. And what is it when it comes, but either the end of a journey, or a passage? It is as great a folly to fear *death* as to fear *old age*; nay, as to fear life itself; for he that would not die ought not to live, since death is the condition of life. Beside that it is a madness to fear a thing that is certain; for where there is no doubt, there is no place for fear.

We are still chiding of Fate, and even those that exact the most rigorous justice betwixt man and man are yet themselves unjust to Providence. "Why was such a one taken away in the prime of his years?" As if it were the number of years that makes death easy to us, and not the temper of the mind. He that would live a little longer to-day, would be as loth to die a hundred years hence. But which is more reasonable for us to obey Nature, or for Nature to obey us? Go we must at last, and no matter how soon. It is the work of Fate to make us live long, but it is the business of virtue to make a short life sufficient. Life is to be measured by action, not by time; a man may die old at thirty, and young at fourscore: nay, the one lives after death, and the other perished before he died. I look upon age among the effects of chance. How long I shall live is in the power of others, but it is in my own how well. The largest space of time is to live till a man is wise. He that dies of old age does no more than go to bed when he is weary. Death is the test of life, and it is that only which discovers what we are, and distinguishes betwixt ostentation and virtue. A man may dispute, cite great authorities, talk learnedly, huff it out, and yet be rotten at heart. But let us soberly attend our business: and since it is uncertain *when*, or *where*, we shall die, let us look for death in all places, and at all times: we can never study that point too much, which we can never come to experiment whether we know it or not. It is a blessed thing to dispatch the business of life before we die, and then to expect death in the possession of a happy life. He is the great man who is willing to die when his life is pleasant to him. An honest life is not a greater good than an honest death. How many brave young men, by an instinct of Nature, are carried on to great actions, and even to the contempt of all hazards!

It is childish to go out of the world groaning and wailing as we came into it. Our bodies must be thrown away, as the secundine that wraps up the infant, the other being only the covering of the soul; we shall then discover the secrets of Nature; the darkness shall be discussed, and our souls irradiated with light and glory: a glory without a shadow; a glory that shall surround us, and from whence we shall look down and see day and night beneath us. If we cannot lift up our eyes toward the lamp of heaven without dazzling, what shall we do when we come to behold the divine light in its illustrious original? That death which we so much dread and decline, is not the determination, but the intermission of a life, which will return again. All those things, that are the very cause of life, are the way to death: we fear it as we do fame; but it is a great folly to fear words. Some people are so impatient of life, that they are still wishing for death; but he that wishes to die does not desire it: let us rather wait God's pleasure, and pray for health and life. If we have a mind to live, why do we wish to die? If we have a mind to die, we may do it without talking of it. Men are a great deal more resolute in the article of *death* itself than they are about the circumstances of it: for it gives a man courage to consider that his fate is inevitable: the slow approaches of death are the most troublesome to us; as we see many a gladiator, who upon his wounds, will direct his adversary's weapon to his very heart, though but timorous perhaps in the combat. There are some that have not the heart either to live or die; that is a sad case. But this we are sure of, "the fear of death is a continual slavery, as the contempt of it is certain liberty."

XXII

CONSOLATIONS AGAINST DEATH, FROM THE PROVIDENCE AND THE NECESSITY OF IT

This life is only a prelude to eternity, where we are to expect another original, and another state of things; we have no prospect of heaven here but at a distance; let us therefore expect our last and decretory hour with courage. The last (I say) to our bodies, but not to our minds: our luggage we leave behind us, and return as naked out of the world as we came into it. The day which we fear as our last is but the birth-day of our eternity; and it is the only way to it. So that what we fear as a rock, proves to be but a port, in many cases to be desired, never to be refused; and he that dies young has only made a quick voyage of it. Some are becalmed, others cut it away before wind; and we live just as we sail: first, we rub our childhood out of sight; our youth next; and then our middle age: after that follows old age, and brings us to the common end of mankind.

It is a great providence that we have more ways out of the world than we have into it. Our security stands upon a point, the very article of death. It draws a great many blessings into a very narrow compass: and although the fruit of it does not seem to extend to the defunct, yet the difficulty of it is more than balanced by the contemplation of the future. Nay, suppose that all the business of this world should be forgotten, or my memory, traduced, what is all this to me? "I have done my duty." Undoubtedly that which puts an end to all other evils, cannot be a very great evil itself, and yet it is no easy thing for flesh and blood to despise life. What if death comes? If it does not stay with us why should we fear it? One hangs himself for a mistress; another leaps the garret-window to avoid a choleric master; a third runs away and stabs himself, rather than he will be brought back again. We see the force even of our infirmities, and shall we not then do greater things for the love of virtue? To suffer death is but the law of nature; and it is a great comfort that it can be done but once;

in the very convulsions of it we have this consolation, that our pain is near an end, and that it frees us from all the miseries of life.

What it is we know not, and it were rash to condemn what we do not understand; but this we presume, either that we shall pass out of this into a better life, where we shall live with tranquillity and splendor, in diviner mansions, or else return to our first principles, free from the sense of any inconvenience. There is nothing immortal, nor many things lasting; by but divers ways everything comes to an end. What an arrogance is it then, when the world itself stands condemned to a dissolution, that man alone should expect to live forever! It is unjust not to allow unto the giver the power of disposing of his own bounty, and a folly only to value the present. Death is as much a debt as money, and life is but a journey towards it: some dispatch it sooner, others later, but we must all have the same period. The thunderbolt is undoubtedly just that draws even from those that are struck with it a veneration.

A great soul takes no delight in staying with the body: it considers whence it came, and knows whither it is to go. The day will come that shall separate this mixture of soul and body, of divine and human; my body I will leave where I found it, my soul I will restore to heaven, which would have been there already, but for the clog that keeps it down: and beside, how many men have been the worse for longer living, that might have died with reputation if they had been sooner taken away! How many disappointments of hopeful youths, that have proved dissolute men! Over and above the ruins, shipwrecks, torments, prisons, that attend long life; a blessing so deceitful, that if a child were in condition to judge of it, and at liberty to refuse it, he would not take it.

What Providence has made necessary, human prudence should comply with cheerfully: as there is a necessity of death, so that necessity is equal and invincible. No man has cause of complaint for that which every man must suffer as well as himself. When we *should* die, we *will not*, and when we *would not* we *must*: but our fate is fixed, and unavoidable is the decree. Why do we then stand trembling when the time comes? Why do we not as well lament that we did not live a thousand years ago, as that we shall not be alive a thousand years hence? It is but traveling the great road, and to the place whither we must all go at last. It is but submitting to the law of Nature, and to that lot which the whole world has suffered that is gone before us; and so must they too that are to come after us. Nay, how many thousands, when our time comes, will expire in the same moment with us! He that will not follow shall be drawn by force: and is it not much better now to do that willingly which we shall otherwise be made to do in spite of our hearts?

The sons of mortal parents must expect a mortal posterity — death is the end of great and small. We are born helpless, and exposed to the injuries of all creatures and of all weathers. The very necessaries of life are deadly to us; we meet with our fate in our dishes, in our cups, and in the very air we breathe; nay, our very birth is inauspicious, for we come into the world weeping, and in the middle of our designs, while we are meditating great matters, and stretching of our thoughts to after ages, death cuts us off, and our longest date is only the revolution of a few years. One man dies at the table; another goes away in his sleep, a third in his mistress's arms, a fourth is stabbed, another is stung with an adder, or crushed with the fall of a house. We have several ways to our end, but the end itself, which is death, is still the same. Whether we die by a sword, by a halter, by a potion, or by a disease, it is all but *death*. A child dies in the swaddling-clouts, and an old man at a hundred — they are both mortal alike, though the one goes sooner than the other. All that lies betwixt the cradle and the grave is uncertain. If we compute the *troubles*, the life even of a child is long: if the *sweetness* of the *passage*, that of an old man is short; the whole is slippery and deceitful, and only death certain; and yet all people complain of that which never deceived any man. Senecio raised himself from a small beginning to a vast fortune, being very well skilled in the faculties both of getting and of keeping, and either of them was sufficient for the doing of his business. He was a man infinitely careful both of his patrimony and of his body. He gave me a morning's visit, (says our author,) and after that visit he went away and spent the rest of the day with a friend of his that was desperately sick. At night, he was merry at supper, and seized immediately after with a quinsy which dispatched him in a few hours. This man that had money at use in all places, and in the very course and height of his prosperity was thus cut off. How foolish a thing is it then for a man to flatter himself with long hopes, and to pretend to dispose of the future: nay, the very present slips through our fingers, and there is not that moment which we can call our own.

How vain a thing is it for us to enter upon projects, and to say to ourselves, "Well, I will go build, purchase, discharge such offices, settle my affairs, and then retire!" We are all of us born to the same casualties — all equally frail and uncertain of to-morrow. At the very altar where we pray for life, we learn to die, by seeing the sacrifices killed before us. But there is no need of a wound, or searching the heart for it, when the noose of a cord, or the smothering of a pillow will do the work. All things have their seasons — they begin, they increase, and they die. The heavens and the earth grow old, and are appointed their periods.

That which we call *death* is but a pause or suspension; and, in truth, a progress to life, only our thoughts look downward upon the body, and not forward upon things to come. All things under the sun are mortal — cities — empires — and the time will come when it shall be a question where they were, and, perchance, whether ever they had a being or not. Some will be destroyed by war, others by luxury, fire, inundations, earthquakes — why should it trouble me then to die, as a forerunner of an universal dissolution? A great mind submits itself to God, and suffers willingly what the law of the universe will otherwise bring to pass upon necessity.

That good old man Bassus, (though with one foot in the grave,) how cheerful a mind does he bear. He lives in the view of death, and contemplates his own end with less concern of thought or countenance, than he would do another man's. It is a hard lesson, and we are a long time a learning of it, to receive our death without trouble, especially in the case of Bassus: in other deaths there is a mixture of hope — a disease may be cured, a fire quenched, a falling house either propped or avoided, the sea may swallow a man and throw him up again, a pardon may interpose twixt the ax and the body — but in the case of old age there is no place for either hope or intercession.

Let us live in our bodies, therefore, as if we were only to lodge in them this night, and to leave them to-morrow. It is the frequent thought of death that must fortify us against the necessity of it. He that has armed himself against poverty, may, perhaps, come to live in plenty. A man may strengthen himself against pain and yet live in a state of health; against the loss of friends, and never lose any, but he that fortifies himself against the fear of death shall most certainly have occasion to employ that virtue. It is the care of a wise and a good man to look to his manners and actions; and rather how well he lives than how long, for to die sooner or later is not the business, but to die well or ill, for "death brings us to immortality."

XXIII

AGAINST IMMODERATE SORROW FOR THE DEATH OF FRIENDS

Next to the encounter of death in our own bodies, the most sensible calamity to an honest man is the death of a friend; and we are not in truth without some generous instances of those that have preferred a friend's life before their own; and yet this affliction, which by nature is so grievous to us, is by virtue and Providence made familiar and easy.

To lament the death of a friend is both natural and just; a sigh or a tear I would allow to his memory: but no profuse or obstinate sorrow. Clamorous and public lamentations are not so much the effects of grief as of vain-glory. He that is sadder in company than alone, shows rather the ambition of his sorrow than the piety of it. Nay, and in the violence of his passion there fall out twenty things that set him a-laughing. At the long-run, time cures all, but it were better done by moderation and wisdom. Some people do as good as set a watch upon themselves, as if they were afraid that their grief would make an escape. The ostentation of grief is many times more than the grief itself. When any body is within hearing, what groans and outcries! when they are alone and private, all is hush and quiet: so soon as any body comes in, they are at it again; and down they throw themselves upon the bed; fall to wringing of their hands, and wishing of themselves dead; which they might have executed by themselves; but their sorrow goes off with the company. We forsake nature, and run over to the practices of the people, that never were the authors of anything that is good. If destiny were to be wrought upon by tears, I would allow you to spend your days and nights in sadness and mourning, tearing of your hair, and beating of your breast; but if Fate be inexorable, and death will keep what it has taken, grief is to no purpose. And yet I would not advise insensibility and hardness; it were inhumanity, and not virtue, not to be moved at the separation of familiar friends and relations: now, in such cases, we cannot command ourselves, we cannot forbear weeping, and we ought not to forbear: but let us not pass the bounds of affection, and run into imitation; within these limits it is some ease to the mind.

A wise man gives way to tears in some cases, and cannot avoid them in others. When one is struck with the surprise of ill-news, as the death of a friend, or the like; or upon the last embrace of an acquaintance under the hand of an executioner, he lies under a natural necessity of weeping and trembling. In another case, we may indulge our sorrow, as upon the memory of a dead friend's conversation or kindness, one may let fall tears of generosity and joy. We favor the one, and we are overcome by the other; and this is well: but we are not upon any terms to force them: they may flow of their own accord, without derogating from the dignity of a wise man; who at the same time both preserves his gravity, and obeys nature. Nay, there is a certain *decorum* even in weeping; for excess of sorrow is as foolish as profuse laughter. Why do we not as well cry, when our trees that we took pleasure in, shed their leaves, as at the loss of our satisfactions; when the next season repairs them, either with the same again, or others in their places. We may *accuse* Fate, but we cannot *alter* it; for it is hard and inexorable, and not to be removed either with reproaches or tears. They may carry *us* to the *dead*, but never bring *them* back again to us. If reason does not put an end to our sorrows, fortune never will: one is pinched with poverty; another solicited with ambition, and fears the very wealth that he coveted. One is troubled for the loss of children; another for the want of them: so that we shall sooner want tears than matter for them; let us therefore spare that for which we have so much occasion. I do confess, that in the very parting of friends there is something of uneasiness and trouble; but it is rather voluntary than natural; and it is custom more than sense that affects us: we do rather impose a sorrow upon ourselves than submit to it; as people cry when they have company, and when nobody looks on, all is well again. To mourn without measure is folly, and not to mourn at all is insensibility. The best temper is betwixt piety and reason; to be sensible, but neither transported nor cast down. He that can put a stop to his tears and pleasures when he will is safe. It is an equal infelicity to be either too soft or too hard: we are overcome by the one, and put to struggle with the other. There is a certain intemperance in that sorrow that passes the rules of modesty; and yet great piety is, in many cases, a dispensation to good manners. The loss of a son or of a friend, cuts a man to the heart, and there is no opposing the first violence of his passion; but when a man comes once to deliver himself wholly up to lamentations, he is to understand, that though some tears deserve compassion, others are yet ridiculous. A grief that is fresh finds pity and comfort, but when it is inveterate it is laughed at, for it is either counterfeit or foolish. Beside that, to weep excessively for the dead is an affront to the living. The most justifiable cause of mourning is to see good men come to ill ends, and virtue oppressed by the iniquity of Fortune. But in this case, too, they either suffer resolutely, and yield us delight in their courage and example, or meanly, and so give us the less trouble for the loss. He that dies cheerfully, dries up my tears; and he that dies whiningly, does not deserve them. I would bear the death of friends and children with the same constancy that I would expect my own, and no more lament the one than fear the other. He that bethinks himself, how often friends have been parted, will find more time lost among the living, than upon the dead; and the most desperate mourners are they that cared least for their friends when they were living; for they think to redeem their credits, for want of kindness to the living, by extravagant ravings after the dead. Some (I know) will have grief to be only the perverse delight of a restless mind, and sorrows and pleasures to be near akin; and there are, I am confident, that find joy even in their tears. But which is more barbarous, to be insensible of grief for the death of a friend, or to fish for pleasure in grief, when a son perhaps is burning, or a friend expiring? To forget one's friend, to bury the memory with the body, to lament out of measure, is all inhuman. He that is gone either would not have his friend tormented, or does not know that he is so: if he does not feel it, it is superfluous; if he does, it is unacceptable to him. If reason cannot prevail, reputation may; for immoderate mourning lessens a man's character: it is a shameful thing for a wise man to make the *weariness* of grieving the *remedy* of it. In time, the most stubborn grief will leave us, if in prudence we do not leave that first.

But do I grieve for my friend's sake or for my own? Why should I afflict myself for the loss of him that is either happy or not at all in being? In the one case it is envy, and in the other it is madness. We are apt to say, "What would I give to see him again, and to enjoy his conversation! I was never sad in his company: my heart leaped whenever I met him; I want him wherever I go." All that is to be said is, "The greater the loss, the greater is the virtue to overcome it." If grieving will do no good, it is an idle thing to grieve; and if that which has befallen one man remains to all, it is as unjust to complain. The whole world is upon the march towards the same point; why do we not cry for ourselves that are to follow, as well as for him that has gone first? Why do we not as well lament beforehand for that which we know will be, and can not possibly but be? He is not *gone*, but *sent before*. As there are many things that he has lost, so there are many things that he does not fear; as anger, jealousy, envy, etc. Is he not more happy in desiring nothing than miserable in what he has lost? We do not mourn for the absent, why then for the dead, who are effectually no other? We have lost one blessing, but we have many left; and shall not all these satisfactions support us against one sorrow?

The comfort of having a friend may be taken away, but not that of having had one. As there is a sharpness in some fruits, and a bitterness in some wines that please us, so there is a mixture in the remembrance of friends, where the loss of their company is sweetened again by the contemplation of their virtues. In some respects, I have lost what I had, and in others, I retain still what I have lost. It is an ill construction of Providence to reflect only upon my friend's being taken away, without any regard to the benefit of his being once given me. Let us therefore make the best of our friends while we have them; for how long we shall keep them is uncertain. I have lost a hopeful son, but how many fathers have been deceived in their expectations! and how many noble families have been destroyed by luxury and riot! He that grieves for the loss of a son, what if he had lost a friend? and yet he that has lost a friend has more cause of joy that he once had him, than of grief that he is taken away. Shall a man bury his friendship with his friend? We are ungrateful for that which is past, in hope of what is to come; as if that which is to come would not quickly be past too. That which is past we are sure of. We may receive satisfaction, it is true, both from the future and what is already past; the one by expectation, and the other by memory; only the one may possibly not come to pass, and it is impossible to make the other not to have been.

But there is no applying of consolation to fresh and bleeding sorrow; the very discourse irritates the grief and inflames it. It is like an unseasonable medicine in a disease; when the first violence is over, it will be more tractable, and endure the handling. Those people whose minds are weakened by long felicity may be allowed to groan and complain, but it is otherwise with those that have led their days in misfortunes. A long course of adversity has this good in it, that though it vexes a body a great while, it comes to harden us at last; as a raw soldier shrinks at every wound, and dreads the surgeon more than an enemy; whereas a *veteran* sees his own body cut and lamed with as little concern as if it were another's. With the same resolution should we stand the shock and cure of all misfortunes; we are never the better for our experience, if we have not yet learned to be miserable. And there is no thought of curing us by the diversion of sports and entertainments; we are apt to fall into relapses; wherefore we had better overcome our sorrow than delude it.

XXIV

CONSOLATION AGAINST BANISHMENT AND BODILY PAIN

It is a masterpiece to draw good out of evil; and, by the help of virtue, to improve misfortunes into blessings. "It is a sad condition," you will say, "for a man to be barred the freedom of his own country." And is not this the case of thousands that we meet every day in the streets? Some for ambition; others, to negotiate, or for curiosity, delight, friendship, study, experience, luxury, vanity, discontent: some to exercise their virtues, others their vices; and not a few to prostitute either their bodies or their eloquence? To pass now from pleasant countries into the worst of islands; let them be never so barren or rocky, the people never so barbarous, or the clime never so intemperate, he that is banished thither shall find many strangers to live there for their pleasure. The mind of man is naturally curious and restless; which is no wonder, considering their divine original; for heavenly things are always in motion: witness the stars, and the orbs, which are perpetually moving, rolling, and changing of place and according to the law and appointment of Nature. But here are no woods, you will say, no rivers, no gold nor pearl, no commodity for traffic or commerce; nay, hardly provision enough to keep the inhabitants from starving. It is very right; here are no palaces, no artificial grottoes, or materials for luxury and excess; but we lie under the protection of Heaven; and a poor cottage for a retreat is more worth than the most magnificent temple, when that cottage is consecrated by an honest man under the guard of his virtue. Shall any man think banishment grievous, when he may take such company along with him! Nor is there any banishment but yields enough for our necessities, and no kingdom is sufficient for superfluities. It is the mind that makes us rich in a desert; and if the body be but kept alive, the soul enjoys all spiritual felicities in abundance. What signifies the being banished from one spot of ground to another, to a man that has his thoughts above, and can look forward and backward, and wherever he pleases; and that, wherever he is, has the same matter to work upon? The body is but the prison or the clog of the mind, subjected to punishments, robberies, diseases; but the mind is sacred and spiritual, and liable to no violence. Is it that, a man shall want garments or covering in banishment? The body is as easily clothed as fed; and Nature has made nothing hard that is necessary. But if nothing will serve us but rich embroideries and scarlet, it is none of Fortune's fault that we are poor, but our own. Nay, suppose a man should have all restored him back again that he has lost, it will come to nothing, for he will want more after that to satisfy his desires than he did before to supply his necessities. Insatiable appetites are not so much a thirst as a disease.

To come lower now; where is the people or nation that have not changed their place of abode? Some by the fate of war; others have been cast by tempests, shipwrecks, or want of provisions, upon unknown coasts. Some have been forced abroad by pestilence, sedition, earthquakes, surcharge of people at home. Some travel to see the world, others for commerce; but, in fine, it is clear, that, upon some reason or other, the whole race of mankind have shifted their quarters; changed their very names as well as their habitations; insomuch that we have lost the very memorials of what they were. All these transportations of people, what are they but public banishments?

The very *founder* of the *Roman empire* was an *exile*: briefly, the whole world has been transplanted, and one mutation treads upon the heel of another. That which one man desires, turns another man's stomach; and he that proscribes me to-day, shall himself be cast out to-morrow. We have, however, this comfort in our misfortune; we have the same nature, the same Providence, and we carry our virtues along with us. And this blessing we owe to that almighty Power, call it what you will; either a *God*, or an *Incorporeal Reason*, a *Divine Spirit*, or *Fate*, and the *unchangeable Course* of *causes* and *effects*: it is, however, so ordered, that nothing can be taken from us but what we can well spare: and that which is most magnificent and valuable continues with us. Wherever we go, we have the heavens over our heads, and no farther from us than they were before; and so long as we can entertain our eyes and thoughts with those glories, what matter is it what ground we tread upon?

In the case of pain or sickness, it is only the body that is affected; it may take off the speed of a footman, or bind the hands of a cobbler, but the mind is still at liberty to hear, learn, teach, advise, and to do other good offices. It is an example of public benefit, a man that is in pain and patient. Virtue may show itself as well in the bed as in the field; and he that cheerfully encounters the terrors of death and corporal anguish, is as great a man as he that most generously hazards himself in a battle. A disease, it is true, bars us of some pleasures, but procures us others. Drink is never so grateful to us as in a burning fever; nor meat, as when we have fasted ourselves sharp and hungry. The patient may be forbidden some sensual satisfaction, but no physician will forbid us the delight of the mind. Shall we call any sick man miserable, because he must give over his intemperance of wine and gluttony, and betake himself to a diet of more sobriety, and less expense; and abandon his luxury, which is the distemper of the mind as well as of the body? It is troublesome, I know, at first, to abstain from the pleasures we have been used to, and to endure hunger and thirst; but in a little time we lose the very appetite, and it is no trouble then to be without that which we do not desire. In diseases there are great pains; but if they be long they remit, and give us some intervals of ease; if short and violent, either they dispatch *us*, or consume *themselves*; so that either their respites make them tolerable, or the extremity makes them short. So merciful is Almighty

God to us, that our torments cannot be very sharp and lasting. The acutest pains are those that affect the nerves, but there is this comfort in them too, that they will quickly make us stupid and insensible. In cases of extremity, let us call to mind the most eminent instances of patience and courage, and turn our thoughts from our afflictions to the contemplation of virtue. Suppose it be the stone, the gout, nay, the rack itself; how many have endured it without so much as a groan or word speaking; without so much as asking for relief, or giving an answer to a question! Nay, they have laughed at the tormentors upon the very torture, and provoked them to new experiments of their cruelty, which they have had still in derision. The *asthma* I look upon as of all diseases the most importunate; the physicians call it the *meditation of death*, as being rather an agony than a sickness; the fit holds one not above an hour, as nobody is long in expiring. Are there not three things grievous in sickness, the fear of death, bodily pain, and the intermission of our pleasures? the first is to be imputed to nature, not to the disease; for we do not die because we are sick, but because we live. Nay, sickness itself has preserved many a man from dying.

XXV

POVERTY TO A WISE MAN IS RATHER A BLESSING THAN A MISFORTUNE

No man shall ever be poor that goes to himself for what he wants; and that is the readiest way to riches. Nature, indeed, will have her due; but yet whatsoever is beyond necessity is precarious, and not necessary. It is not her business to gratify the palate, but to satisfy a craving stomach. Bread, when a man is hungry, does his work, let it be never so coarse; and water when he is dry; let his thirst be quenched, and Nature is satisfied, no matter whence it comes, or whether he drinks in gold, silver, or in the hollow of his hand. To promise a man riches, and to teach him poverty, is to deceive him: but shall I call him poor that wants nothing; though he maybe beholden for it to his patience, rather than to his fortune? Or shall any man deny him to be rich, whose riches can never be taken away? Whether is it better to have much or enough? He that has much desires more, and shows that he has not yet enough; but he that has enough is at rest. Shall a man be reputed the less rich for not having that for which he shall be banished; for which his very wife, or son, shall poison him: that which gives him security in war, and quiet in peace; which he possesses without danger, and disposes of without trouble? No man can be poor that has enough; nor rich, that covets more than he has. Alexander, after all his conquests, complained that he wanted more worlds; he desired something more, even when he had gotten all: and that which was sufficient for human nature was not enough for one man. Money never made any man rich; for the more he had, the more he still coveted. The richest man that ever lived is poor in my opinion, and in any man's may be so: but he that keeps himself to the stint of Nature, does neither feel poverty nor fear it; nay, even in poverty itself there are some things superfluous. Those which the world calls happy, their felicity is a false splendor, that dazzles the eyes of the vulgar; but our rich man is glorious and happy within. There is no ambition in hunger or thirst: let there be food, and no matter for the table, the dish, and the servants, nor with what meats nature is satisfied. Those are the torments of luxury, that rather stuff the stomach than fill it: it studies rather to cause an appetite than to allay it. It is not for us to say, "This is not handsome; that is common; the other offends my eye." Nature provides for health, not delicacy. When the trumpet sounds a charge, the poor man knows that he is not aimed at; when they cry out *fire*, his body is all he has to look after: if he be to take a journey, there is no blocking up of streets, and thronging of passages, for a parting compliment: a small matter fills his belly, and contents his mind: he lives from hand to mouth, without caring or fearing for to-morrow. The temperate rich man is but his counterfeit; his wit is quicker and his appetite calmer.

No man finds poverty a trouble to him, but he that thinks it so; and he that thinks it so, makes it so. Does not a rich man travel more at ease with less luggage, and fewer servants? Does he not eat many times as little and as coarse in the field as a poor man? Does he not for his own pleasure, sometimes, and for variety, feed upon the ground, and use only earthen vessels? Is not he a madman then, that always fears what he often desires, and dreads the thing that he takes delight to imitate: he that would know the worst of poverty, let him but compare the looks of the rich and of the poor, and he shall find the poor man to have a smoother brow, and to be more merry at heart; or if any trouble befalls him, it passes over like a cloud: whereas the other, either his good humor is counterfeit, or his melancholy deep and ulcerated, and the worse, because he dares not publicly own his misfortune; but he is forced to play the part of a happy man even with a cancer in his heart. His felicity is but personated; and if he were but stripped of his ornaments, he would be contemptible. In buying of a horse, we take off his clothes and his trappings, and examine his shape and body for fear of being cozened; and shall we put an estimate upon a man for being set off by his fortune and quality? Nay, if we see anything of ornament about him, we are to suspect him the more for some infirmity under it. He that is not content in poverty, would not be so neither in plenty; for the fault is not in the thing, but in the mind. If that be sickly, remove him from a kennel to a palace, he is at the same pass; for he carries his disease along with him.

What can be happier than the condition both of mind and of fortune from which we cannot fall — what can be a greater felicity than in a covetous, designing age, for a roan to live safe among informers and thieves? It puts a poor man into the very condition of Providence, that gives all, without reserving anything to itself. How happy is he that owes nothing but to himself, and only that which he can easily refuse or easily pay! I do not reckon him poor that has but a little, but he is so that covets more — it is a fair degree of plenty to have what is necessary. Whether had a man better find satiety in want, or hunger in plenty? It is not the augmenting of our fortunes, but the abating of our appetites that makes us rich.

Why may not a man as well contemn riches in his own coffers as in another man's, and rather hear that they are his than feel them to be so, though it is a great matter not to be corrupted even by having them under the same roof. He is the greater man that is honestly poor in the middle of plenty — but he is the more secure that is free from the temptation of that plenty, and has the least matter for another to design upon. It is no great business for a poor man to preach the contempt of riches, or for a rich man to extol the benefits of poverty, because we do not know how either the one or the other would behave himself in the contrary condition. The best proof is the doing of it by choice and not by necessity; for the practice of poverty in jest is a preparation toward the bearing of it in earnest;

but it is yet a generous disposition so to provide for the worst of fortunes as what may be easily borne — the premeditation makes them not only tolerable but delightful to us, for there is that in them without which nothing can be comfortable, that is to say, security. If there were nothing else in poverty but the certain knowledge of our friends, it were yet a most desirable blessing, when every man leaves us but those that love us. It is a shame to place the happiness of life in gold and silver, for which bread and water is sufficient; or, at the worst, hunger puts an end to hunger.

For the honor of *poverty*, it was both the *foundation* and the *cause of the Roman empire*; and no man was ever yet so poor but he had enough to carry him to his journey's end.

All I desire is that my property may not be a burden to myself, or make me so to others; and that is the best state of fortune that is neither directly necessitous, nor far from it. A mediocricity of fortune with a gentleness of mind, will preserve us from fear or envy, which is a desirable condition, for no man wants power to do mischief. We never consider the blessing of coveting nothing, and the glory of being full in ourselves, without depending upon Fortune. With parsimony a little is sufficient and without it nothing; whereas frugality makes a poor man rich. If we lose an estate, we had better never have had it — he that has least to lose has least to fear, and those are better satisfied whom Fortune never favored, than those whom she has forsaken.

The state is most commodious that lies betwixt poverty and plenty. Diogenes understood this very well when he put himself into an incapacity of losing any thing. That course of life is most commodious which is both safe and wholesome — the body is to be indulged no farther than for health, and rather mortified than not kept in subjection to the mind. It is necessary to provide against hunger, thirst, and cold; and somewhat for a covering to shelter us against other inconveniences; but not a pin matter whether it be of turf or of marble — a man may lie as warm and as dry under a thatched as under a gilded roof. Let the mind be great and glorious, and all other things are despicable in comparison. "The future is uncertain, and I had rather beg of myself not to desire any thing, than of Fortune to bestow it."

ANGER

I

ANGER DESCRIBED, IT IS AGAINST NATURE,
AND ONLY TO BE FOUND IN MAN

We are here to encounter the most outrageous, brutal, dangerous, and intractable of all passions; the most loathsome and unmannerly; nay, the most ridiculous too; and the subduing of this monster will do a great deal toward the establishment of human peace. It is the method of *physicians* to begin with a description of the disease, before they meddle with the cure: and I know not why this may not do as well in the distempers of the mind as in those of the body.

The *Stoics* will have *anger* to be a "desire of punishing another for some injury done." Against which it is objected, that we are many times angry with those that never did hurt us, but possibly may, though the harm be not as yet done. But I say, that they hurt us already in conceit: and the very purpose of it is an injury in thought before it breaks out into act. It is opposed again, that if anger were a *desire of punishing*, mean people would not be angry with great ones that are out of their reach; for no man can be said to desire any thing which he judges impossible to compass. But I answer to this, That *anger* is the *desire*, not the *power* and *faculty* of *revenge*; neither is any man so low, but that the greatest man alive may peradventure lie at his mercy.

Aristotle takes *anger* to be, "a desire of paying sorrow for sorrow;" and of plaguing those that have plagued us. It is argued against both, that beasts are angry; though neither provoked by any injury, nor moved with a desire of any body's grief or punishment. Nay, though they cause it, they do not design or seek it. Neither is *anger* (how unreasonable soever in itself) found anywhere but in reasonable creatures. It is true, the beasts have an impulse of rage and fierceness; as they are more affected also than men with some pleasures; but we may as well call them luxurious and ambitious as angry. And yet they are not without certain images of human affections. They have their likings and their loathings; but neither the passions of reasonable nature, nor their virtues, nor their vices. They are moved to fury by some objects; they are quieted by others; they have their terrors and their disappointments, but without reflection: and let them be never so much irritated or affrighted, so soon as ever the occasion is removed they fall to their meat again, and lie down and take their rest. Wisdom and thought are the goods of the mind, whereof brutes are wholly incapable; and we are as unlike them within as we are without: they have an odd kind of fancy, and they have a voice too; but inarticulate and confused, and incapable of those variations which are familiar to us.

Anger is not only a vice, but a vice point-blank against nature, for it divides instead of joining; and in some measure, frustrates the end of Providence in human society. One man was born to help another; anger makes us destroy one another; the one unites, the other separates; the one is beneficial to us, the other mischievous; the one succors even strangers, the other destroys even the most intimate friends; the one ventures all to save another, the other ruins himself to undo another. Nature is bountiful, but anger is pernicious: for it is not fear, but mutual love that binds up mankind.

There are some motions that look like anger, which cannot properly be called so; as the passion of the people against the *gladiators*, when they hang off, and will not make so quick a dispatch as the spectators would have them: there is something in it of the humor of children, that if they get a fall, will never leave bawling until the naughty ground is beaten, and then all is well again. They are angry without any cause or injury; they are deluded by an imitation of strokes, and pacified with counterfeit tears. A false and a childish sorrow is appeased with as false and as childish a revenge. They take it for a contempt, if the *gladiators* do not immediately cast themselves upon the sword's point. They look presently about them from one to another, as who should say; "Do but see, my masters, how these rogues abuse us."

To descend to the particular branches and varieties would be unnecessary and endless. There is a stubborn, a vindictive, a quarrelsome, a violent, a froward, a sullen, a morose kind of anger; and then we have this variety in complication too. One goes no further than words; another proceeds immediately to blows, without a word speaking; a third sort breaks out into cursing and reproachful language; and there are that content themselves with chiding and complaining. There is a conciliable anger and there is an implacable; but in what form or degree soever it appears, all anger, without exception, is vicious.

II

THE RISE OF ANGER

The question will be here, whether *anger* takes its rise from impulse or judgment; that is, whether it be moved of its own accord, or, as many other things are, from within us, that arise we know not how? The clearing of this point will lead us to greater matters.

The *first* motion of *anger* is in truth involuntary, and only a kind of menacing preparation towards it. The *second* deliberates; as who should say, "This injury should not pass without a revenge," and there it stops. The *third* is impotent; and, right or wrong, resolves upon vengeance. The *first motion* is not to be avoided, nor indeed the *second*, any more than yawning for company; custom and care may lessen it, but reason itself cannot overcome it. The *third*, as it rises upon consideration, it must fall so too, for that motion which proceeds with judgment may be taken away with judgment. A man thinks himself injured, and hath a mind to be revenged, but for some reason lets it rest. This is not properly *anger*, but an *affection overruled by reason*; a kind of proposal disapproved — and what are reason and affection, but only changes of the mind for the better or for the worse? Reason deliberates before it judges; but anger passes sentence without deliberation. Reason only attends the matter in hand; but anger is startled at every accident; it passes the bounds of reason, and carries it away with it. In short, "anger is an agitation of the mind that proceeds to the resolution of a revenge, the mind assenting to it."

There is no doubt but anger is moved by the species of an injury; but whether that motion be voluntary or involuntary is the point in debate; though it seems manifest to me that *anger* does nothing but where the mind goes along with it, for, first, to take an offence, and then to meditate a revenge, and after that to lay both propositions together, and say to myself, "This injury ought not to have been done; but as the case stands, I must do myself right." This discourse can never proceed without the concurrence of the will.

The first motion indeed is single; but all the rest is deliberation and superstructure — there is something understood and condemned — an indignation conceived and a revenge propounded. This can never be without the agreement of the mind to the matter in deliberation. The end of this question is to know the nature and quality of *anger*. If it be bred in us it will never yield to reason, for all involuntary motions are inevitable and invincible; as a kind of horror and shrugging upon the sprinkling of cold water; the hair standing on end at ill news; giddiness at the sight of a precipice; blushing at lewd discourse. In these cases reason can do no good, but *anger* may undoubtedly be overcome by caution and good counsel, for it is a *voluntary vice*, and not of the condition of those accidents that befall us as frailties of our humanity, amongst which must be reckoned the first motions of the mind after the opinion of an injury received, which it is not in the power of human nature to avoid, and this is it that affects us upon the stage, or in a story.

Can any man read the death of Pompey, and not be touched with an indignation? The sound of a trumpet rouses the spirits and provokes courage. It makes a man sad to see the shipwreck even of an enemy; and we are much surprised by fear in other cases — all these motions are not so much affections as preludes to them. The clashing of arms or the beating of a drum excites a war-horse: nay, a song from Xenophantes would make Alexander take his sword in his hand.

In all these cases the mind rather suffers than acts, and therefore it is not an affection *to be moved*, but *to give way* to that motion, and to follow willingly what was started by chance — these are not affections, but impulses of the body. The bravest man in the world may look pale when he puts on his armor, his knees knock, and his heart work before the battle is joined: but these are only *motions*; whereas *anger* is an *excursion*, and proposes revenge or punishment, which cannot be without the mind. As fear flies, so anger assaults; and it is not possible to resolve, either upon violence or caution, without the concurrence of the will.

III

ANGER MAY BE SUPPRESSED

It is an idle thing to pretend that we cannot govern our *anger*; for some things that we do are much harder than others that we ought to do; the wildest affections may be tamed by discipline, and there is hardly anything which the mind will do but it may do. There needs no more argument in this case than the instances of several persons, both powerful and impatient, that have gotten the absolute mastery of themselves in this point.

Thrasippus in his drink fell foul upon the cruelties of Pisistratus; who, when he was urged by several about him to make an example of him, returned this answer, "Why should I be angry with a man that stumbles upon me blindfold?" In effect most of our quarrels are of our own making, either by mistake or by aggravation. Anger comes sometimes upon us, but we go oftener to it, and instead of rejecting it we call it.

Augustus was a great master of his passion: for Timagenus, an historian, wrote several bitter things against his person and his family: which passed among the people plausibly enough, as pieces of rash wit commonly do. Caesar advised him several times to forbear; and when that would not do, forbade him his roof. After this, Asinius Pollio gave him entertainment; and he was so well beloved in the city, that every man's house was open to him. Those things that he had written in honor of Augustus, he recited and burnt, and publicly professed himself Caesar's enemy. Augustus, for all this, never fell out with any man that received him; only once, he told Pollio, that he had taken a *snake* into his bosom: and as Pollio was about to excuse himself; "No," says Caesar, interrupting him, "make your best of him." And offering to cast him off at that very moment, if Caesar pleased: "Do you think," says Caesar, "that I will ever contribute to the parting of you, that made you friends?" for Pollio was angry with him before, and only entertained him now because Caesar had discarded him.

The moderation of Antigonus was remarkable. Some of his soldiers were railing at him one night, where there was but a hanging betwixt them. Antigonus overheard them, and putting it gently aside; "Soldiers," says he, "stand a little further off, for fear the king should hear you." And we are to consider, not only violent examples, but moderate, where there wanted neither cause of displeasure nor power of revenge: as in the case of Antigonus, who the same night hearing his soldiers cursing him for bringing them into so foul a way, he went to them, and without telling them who he was, helped them out of it. "Now," says he, "you may be allowed to curse him that brought you into the mire, provided you bless him that took you out of it."

It was a notable story that of Vedius Pallio, upon his inviting of Augustus to supper. One of his boys happened to break a glass: and his master, in a rage, commanded him to be thrown in a pond to feed his lampreys. This action of his might be taken for *luxury*, though, in truth, it was cruelty. The boy was seized, but brake loose and threw himself at Augustus' feet, only desiring that he might not die that death. Caesar, in abhorrence of the barbarity, presently ordered all the rest of the glasses to be broken, the boy to be released, and the pond to be filled up, that there might be no further occasion for an inhumanity of that nature. This was an authority well employed. Shall the breaking of a glass cost a man his life? Nothing but a predominant fear could ever have mastered his choleric and sanguinary disposition. This man deserved to die a thousand deaths, either for eating human flesh at second-hand in his *lampreys*, or for keeping of his fish to be so fed.

It is written of Praexaspes (a favorite of Cambyses, who was much given to wine) that he took the freedom to tell this prince of his hard drinking, and to lay before him the scandal and the inconveniences of his excesses; and how that, in those distempers, he had not the command of himself. "Now," says Cambyses, "to show you your mistake, you shall see me drink deeper than ever I did, and yet keep the use of my eyes, and of my hands, as well as if I were sober." Upon this he drank to a higher pitch than ordinary, and ordered Praexaspes' son to go out, and stand on the other side of the threshold, with his left arm over his head; "And," says he, "if I have a good aim, have at the heart of him." He shot, and upon cutting up the young man, they found indeed that the arrow had struck him through the middle of the heart. "What do you think now," says Cambyses, "is my hand steady or not?" "Apollo himself," says Praexaspes, "could not have outdone it." It may be a question now, which was the greater impiety, the murder itself, or the commendation of it; for him to take the heart of his son, while it was yet reeking and panting under the wound, for an occasion of flattery: why was there not another experiment made upon the father, to try if Cambyses could not have yet mended his shot? This was a most unmanly violation of hospitality; but the approbation of the act was still worse than the crime itself. This example of Praexaspes proves sufficiently that a man may repress his anger; for he returned not one ill word, no not so much as a complaint; but he paid dear for his good counsel. He had been wiser, perhaps, if he had let the king alone in his cups, for he had better have drunk wine than blood. It is a dangerous office to give good advice to intemperate princes.

Another instance of anger suppressed, we have in Harpagus, who was commanded to expose Cyrus upon a mountain. But the child was preserved; which, when Astyages came afterwards to understand, he invited Harpagus to a dish of meat; and when he had eaten his fill, he told him it was a piece of his son, and asked him how he liked the seasoning. "Whatever pleases your Majesty," says Harpagus, "must please me:" and he made no more words of it. It is most certain, that we might govern our anger if we would; for the same thing that galls us at home gives us no offence at all abroad; and what is the reason of it, but that we are patient in one place, and froward in another?

It was a strong provocation that which was given to Philip of Macedon, the father of Alexander. The Athenians sent their ambassadors to him, and they were received with this compliment, "Tell me, gentlemen," says Philip, "what is there that I can do to oblige the Athenians?" Democharas, one of the ambassadors, told him, that they would take it for a great obligation if he would be pleased to hang himself. This insolence gave an indignation to the by-standers; but Philip bade them not to meddle with him, but even to let that foul-mouthed fellow go as he came. "And for you, the rest of the ambassadors," says he, "pray tell the Athenians, that it is worse to speak such things than to hear and forgive them." This wonderful patience under contumelies was a great means of Philip's security.

IV

IT IS A SHORT MADNESS, AND A DEFORMED VICE

He was much in the right, whoever it was, that first called *anger a short madness*; for they have both of them the same symptoms; and there is so wonderful a resemblance betwixt the transports of *choler* and those of *frenzy*, that it is a hard matter to know the one from the other. A bold, fierce, and threatening countenance, as pale as ashes, and, in the same moment, as red as blood; a glaring eye, a wrinkled brow, violent motions, the hands restless and perpetually in action, wringing and menacing, snapping of the joints, stamping with the feet, the hair starting, trembling of the lips, a forced and squeaking voice; the speech false and broken, deep and frequent sighs, and ghastly looks; the veins swell, the heart pants, the knees knock; with a hundred dismal accidents that are common to both distempers. Neither is *anger* a bare resemblance only of madness, but many times an irrevocable transition into the thing itself. How many persons have we known, read, and heard of, that have lost their wits in a passion, and never came to themselves again? It is therefore to be avoided, not only for moderation's sake, but also for health. Now, if the outward appearance of anger be so foul and hideous, how deformed must that miserable mind be that is harassed with it? for it leaves no place either for counsel or friendship, honesty or good manners; no place either for the exercise of reason, or for the offices of life. If I were to describe it, I would draw a tiger bathed in blood, sharp set, and ready to take a leap at his prey; or dress it up as the poets represent the furies, with whips, snakes, and flames; it should be sour, livid, full of scars, and wallowing in gore, raging up and down, destroying, grinning, bellowing, and pursuing; sick of all other things, and most of all, itself. It turns beauty into deformity, and the calmest counsels into fierceness: it disorders our very garments, and fills the mind with horror. How abominable is it in the soul then, when it appears so hideous even through the bones, the skin and so many impediments! Is not he a madman that has lost the government of himself, and is tossed hither and thither by his fury as by a tempest? the executioner and the murderer of his nearest friends? The smallest matter moves it, and makes us unsociable and inaccessible. It does all things by violence, as well upon itself as others; and it is, in short; the master of all passions.

There is not any creature so terrible and dangerous by nature, but it becomes fiercer by anger. Not that beasts have human affections, but certain impulses they have which come very near them. The boar foams, champs, and whets his tusks; the bull tosses his horns in the air, bounds, and tears up the ground with his feet; the lion roars and swinges himself with his tail; the serpent swells; and there is a ghastly kind of fellness in the aspect of a mad dog. How great a wickedness is it now to indulge a violence, that does not only turn a man into a beast, but makes even the most outrageous of beasts themselves to be more dreadful and mischievous! A vice that carries along with it neither pleasure nor profit, neither honor nor security; but on the contrary, destroys us to all the comfortable and glorious purposes of our reasonable being. Some there are, that will have the root of it to be the greatness of mind. And, why may we not as well entitle *impudence* to *courage*, whereas the one is proud, the other brave; the one is gracious and gentle, the other rude and furious? At the same rate we may ascribe magnanimity to avarice, luxury, and ambition, which are all but splendid impotences, without measure and without foundation. There is nothing great but what is virtuous, nor indeed truly great, but what is also composed and quiet. Anger, alas! is but a wild impetuous blast, an empty tumor, the very infirmity of woman and children; a brawling, clamorous evil: and the more noise the less courage; as we find it commonly, that the boldest tongues have the faintest hearts.

V

ANGER IS NEITHER WARRANTABLE NOR USEFUL

In the first place, Anger is *unwarrantable* as it is *unjust*: for it falls many times upon the wrong person, and discharges itself upon the innocent instead of the guilty: beside the disproportion of making the most trivial offences to be capital, and punishing an inconsiderate word perhaps with torments, fetters, infamy, or death. It allows a man neither time nor means for defence, but judges a cause without hearing it, and admits of no mediation. It flies into the face of truth itself, if it be of the adverse party; and turns obstinacy in an error, into an argument of justice. It does every thing with agitation and tumult; whereas reason and equity can destroy whole families, if there be occasion for it, even to the extinguishing of their names and memories, without any indecency, either of countenance or action.

Secondly, It is unsociable to the highest point; for it spares neither friend nor foe; but tears all to pieces, and casts human nature into a perpetual state of war. It dissolves the bond of mutual society, insomuch that our very companions and relations dare not come near us; it renders us unfit for the ordinary offices of life: for we can neither govern our tongues, our hands, nor any part of our body. It tramples upon the laws of hospitality, and of nations, leaves every man to be his own carver, and all things, public and private, sacred and profane, suffer violence.

Thirdly, It is to no purpose. "It is a sad thing," we cry, "to put up with these injuries, and we are not able to bear them;" as if any man that can bear *anger* could not bear an *injury*, which is much more supportable. You will say that anger does some good yet, for it keeps people in awe, and secures a man from contempt; never considering, that it is more dangerous to be feared than despised. Suppose that an angry man could do as much as he threatens; the more terrible, he is still the more odious; and on the other side, if he wants power, he is the more despicable for his anger; for there is nothing more wretched than a choleric huff, that makes a noise, and nobody cares for it.

If anger would be valuable because men are afraid of it, why not an adder, a toad, or a scorpion as well? It makes us lead the life of gladiators; we live, and we fight together. We hate the happy, despise the miserable, envy our superiors, insult our inferiors, and there is nothing in the world which we will not do, either for pleasure or profit. To be angry at offenders is to make ourselves the common enemies of mankind, which is both weak and wicked; and we may as well be angry that our thistles do not bring forth apples, or that every pebble in our ground is not an oriental pearl. If we are angry both with young men and with old, because they do offend, why not with infants too, because they will offend? It is laudable to rejoice for anything that is well done; but to be transported for another man's doing ill, is narrow and sordid. Nor is it for the dignity of virtue to be either angry or sad.

It is with a tainted mind as with an ulcer, not only the touch, but the very offer at it, makes us shrink and complain; when we come once to be carried off from our poise, we are lost. In the choice of a sword, we take care that it be wieldy and well mounted; and it concerns us as much to be wary of engaging in the excesses of ungovernable passions. It is not the speed of a horse altogether that pleases us unless we find that he can stop and turn at pleasure. It is a sign of weakness, and a kind of stumbling, for a man to run when he intends only to walk; and it behoves us to have the same command of our mind that we have of our bodies. Besides that the greatest punishment of an injury is the conscience of having done it; and no man suffers more than he that is turned over to the pain of a repentance. How much better is it to compose injuries than to revenge them? For it does not only spend time, but the revenge of one injury exposes to more. In fine, as it is unreasonable to be angry at a crime, it is as foolish to be angry without one.

But "may not an honest man then be allowed to be angry at the murder of his father, or the ravishing of his sister or daughter before his face?" No, not at all. I will defend my parents, and I will repay the injuries that are done them; but it is my piety and not my anger, that moves me to it. I will do my duty without fear or confusion, I will not rage, I will not weep; but discharge the office of a good man without forfeiting the dignity of a man. If my father be assaulted, I will endeavor to rescue him; if he be killed, I will do right to his memory; find all this, not in any transport of passion, but in honor and conscience. Neither is there any need of anger where reason does the same thing.

A man may be temperate, and yet vigorous, and raise his mind according to the occasion, more or less, as a stone is thrown according to the discretion and intent of the caster. How outrageous have I seen some people for the loss of a monkey or a spaniel! And were it not a shame to have the same sense for a friend that we have for a puppy; and to cry like children, as much for a bauble as for the ruin of our country? This is not the effect of reason, but of infirmity. For a man indeed to expose his person for his prince, or his parents, or his friends, out of a sense of honesty, and judgment of duty, it is, without dispute, a worthy and a glorious action; but it must be done then with sobriety, calmness, and resolution.

It is high time to convince the world of the indignity and uselessness of this passion, when it has the authority and recommendation of no less than Aristotle himself, as an affection very much conducing to all heroic actions that require heat and vigor: now, to show, on the other side, that it is not in any case profitable, we shall lay open the obstinate and unbridled madness of it: a wickedness neither sensible of infamy nor of glory, without either modesty or fear; and if it passes once from anger into a hardened hatred, it is incurable. It is either stronger than reason, or it is weaker. If stronger, there is no contending with it; if weaker, reason will do the business without it. Some will have it that an angry man is good-natured and sincere; whereas, in truth, he only lays himself open out of heedlessness and want of caution. If it were in itself good the more of it the better; but in this case, the more the worse; and a wise man does his duty, without the aid of anything that is ill. It is objected by some, that those are the most generous creatures which are the most prone to anger. But, first, *reason* in *man* is *impetuous* in *beasts*. Secondly, without discipline it runs into audaciousness and temerity; over and above that, the same thing does not help all. If anger helps the lion, it is fear that saves the stag, swiftness the hawk, and flight the pigeon: but man has God for his example (who is never angry) and not the *creatures*. And yet it is not amiss sometimes to counterfeit anger; as upon the stage; nay, upon the bench, and in the pulpit, where the imitation of it is more effectual than the thing itself.

But it is a great error to take this passion either for a companion or for an assistant to virtue; that makes a man incapable of those necessary counsels by which virtue is to govern herself. Those are false and inauspicious powers, and destructive of themselves, which arise only from the accession and fervor of disease. Reason judges according to right; anger will have every thing seem right, whatever it does, and when it has once pitched upon a mistake, it is never to be convinced, but prefers a pertinacity, even in the greatest evil, before the most necessary repentance.

Some people are of opinion that anger inflames and animates the soldier; that it is a spur to bold and arduous undertakings; and that it were better to moderate than to wholly suppress it, for fear of dissolving the spirit and force of the mind. To this I answer, that virtue does not need the help of vice; but where there is any ardor of mind necessary, we may rouse ourselves, and be more or less brisk and vigorous as there is occasion: but all without anger still. It is a mistake to say, that we may make use of anger as a common soldier, but not as a commander; for if it hears reason, and follows orders, it is not properly anger; and if it does not, it is contumacious and mutinous. By this argument a man must be angry to be valiant; covetous to be industrious; timorous to be safe, which makes our reason confederate with our affections. And it is all one whether passion be inconsiderate without reason, or reason ineffectual without passion; since the one cannot be without the other. It is true, the less the passion, the less is the mischief; for a little passion is the smaller evil. Nay, so far is it from being of use or advantage in the field, that it is in place of all others where it is the most dangerous; for the actions of war are to be managed with order and caution, not precipitation and fancy; whereas anger is heedless and heady, and the virtue only of *barbarous nations*; which, though their bodies were much stronger and more hardened, were still worsted by the moderation and discipline of the Romans. There is not upon the face of the earth a bolder or a more indefatigable nation than the Germans; not a braver upon a charge, nor a hardier against colds and heats; their only delights and exercise is in arms, to the utter neglect of all things else: and, yet upon the encounter, they are broken and destroyed through their own undisciplined temerity, even by the most effeminate of men. The huntsman is not angry with the wild boar when he either pursues or receives him; a good swordsman watches his opportunity, and keeps himself upon his guard, whereas passion lays a man open: nay, it is one of the prime lessons in a fencing-school to learn not to be angry. If Fabius had been *choleric*, Rome had been *lost*; and before he conquered *Hannibal* he overcame *himself*. If Scipio had been *angry*, he would never have left Hannibal and his army (who were the proper objects of his displeasure) to carry the war into Afric and so compass his end by a more temperate way. Nay, he was so slow, that it was charged upon him for want of mettle and resolution. And what did the *other* Scipio? (Africanus I mean:) how much time did he spend before Numantia, to the common grief both of his country and himself? Though he reduced it at last by so miserable a famine, that the inhabitants laid violent hands upon themselves, and left neither man, woman, nor child, to survive the ruins of it. If anger makes a man fight better, so does wine, frenzy, nay, and fear itself; for the greatest coward in despair does the greatest wonders. No man is courageous in his anger that was not so without it. But put the case, that anger by accident may have done some good, and so have fevers removed some distempers; but it is an odious kind of remedy that makes us indebted to a disease for a cure. How many men have been preserved by poison; by a fall from a precipice; by a shipwreck; by a tempest! does it therefore follow that we are to recommend the practice of these experiments?

"But in case of an exemplary and prostitute dissolution of manners, when Clodius shall be preferred, and Cicero rejected; when loyalty shall be broken upon the wheel, and treason sit triumphant upon the bench; is not this a subject to move the choler of any virtuous man?" No, by no means, virtue will never allow of the correcting of one vice by another; or that anger, which is the greater crime of the two, should presume to punish the less. It is the natural property of virtue to make a man serene and cheerful; and it is not for the dignity of a philosopher to be transported either with grief or anger; and then the end of anger is sorrow, the constant effect of disappointment and repentance. But, to my purpose. If a man should be angry at wickedness, the greater the wickedness is, the greater must be his anger; and, so long as there is wickedness in the world he must never be pleased: which makes his quiet dependent upon the humor or manners of others.

There passes not a day over our heads but he that is choleric shall have some cause or other of displeasure, either from men, accidents, or business. He shall never stir out of his house but he shall meet with criminals of all sorts; prodigal, impudent, covetous, perfidious, contentious, children persecuting their parents, parents cursing their children, the innocent accused, the delinquent acquitted, and the judge practicing that in his chamber which he condemns upon the bench. In fine, wherever there are men there are faults; and upon these terms, Socrates himself should never bring the same countenance home again that he carried out with him.

If anger was sufferable in any case, it might be allowed against an incorrigible criminal under the hand of justice: but punishment is not matter of anger but of caution. The law is without passion, and strikes malefactors as we do serpents and venomous creatures, for fear of greater mischief. It is not for the dignity of a judge, when he comes to pronounce the fatal sentence, to express any motions of anger in his looks, words, or gestures: for he condemns the vice, not the man; and looks upon the wickedness without anger, as he does upon the prosperity of wicked men without envy. But though he be not angry, I would have him a little moved in point of humanity; but yet without any offence, either to his place or wisdom. Our passions vary, but reason is equal; and it were a great folly for that which is stable, faithful, and sound, to repair for succor to that which is uncertain, false, and distempered. If the offender be incurable, take him out of the world, that if he will not be good he may cease to be evil; but this must be without anger too. Does any man hate an arm, or a leg, when he cuts it off; or reckon *that* a passion which is only a miserable cure? We knock mad dogs on the head, and remove scabbed sheep out of the fold: and this is not anger still, but reason, to separate the sick from the sound. Justice cannot be angry; nor is there any need of an angry magistrate for the punishment of foolish and wicked men. The power of life and death must not be managed with passion. We give a horse the spur that is restive or jadish, and tries to cast his rider; but this is without anger too, and only to take down his stomach, and bring him, by correction, to obedience.

It is true, that correction is necessary, yet within reason and bounds; for it does not hurt, but profits us under an appearance of harm. Ill dispositions in the mind are to be dealt with as those in the body: the physician first tries purging and abstinence; if this will not do, he proceeds to bleeding, nay, to dismembering rather than fail; for there is no operation too severe that ends in health. The public magistrate begins with persuasion, and his business is to beget a detestation for vice, and a veneration for virtue; from thence, if need be, he advances to admonition and reproach, and then to punishments; but moderate and revocable, unless the wickedness be incurable, and then the punishment must be so too. There is only this difference, the physician when he cannot save his patient's life, endeavors to make his death easy; but the magistrate aggravates the death of the criminal with infamy and disgrace; not as delighting in the severity of it, (for no good man can be so barbarous) but for example, and to the end that they that will do no good living may do some dead. The end of all correction is either the amendment of wicked men, or to prevent the influence of ill example: for men are punished with a respect to the future; not to expiate offenses committed, but for fear of worse to come. Public offenders must be a terror to others; but still, all this while, the power of life and death must not be managed with passion. The medicine, in the mean time must be suited to the disease; infamy cures one, pain another, exile cures a third, beggary a fourth; but there are some that are only to be cured by the gibbet. I would be no more angry with a thief, or a traitor, than I am angry with myself when I open a vein. All punishment is but a moral or civil remedy. I do not do anything that is very ill, but yet I transgress often. Try me first with a private reprehension, and then with a public; if that will not serve, see what banishment will do; if not that neither, load me with chains, lay me in prison: but if I should prove wicked for wickedness' sake, and leave no hope of reclaiming me, it would be a kind of mercy to destroy me. Vice is incorporated with me; and there is no remedy but the taking of both away together; but still without anger.

VI

ANGER IN GENERAL, WITH THE
DANGER AND EFFECTS OF IT

There is no surer argument of a great mind than not to be transported to anger by any accident; the clouds and the tempests are formed below, but all above is quiet and serene; which is the emblem of a brave man, that suppresses all provocations, and lives within himself, modest, venerable, and composed: whereas anger is a turbulent humor, which, at first dash, casts off all shame, without any regard to order, measure, or good manners; transporting a man into misbecoming violences with his tongue, his hands, and every part of his body. And whoever considers the foulness and the brutality of this vice, must acknowledge that there is no such monster in Nature as one man raging against another, and laboring to sink that which can never be drowned but with himself for company. It renders us incapable either of discourse or of other common duties. It is of all passions the most powerful; for it makes a man that is in love to kill his mistress, the ambitious man to trample upon his honors, and the covetous to throw away his fortune.

There is not any mortal that lives free from the danger of it; for it makes even the heavy and the good-natured to be fierce and outrageous: it invades us like a pestilence, the lusty as well as the weak; and it is not either strength of body, or a good diet, that can secure us against it; nay, the most learned, and men otherwise of exemplary sobriety, are infected with it. It is so potent a passion that Socrates durst not trust himself with it. "Sirrah," says he to his man, "now would I beat you, if I were not angry with you!" There is no age or sect of men that escapes it. Other vices take us one by one; but this, like an *epidemical contagion*, sweeps all: men, women, and children, princes and beggars, are carried away with it in shoals and troops as one man.

It was never seen that a whole nation was in love with one woman, or unanimously bent upon one vice: but here and there some particular men are tainted with some particular crimes; whereas in anger, a single word many times inflames the whole multitude, and men betake themselves presently to fire and sword upon it; the rabble take upon them to give laws to their governors; the common soldiers to their officers, to the ruin, not only of private families, but of kingdoms: turning their arms against their own leaders, and choosing their own generals. There is no public council, no putting things to the vote; but in a rage the mutineers divide from the senate, name their head, force the nobility in their own houses, and put them to death with their own hands. The laws of nations are violated, the persons of public ministers affronted, whole cities infected with a general madness, and no respite allowed for the abatement or discussing of this public tumor. The ships are crowded with tumultuary soldiers; and in this rude and ill-boding manner they march, and act under the conduct only of their own passions. Whatever comes next serves them for arms, until at last they pay for their licentious rashness with the slaughter of the whole party: this is the event of a heady and inconsiderate war.

When men's minds are struck with the opinion of an injury, they fall on immediately wheresoever their passion leads them, without either order, fear, or caution: provoking their own mischief; never at rest till they come to blows; and pursuing their revenge, even with their bodies, upon the points of their enemies' weapons. So that the anger itself is much more hurtful for us than the injury that provokes it; for the one is bounded, but where the other will stop, no man living knows. There are no greater slaves certainly, than those that serve anger; for they improve their misfortunes by an impatience more insupportable than the calamity that causes it.

Nor does it rise by degrees, as other passions, but flashes like gunpowder, blowing up all in a moment. Neither does it only press to the mark, but overbears everything in the way to it. Other vices drive us, but this hurries us headlong; other passions stand firm themselves, though perhaps we cannot resist them; but this consumes and destroys itself: it falls like thunder or a tempest, with an irrevocable violence, that gathers strength in the passage, and then evaporates in the conclusion. Other vices are unreasonable, but this is unhealthful too; other distempers have their intervals and degrees, but in this we are thrown down as from a precipice: there is not anything so amazing to others, or so destructive to itself; so proud and insolent if it succeeds, or so extravagant if it be disappointed. No repulse discourages it, and, for want of other matter to work upon, it falls foul upon itself; and, let the ground be never so trivial, it is sufficient for the wildest outrage imaginable. It spares neither age, sex, nor quality.

Some people would be luxurious perchance, but that they are poor; and others lazy, if they were not perpetually kept at work. The simplicity of a country life, keeps many men in ignorance of the frauds and impieties of courts and camps: but no nation or condition of men is exempt from the impressions of anger; and it is equally dangerous, as well in war as in peace. We find that elephants will be made familiar; bulls will suffer children to ride upon their backs, and play with their horns; bears and lions, by good usage, will be brought to fawn upon their masters; how desperate a madness is it then for men, after the reclaiming of the fiercest of beasts, and the bringing of them to be tractable and domestic, to become yet worse than beasts one to another! Alexander had two friends, Clytus and Lysimachus; the one he exposed to a lion, the other to himself; and he that was turned loose to the beast escaped. Why do we not rather make the best of a short life, and render ourselves amiable to all while we live, and desirable when we die?

Let us bethink ourselves of our mortality, and not squander away the little time that we have upon animosities and feuds, as if it were never to be at an end. Had we not better enjoy the pleasure of our own life than to be still contriving how to gall and torment another's? in all our brawlings and contentions never so much as dreaming of our weakness. Do we not know that these implacable enmities of ours lie at the mercy of a fever, or any petty accident, to disappoint? Our fate is at hand, and the very hour that we have set for another man's death may peradventure be prevented by our own. What is it that we make all this bustle for, and so needlessly disquiet our minds? We are offended with our servants, our masters, our princes, our clients: it is but a little patience, and we shall be all of us equal; so that there is no need either of ambushes or of combats. Our wrath cannot go beyond death; and death will most undoubtedly come whether we be peevish or quiet. It is time lost to take pains to do that which will infallibly be done without us. But suppose that we would only have our enemy banished, disgraced, or damaged, let his punishment be more or less, it is yet too long, either for him to be inhumanly tormented, or for us ourselves to be most barbarously pleased with it. It holds in anger as in mourning, it must and it will at last fall of itself; let us look to it then betimes, for when it is once come to an ill habit, we shall never want matter to feed it; and it is much better to overcome our passions than to be overcome by them. Some way or other, either our parents, children, servants, acquaintance, or strangers, will be continually vexing us. We are tossed hither and thither by our affections, like a feather in a storm, and by fresh provocations the madness becomes perpetual. Miserable creatures! that ever our precious hours should be so ill employed! How prone and eager are we in our hatred, and how backward in our love! Were it not much better now to be making of friendships, pacifying of enemies, doing of good offices both public and private, than to be still meditating of mischief, and designing how to wound one man in his fame, another in his fortune, a third in his person? the one being so easy, innocent, and safe, and the other so difficult, impious, and hazardous. Nay, take a man in chains, and at the foot of his oppressor; how many are there, who, even in this case, have maimed themselves in the heat of their violence upon others.

This untractable passion is much more easily kept out than

governed when it is once admitted; for the stronger will give laws to the weaker; and make reason a slave to the appetite. It carries us headlong; and in the course of our fury, we have no more command of our minds, than we have of our bodies down a precipice: when they are once in motion, there is no stop until they come to the bottom. Not but that it is possible for a man to be warm in winter, and not to sweat in the summer, either by the benefit of the place, or the hardiness of the body: and in like manner we may provide against anger. But certain it is, that virtue and vice can never agree in the same subject; and one may as well be a sick man and a sound at the same time, as a good man, and an angry. Besides, if we will needs be quarrelsome, it must be either with our superior, our equal, or inferior. To contend with our superior is folly and madness: with our equals, it is doubtful and dangerous: and with our inferiors, it is base. For does any man know but that he that is now our enemy may come hereafter to be our friend, over and above the reputation of clemency and good nature? And what can be more honorable or comfortable, than to exchange a feud for a friendship? The people of Rome never had more faithful allies than those that were at first the most obstinate enemies; neither had the *Roman Empire* ever arrived at that height of power, if Providence had not mingled the vanquished with the conquerors.

There is an end of the contest when one side deserts it; so that the paying of anger with benefits puts a period to the controversy. But, however, if it be our fortune to transgress, let not our anger descend to the children, friends or relations, even of our bitterest enemies. The very cruelty of Sylla was heightened by that instance of incapacitating the issue of the proscribed. It is inhuman to entail the hatred we have for the father upon his posterity.

A good and a wise man is not to be an *enemy* of wicked men, but a *reprover* of them; and he is to look upon all the drunkards, the lustful, the thankless, covetous, and ambitious, that he meets with, not otherwise than as a physician looks upon his patients; for he that will be angry with *any man* must be displeased with *all*; which were as ridiculous as to quarrel with a body for stumbling in the dark; with one that is deaf, for not doing as you bid him; or with a school-boy for loving his play better than his book. Democritus *laughed*, and Heraclitus *wept*, at the folly and wickedness of the world, but we never read of any *angry philosopher*.

This is undoubtedly the most detestable of vices, even compared with the worst of them. Avarice scrapes and gathers together that which somebody may be the better for: but anger lashes out, and no man comes *off* gratis. An angry master makes one servant run away, and another hang himself; and his choler causes him a much greater loss than he suffered in the occasion of it. It is the cause of mourning to the father, and of divorce to the husband: it makes the magistrate odious, and gives the candidate a repulse. And it is worse than luxury too, which only aims at its proper pleasure; whereas the other is bent upon another body's pain.

The malevolent and the envious content themselves only to *wish* another man miserable; but it is the business of anger to *make* him so, and to wreck the mischief itself; not so much desiring the hurt of another, as to inflict it. Among the powerful, it breaks out into open war, and into a private one with the common people, but without force or arms. It engages us in treacheries, perpetual troubles and contentions: it alters the very nature of a man, and punishes itself in the persecution of others. Humanity excites us to love, this to hatred; that to be beneficial to others, this to hurt them: beside, that, though it proceeds from too high a conceit of ourselves, it is yet, in effect, but a narrow and contemptible affection; especially when it meets with a mind that is hard and impenetrable, and returns the dart upon the head of him that casts it.

To take a farther view, now, of the miserable consequences and sanguinary effects of this hideous distemper; from hence come slaughters and poisons, wars, and desolations, the razing and burning of cities; the unpeopling of nations, and the turning of populous countries into deserts, public massacres and regicides; princes led in triumph; some murdered in their bed-chambers; others stabbed in the senate or cut off in the security of their spectacles and pleasures. Some there are that take anger for a princely quality; as Darius, who, in his expedition against the Scythians, being besought by a nobleman, that had three sons, that he would vouchsafe to accept of two of them into his service, and leave the third at home for a comfort to his father. "I will do more for you than that," says Darius, "for you shall have them all three again;" so he ordered them to be slain before his face, and left him their bodies. But Xerxes dealt a little better with Pythius, who had five sons, and desired only one of them for himself. Xerxes bade him take his choice, and he named the *eldest*, whom he immediately commanded to be cut in halves; and one half of the body to be laid on each side of the way when his army was to pass betwixt them; undoubtedly a most auspicious sacrifice; but he came afterward to the end that he deserved; for he lived to see that prodigious power scattered and broken: and instead of military and victorious troops, to be encompassed with carcasses. But these, you will say, were only barbarous princes that knew neither civility nor letters; and these savage cruelties will be imputed perchance to their rudeness of manners, and want of discipline. But what will you say then of Alexander the Great, that was trained up under the institution of Aristotle himself, and killed Clytus, his favorite and schoolfellow, with his *own hand*, under his *own roof*, and *over the freedom of a cup of wine*? And what was his crime? He was loth to degenerate from a Macedonian *liberty* into a Persian *slavery*; that is to say, he could not *flatter*.

Lysimachus, another of his friends, he exposed to a lion; and this very Lysimachus, after he had escaped this danger, was never the more merciful when he came to reign himself; for he cut off the ears and nose of his friend Telesphorous; and when he had so disfigured him that he had no longer the face of a man, he threw him into a dungeon, and there kept him to be showed for a monster, as a strange sight. The place was so low that he was fain to creep upon all fours, and his sides were galled too with the straitness of it. In this misery he lay half-famished in his own filth; so odious, so terrible, and so loathsome a spectacle, that the horror of his condition had even extinguished all pity for him. "Nothing was ever so unlike a mar as the poor wretch that suffered this, saving the tyrant that acted it."

Nor did this merciless hardness only exercise itself among foreigners, but the fierceness of their outrages and punishments, as well as their vices, brake in upon the Romans. C. Marius, that had his statue set up everywhere, and was adored as a God, L. Sylla commanded his bones to be broken, his eyes to be pulled out, his hands to be cut off; and, as if every wound had been a several death, his body to be torn to pieces, and Catiline was the executioner. A *cruelty* that was only fit for Marius to *suffer*, Sylla to *command*, and Catiline to *act*; but most dishonorable and fatal to the commonwealth, to fall indifferently upon the sword's point both of citizens and of enemies.

It was a severe instance, that of Piso too. A soldier that had leave to go abroad with his comrade, came back to the camp at his time, but without his companion. Piso condemned him to die, as if he had killed him, and appoints a centurion to see the execution. Just as the headsman was ready to do his office, the other soldier appeared, to the great joy of the whole field, and the centurion bade the executioner hold his hand. Hereupon Piso, in a rage, mounts the *tribunal*, and sentences all three to death: the one because he was *condemned*, the *other* because it was for *his sake* that his fellow-soldier was *condemned*, the *centurion* for not obeying the *order* of his *superior*. An ingenious piece of inhumanity, to contrive how to make three criminals, where effectively there were none.

There was a Persian king that caused the noses of a whole nation to be cut off, and they were to thank him that he spared their heads. And this, perhaps, would have been the fate of the Macrobii, (if Providence had not hindered it,) for the freedom they used to Cambyses' ambassadors, in not accepting the slavish terms that were offered them. This put Cambyses into such a rage, that he presently listed into his service every man that was able to bear arms; and, without either provisions or guides, marched immediately through dry and barren deserts, and where never any man had passed before him, to take his revenge. Before he was a third part of the way, his provisions failed him. His men, at first, made shift with the buds of trees, boiled leather, and the like; but soon after there was not so much as a root or a plant to be gotten, nor a living creature to be seen; and then by lot every tenth man was to die for a nourishment to the rest, which was still worse than the famine. But yet this passionate king went on so far, until one part of his army was lost, and the other devoured, and until he feared that he himself might come to be served with the same sauce. So that at last he ordered a retreat, wanting no delicates all this while for himself, while his soldiers were taking their chance who should die miserably, or live worse. Here was an anger taken up against a whole nation, that neither deserved any ill from him, nor was so much as known to him.

VII

THE ORDINARY GROUNDS AND OCCASIONS OF ANGER

In this wandering state of life we meet with many occasions of trouble and displeasure, both great and trivial; and not a day passes but, from men or things, we have some cause or other for offense; as a man must expect to be jostled, dashed, and crowded, in a populous city. One man deceives our expectation; another delays it; and a third crosses it; and if everything does not succeed to our wish, we presently fall out either with the person, the business, the place, our fortune, or ourselves. Some men value themselves upon their wit, and will never forgive anyone that pretends to lessen it; others are inflamed by wine: and some are distempered by sickness, weariness, watchings, love, care, etc. Some are prone to it, by heat of constitution; but moist, dry, and cold complexions are more liable to other affections; as suspicion, despair, fear, jealousy, etc. But most of our quarrels are of our own contriving. One while we suspect upon mistake; and another while we make a great matter of trifles. To say the truth, most of those things that exasperate us are rather subjects of disgust than of mischief: there is a large difference betwixt opposing a man's satisfaction and not assisting it: betwixt *taking away* and *not giving*; but we reckon upon *denying* and *deferring* as the same thing; and interpret another's being *for himself* as if he were *against us*. Nay, we do many times entertain an ill opinion of well doing, and a good one of the contrary: and we hate a man for doing that very thing which we should hate him for on the other side, if he did not do it.

We take it ill to be opposed when there is a father perhaps, a brother, or a friend, in the case against us; when we should rather love a man for it; and only wish that he could be honestly of our party. We approve of the fact, and detest the doer of it. It is a base thing to hate the person whom we cannot but commend; but it is a great deal worse yet if we hate him for the very thing that deserves commendation. The things that we desire, if they be such as cannot be given to one without being taken away from another, must needs set those people together by the ears that desire the same thing. One man has a design upon my mistress, another upon mine inheritance; and that which should make friends makes enemies, our being all of a mind. The general cause of anger is the sense or opinion of an *injury*; that is, the opinion either of an injury simply done, or of an injury done, which we have not deserved. Some are naturally given to anger, others are provoked to it by occasion; the anger of women and children is commonly sharp, but not lasting: old men are rather querulous and peevish. Hard labor, diseases, anxiety of thought, and whatsoever hurts the body or the mind, disposes a man to be froward, but we must not add fire to fire.

He that duly considers the subject-matter of all our controversies and quarrels, will find them low and mean, not worth the thought of a generous mind; but the greatest noise of all is about *money*. This is it that sets fathers and children together by the ears, husbands and wives; and makes way for sword and poison. This is it that tires out courts of justice, enrages princes, and lays cities in the dust, to seek for gold and silver in the ruins of them. This is it that finds work for the judge to determine which side is least in the wrong; and whose is the more plausible avarice, the plaintiff's or the defendant's. And what is it that we contend for all this while, but those baubles that make us cry when we should laugh? To see a rich old cuff, that has nobody to leave his estate to, break his heart for a handful of dirt; and a gouty usurer, that has no other use of his fingers left him but to count withal; to see him, I say in the extremity of his fit, wrangling for the odd money in his interest. If all that is precious in Nature were gathered into one mass, it were not worth the trouble of a sober mind. It were endless to run over all those ridiculous passions that are moved about meats and drinks, and the matter of our luxury; nay, about words, looks, actions, jealousies, mistakes, which are all of them as contemptible fooleries as those very baubles that children scratch and cry for. There is nothing great or serious in all that which we keep such a clutter about; the madness of it is, that we set too great a value upon trifles. One man flies out upon a salute, a letter, a speech, a question, a gesture, a wink, a look. An action moves one man; a word affects another; one man is tender of his family; another of his person; one sets up for an orator, another for a philosopher: this man will not bear pride, nor that man opposition. He that plays the tyrant at home, is gentle as a lamb abroad. Some take offense if a man ask a favor of them, and others, if he does not. Every man has his weak side; let us learn which that is, and take a care of it; for the same thing does not work upon all men alike. We are moved like beasts at the idle appearances of things, and the fiercer the creature, the more is it startled. The sight of a red coat enrages a bull; a shadow provokes the asp; nay, so unreasonable are some men, that they take moderate benefits for injuries, and squabble about it with their nearest relations: "They have done this and that for others," they cry; "and they might have dealt better with us if they had pleased." Very good! and if it be less than we looked for, it may be yet more than we deserve. Of all unquiet humors this is the worst, that will never suffer any man to be happy, so long as he sees a happier man than himself. I have known some men so weak as to think themselves contemned if a horse did but play the jade with *them*, that is yet obedient to *another rider*. A brutal folly to be offended at a mute animal; for no injury can be done us without the concurrence of reason. A beast may hurt us, as a sword or a stone, and no otherwise. Nay, there are that will complain of "foul weather, a raging sea, a biting winter," as if it were expressly directed to them; and this they charge upon Providence, whose operations are all of them so far from being injurious, that they are beneficial to us.

How vain and idle are many of those things that make us stark mad! A resty horse, the overturning of a glass, the falling of a key, the dragging of a chair, a jealousy, a misconstruction. How shall that man endure the extremities of hunger and thirst that flies out into a rage for putting of a little too much water in his wine? What haste is there to lay a servant by the heels, or break a leg or an arm immediately for it, as if he were not to have the same power over him an hour after, that he has at that instant? The answer of a servant, a wife, a tenant, puts some people out of all patience; and yet they can quarrel with the government, for not allowing them the same liberty in public, which they themselves deny to their own families. If they say nothing, it is contumacy: if they speak or laugh, it is insolence. As if a man had his ears given him only for music; whereas we must suffer all sorts of noises, good and bad, both of man and beast. How idle is it to start at the tinkling of a bell, or the creaking of a door, when, for all this delicacy, we must endure thunder! Neither are our eyes less curious and fantastical than our ears. When we are abroad, we can bear well enough with foul ways, nasty streets, noisome ditches; but a spot upon a dish at home, or an unswept hearth, absolutely distracts us. And what is the reason, but that we are patient in the one place, and fantastically peevish in the other? Nothing makes us more intemperate than luxury, that shrinks at every stroke, and starts at every shadow. It is death to some to have another sit above them, as if a body were ever the more or the less honest for the cushion. But they are only weak creatures that think themselves wounded if they be but touched. One of the Sybarites, that saw a fellow hard at work a digging, desired him to give over, for it made him weary to see him: and it was an ordinary complaint with him, that "he could take no rest because the rose-leaves lay double under him." When we are once weakened with our pleasures, everything grows intolerable. And we are angry as well with those things that cannot hurt us as with those that do. We tear a book because it is blotted; and our clothes, because they are not well made: things that neither deserve our anger nor feel it: the tailor, perchance, did his best, or, however, had no intent to displease us: if so, first, why should we be angry at all? Secondly, why should we be angry with the thing for the man's sake? Nay, our anger extends even to dogs, horses, and other beasts.

It was a blasphemous and a sottish extravagance, that of Caius Caesar, who challenged Jupiter for making such a noise with his *thunder*, that he could not hear his mimics, and so invented a machine in imitation of it to oppose *thunder* to *thunder*; a brutal conceit, to imagine, either that he could reach the Almighty, or that the Almighty could not reach him!

And every jot as ridiculous, though not so impious, was that of Cyrus; who, in his design upon Babylon, found a river in his way that put a stop to his march: the current was strong, and carried away one of the horses that belonged to his own chariot: upon this he swore, that since it had obstructed *his* passage, it should never hinder any body's else; and presently set his whole army to work upon it, which diverted it into a hundred and fourscore channels, and laid it dry. In this ignoble and unprofitable employment he lost his time, and the soldiers their courage, and gave his adversaries an opportunity of providing themselves, while he was waging war with a river instead of an enemy.

VIII

ADVICE IN THE CASES OF CONTUMELY AND REVENGE

Of provocations to anger there are two sorts; there is an *injury*, and there is a *contumely*. The former in its own nature is the heavier; the other slight in itself, and only troublesome to a wounded imagination. And yet some there are that will bear blows, and death itself, rather than contumelious words. A contumely is an indignity below the consideration of the very law; and not worthy either of a revenge, or so much as a complaint. It is only the vexation and infirmity of a weak mind, as well as the practice of a haughty and insolent nature, and signifies no more to a wise and sober man than an idle dream, that is no sooner past than forgotten. It is true, it implies contempt; but what needs any man care for being contemptible to others, if he be not so to himself? For a child in the arms to strike the mother, tear her hair, claw the face of her, and call her names, that goes for nothing with us, because the child knows not what he does. Neither are we moved at the impudence and bitterness of a *buffoon*, though he fall upon his own master as well as the guests; but, on the contrary, we encourage and entertain the freedom.

Are we not mad then, to be delighted and displeased with the same thing, and to take that as an *injury* from one man, which passes only for a *raillery* from another? He that is wise will behave himself toward all men as we do to our children; for they are but children too, though they have gray hairs: they are indeed of a larger size, and their errors are grown up with them; they live without rule, they covet without choice, they are timorous and unsteady; and if at any time they happen to be quiet, it is more out of fear than reason. It is a wretched condition to stand in awe of everybody's tongue; and whosoever is vexed at a reproach would be proud if he were commended. We should look upon contumelies, slanders, and ill words, only as the clamor of enemies, or arrows shot at a distance, that make a clattering upon our arms, but do no execution. A man makes himself less than his adversary by fancying that he is contemned.

Things are only ill that are ill taken; and it is not for a man of worth to think himself better or worse for the opinion of others. He that thinks himself injured, let him say, "Either I have deserved this, or I have not. If I have, it is a judgment; if I have not, it is an injustice: and the doer of it has more reason to be ashamed than the sufferers."

Nature has assigned every man his post, which he is bound in honor to maintain, let him be never so much pressed. Diogenes was disputing of anger, and an insolent young fellow, to try if he could put him beside his philosophy, spit in his face: "Young man," says Diogenes, "this does not make me angry yet; but I am in some doubt whether I should be so or not." Some are so impatient that they cannot bear a contumely, even from a woman; whose very beauty, greatness, and ornaments, are all of them little enough to vindicate her from any indecencies, without much modesty and discretion; nay, they will lay it to heart even from the meanest of servants. How wretched is that man whose peace lies at the mercy of the people?

A physician is not angry at the intemperance of a mad patient; nor does he take it ill to be railed at by a man in a fever; just so should a wise man treat all mankind as a physician does his patient; and looking upon them only as sick and extravagant, let their words and actions, whether good or bad, go equally for nothing, attending still his duty even in the coarsest offices that may conduce to their recovery. Men that are proud, froward, and powerful, he values their scorn as little as their quality, and looks upon them no otherwise than as people in the excess of a fever. If a beggar worships him, or if he takes no notice of him, it is all one to him; and with a rich man he makes it the same case. Their honors and their injuries he accounts much alike; without rejoicing at the one, or grieving at the other.

In these cases, the rule is to pardon all offenses, where there is any sign of repentance, or hope of amendment. It does not hold in injuries as in benefits, the requiting of the one with the other; for it is a shame to overcome in the one, and in the other to be overcome. It is the part of a great mind to despise injuries; and it is one kind of revenge to neglect a man as not worth it: for it makes the first aggressor too considerable. Our philosophy, methinks, might carry us up to the bravery of a generous mastiff, that can hear the barking of a thousand curs without taking any notice of them. He that receives an injury from his superior, it is not enough for him to bear it with patience, and without any thought of revenge, but he must receive it with a cheerful countenance, and look as if he did not understand it too; for if he appear too sensible, he shall be sure to have more of it. "It is a damned humor in great men, that whom they wrong they will hate."

It is well answered of an old courtier, that was asked how he kept so long in favor? "Why," says he, "by receiving injuries, and crying your humble servant for them." Some men take it for an argument of greatness to have revenge in their power; but so far is he that is under the dominion of anger from being great, that he is not so much as free. Not but that anger is a kind of pleasure to some in the act of revenge; but the very *word* is *inhuman*, though it may pass for *honest*. "Virtue," in short, "is impenetrable, and revenge is only the confession of an infirmity."

It is a fantastical humor, that the same jest in private should make us merry, and yet enrage us in public; nay, we will not allow the liberty that we take. Some railleries we account pleasant, others bitter: a conceit upon a *squint-eye*, a *hunch-back*, or any personal defect, passes for a reproach. And why may we not as well hear it as see it? Nay, if a man imitates our gait, speech, or any natural imperfection, it puts us out of all patience; as if the counterfeit were more grievous than the doing of the thing itself. Some cannot endure to hear of their age, nor others of their poverty; and they make the thing the more taken notice of the more they desire to hide it. Some bitter jest (for the purpose) was broken upon you at the table: keep better company then. In the freedom of cups, a sober man will hardly contain himself within bounds. It sticks with us extremely sometimes, that the porter will not let us in to his great master. Will any but a madman quarrel with a cur for barking, when he may pacify him with a crust? What have we to do but to keep further off, and laugh at him? Fidus Cornelius (a tall slim fellow) fell downright a-crying in the senate-house at Corbulo's saying that "he looked like an ostrich." He was a man that made nothing of a lash upon his life and manners; but it was worse than death to him a reflection upon his person. No man was ever ridiculous to others that laughed at himself first: it prevents mischief, and it is a spiteful disappointment of those that take pleasure in such abuses. Vatinius, (a man that was made up for scorn and hatred, scurrilous and impudent to the highest degree, but most abusively witty and with all this he was diseased, and deformed to extremity), his way, was always to make sport with himself, and so he prevented the mockeries of other people. There are none more abusive to others than they that lie most open to it themselves; but the humor goes round, and he that laughs at me to-day will have somebody to laugh at him to-morrow, and revenge my quarrel. But, however, there are some liberties that will never go down with some men.

Asiaticus Valerius, (one of Caligula's particular friends, and a man of stomach, that would not easily digest an affront) Caligula told him in public what kind of bedfellow his wife was. Good God! that ever any man should hear this, or a prince speak it, especially to a man of consular authority, a friend, and a husband: and in such a manner too as at once to own his disgust and his adultery. The tribune Chaereas had a weak broken voice, like an hermaphrodite; when he came to Caligula for the *word*, he would give him sometimes *Venus*, otherwhiles *Priapus*, as a slur upon him both ways. Valerius was afterwards the principal instrument in the conspiracy against him; and Chaereas, to convince him of his manhood, at one blow cleft him down the chin with his sword. No man was so forward as Caligula to *break* a jest, and no man so unwilling to *bear* it.

IX

CAUTIONS AGAINST ANGER IN THE MATTER OF EDUCATION, CONVERSE, AND OTHER GENERAL RULES OF PREVENTING IT, BOTH IN OURSELVES AND OTHERS

All that we have to say in particular upon this subject lies under these two heads: first, that we do not *fall* into anger; and secondly, that we do not *transgress in it*. As in the case of our bodies, we have some medicines to preserve us when we are well, and others to recover us when we are sick; so it is one thing not to admit it, and another thing to overcome it. We are, in the first place, to avoid all provocations, and the beginnings of anger: for if we be once down, it is a hard task to get up again. When our passion has got the better of our reason, and the enemy is received into the gate, we cannot expect that the conqueror should take conditions from the prisoner. And, in truth, our reason, when it is thus mastered, turns effectually into passion. A careful education is a great matter; for our minds are easily formed in our youth, but it is a harder business to cure ill habits: beside that, we are inflamed by climate, constitution, company, and a thousand other accidents, that we are not aware of.

The choice of a good nurse, and a well-natured tutor, goes a great way: for the sweetness both of the blood and of the manners will pass into the child. There is nothing breeds anger more than a soft and effeminate education; and it is very seldom seen that either the mother's or the school-master's darling ever comes to good. But *my young master*, when he comes into the world, behaves himself like a choleric coxcomb; for flattery, and a great fortune, nourish touchiness. But it is a nice point so to check the seeds of anger in a child as not to take off his edge, and quench his spirits; whereof a principal care must be taken betwixt license and severity, that he be neither too much emboldened nor depressed. Commendation gives him courage and confidence; but then the danger is, of blowing him up into insolence and wrath: so that when to use the bit, and when the spur, is the main difficulty. Never put him to a necessity of begging anything basely: or if he does, let him go without it. Inure him to a familiarity where he has any emulation; and in all his exercises let him understand that it is generous to overcome his competitor, but not to hurt him. Allow him to be pleased when he does well, but not transported; for that will puff him up into too high a conceit of himself. Give him nothing that he cries for till the dogged fit is over, but then let him have it when he is quiet; to show him that there is nothing to be gotten by being peevish. Chide him for whatever he does amiss, and make him betimes acquainted with the fortune that he was born to. Let his diet be cleanly, but sparing; and clothe him like the rest of his fellows: for by placing him upon that equality at first, he will be the less proud afterward: and, consequently the less waspish and quarrelsome.

In the next place, let us have a care of temptations that we cannot resist, and provocations that we cannot bear; and especially of sour and exceptious company: for a cross humor is contagious. Nor is it all that a man shall be the better for the example of a quiet conversation; but an angry disposition is troublesome, because it has nothing else to work upon. We should therefore choose a sincere, easy, and temperate companion, that will neither provoke anger nor return it; nor give a man any occasion of exercising his distempers. Nor is it enough to be gentle, submissive, and humane, without integrity and plain-dealing; for flattery is as offensive on the other side. Some men would take a curse from you better than a compliment. Caelius, a passionate orator, had a friend of singular patience that supped with him, who had no way to avoid a quarrel but by saying *amen* to all that Caelius said. Caelius, taking this ill: "Say something against me," says he, "that you and I may be two;" and he was angry with him because he would not: but the dispute fell, as it needs must, for want of an opponent.

He that is naturally addicted to anger, let him use a moderate diet, and abstain from wine; for it is but adding fire to fire. Gentle exercises, recreations, and sports, temper and sweeten the mind. Let him have a care also of long and obstinate disputes; for it is easier not to begin them than to put an end to them. Severe studies are not good for him either, as *law, mathematics*; too much attention preys upon the spirits, and makes him eager: but *poetry, history* and those lighter entertainments, may serve him for diversion and relief. He that would be quiet, must not venture at things out of his reach, or beyond his strength; for he shall either stagger under the burden, or discharge it upon the next man he meets; which is the same case in civil and domestic affairs. Business that is ready and practicable goes off with ease; but when it is too heavy for the bearer, they fall both together. Whatsoever we design, we should first take a measure of ourselves, and compare our force with the undertaking; for it vexes a man not to go through with his work: a repulse inflames a generous nature, as it makes one that is *phlegmatic, sad*. I have known some that have advised looking in a glass when a man is in the fit, and the very spectacle of his own deformity has cured him. Many that are troublesome in their drink, and know their own infirmity, give their servant order beforehand to take them away by force for fear of mischief, and not to obey their masters themselves when they are hot-headed. If the thing were duly considered we should need no other cure than the bare consideration of it. We are not angry at madmen, children, and fools, because they do not know what they do: and why should not imprudence have an equal privilege in other cases? If a horse kick, or a dog bite, shall a man kick or bite again? The one, it is true, is wholly void of reason, but it is also an equivalent darkness of mind that possesses the other. So long as we are among men, let us cherish humanity, and so live that no man may be either in fear or in danger of us. Losses, injuries, reproaches, calumnies, they are but short inconveniences, and we should bear them with resolution. Beside that, some people are above our anger, others below it. To contend with our superiors were a folly, and with our inferiors an indignity.

There is hardly a more effectual remedy against anger than patience and consideration. Let but the first fervor abate, and that mist which darkens the mind will be either lessened or dispelled; a day, nay, an hour, does much in the most violent cases, and perchance totally suppresses it; time discovers the truth of things, and turns that into judgment which at first was anger. Plato was about to strike his servant, and while his hand was in the air, he checked himself, but still held it in that menacing posture. A friend of his took notice of it, and asked him what he meant? "I am now," says Plato, "punishing of an angry man;" so that he had left his servant to chastise himself. Another time his servant having committed a great fault: "Speusippus," says he, "do you beat that fellow, for I am angry," so that he forebore striking him for the very reason that would have made another man have done it. "I am angry," says he, "and shall go further than becomes me." Nor is it fit that a servant should be in his power that is not his own master. Why should any one venture now to trust an angry man with a revenge, when Plato durst not trust himself? Either he must govern that, or that will undo him. Let us do our best to overcome it, but let us, however, keep it close, without giving it any vent. An angry man, if he gives himself liberty at all times, will go too far. If it comes once to show itself in the eye or countenance, it has got the better of us. Nay, we should so oppose it as to put on the very contrary dispositions; calm looks, soft and slow speech, an easy and deliberate march, and by little and little, we may possibly bring our thoughts into sober conformity with our actions. When Socrates was angry, he would take himself in it, and *speak low*, in opposition to the motions of his displeasure. His friends would take notice of it; and it was not to his disadvantage neither, but rather to his credit, that so many should *know* that he was angry, and nobody *feel* it; which could not have been, if he had not given his friends the same liberty of admonition which he himself took. And this course should we take; we should desire our friends not to flatter us in our follies, but to treat us with all liberties of reprehension, even when we are least willing to bear it, against so powerful and so insinuating an evil; we should call for help while we have our eyes in our head, and are yet masters of ourselves. Moderation is profitable for subjects, but more for princes, who have the means of executing all that their anger prompts them to. When that power comes once to be exercised to a common mischief, it can never long continue; a common fear joining in one cause all their divided complaints. In a word now, how we may prevent, moderate, or master this impotent passion in others.

It is not enough to be sound ourselves, unless we endeavor to make others so, wherein we must accommodate the remedy to the temper of the patient. Some are to be dealt with by artifice and address: as, for example, "Why will you gratify your enemies to show yourself so much concerned? It is not worth your anger: it is below you: I am as much troubled at it myself as you can be; but you had better say nothing, and take your time to be even with them." Anger in some people is to be openly opposed; in others, there must be a little yielding, according to the disposition of the person. Some are won by entreaties, others are gained by mere shame and conviction, and some by delay; a dull way of cure for a violent distemper, but this must be the last experiment. Other affections may be better dealt with at leisure; for they proceed gradually: but this commences and perfects itself in the same moment. It does not, like other passions, solicit and mislead us, but it runs away with us by force, and hurries us on with an irresistible temerity, as well to our own as to another's ruin: not only flying in the face of him that provokes us, but like a torrent, bearing down all before it. There is no encountering the first heat and fury of it: for it is deaf and mad, the best way is (in the beginning) to give it time and rest, and let it spend itself: while the passion is too hot to handle, we may deceive it; but, however, let all instruments of revenge be put out of the way. It is not amiss sometimes to pretend to be angry too; and join with him, not only in the opinion of the injury, but in the seeming contrivance of a revenge. But this must be a person then that has some authority over him. This is a way to get time, and, by advising upon some greater punishment to delay the present. If the passion be outrageous, try what shame or fear can do. If weak, it is no hard matter to amuse it by strange stories, grateful news, or pleasant discourses. Deceit, in this case, is friendship; for men must be cozened to be cured.

The injuries that press hardest upon us are those which either we have not deserved, or not expected, or, at least, not in so high a degree. This arises from the love of ourselves: for every man takes upon him, like a prince, in this case, to practice all liberties, and to allow none, which proceeds either from ignorance or insolence. What news is it for people to do ill things? for an enemy to hurt us; nay, for a friend or a servant to transgress, and to prove treacherous, ungrateful, covetous, impious? What we find in one man we may in another, and there is more security in fortune than in men. Our joys are mingled with fear, and a tempest may arise out of a calm; but a skilful pilot is always provided for it.

X

AGAINST RASH JUDGMENT

It is good for every man to fortify himself on his weak side: and if he loves his peace he must not be inquisitive, and hearken to tale-bearers; for the man that is over-curious to hear and see everything, multiplies troubles to himself: for a man does not feel what he does not know. He that is listening after private discourse, and what people say of him, shall never be at peace. How many things that are innocent in themselves are made injuries yet by misconstruction! Wherefore, some things we are to pause upon, others to laugh at, and others again to pardon. Or, if we cannot avoid the sense of indignities, let us however shun the open profession of it, which may easily be done, as appears by many examples of those that have suppressed their anger under the awe of a greater fear. It is a good caution not to believe any thing until we are very certain of it; for many probable things prove false, and a short time will make evidence of the undoubted truth. We are prone to believe many things which we are willing to hear, and so we conclude, and take up a prejudice before we can judge. Never condemn a friend unheard; or without letting him know his accuser, or his crime. It is a common thing to say, "Do not you tell that you had it from me: for if you do, I will deny it, and never tell you any thing again:" by which means friends are set together by the ears, and the informer slips his neck out of the collar. Admit no stories upon these terms: for it is an unjust thing to believe in private and to be angry openly. He that delivers himself up to guess and conjecture runs a great hazard; for there can be no suspicion without some probable grounds; so that without much candor and simplicity, and making the best of every thing, there is no living in society with mankind. Some things that offend us we have by report; others we see or hear. In the first case, let us not be too credulous: some people frame stories that they may deceive us; others only tell what they hear, and are deceived themselves: some make it their sport to do ill offices, others do them only to pick a thank: there are some that would part the dearest friends in the world; others love to do mischief, and stand aloof off to see what comes of it. If it be a small matter, I would have witnesses; but if it be a greater, I would have it upon oath, and allow time to the accused, and counsel too, and hear over and over again.

In those cases where we ourselves are witnesses, we should take into consideration all the circumstances. If a *child*, it was *ignorance*: if a *woman*, a *mistake*: if done by *command* a *necessity*; if a *man* be injured, it is but *quod pro quo*: if a *judge*, he *knows* what he does: if a *prince*, I must *submit*; either if *guilty*, to *justice*, or if *innocent*, to *fortune*: if a *brute*, I make myself one by *imitating* it: if a *calamity* or *disease*, my best relief is *patience*: if *providence*, it is both *impious* and *vain* to be *angry* at it: if a *good* man, I will make the *best* of it: if a *bad*, I will never *wonder* at it. Nor is it only by *tales* and *stories* that we are inflamed, but *suspicions*, *countenances*, nay, a *look* or a *smile*, is enough to blow us up. In these cases, let us suspend our displeasure, and plead the cause of the absent. "Perhaps he is innocent; or, if not, I have time to consider of it and may take my revenge at leisure:" but when it is once *executed* it is not to be *recalled*. A jealous head is apt to take that to himself which was never meant him. Let us therefore trust to nothing but what we see, and chide ourselves where we are over-credulous. By this course we shall not be so easily imposed upon, nor put to trouble ourselves about things not worth the while: as the loitering of a servant upon an errand, and the tumbling of a bed, or the spilling of a glass of drink.

It is a madness to be disordered at these fooleries; we consider the thing done, and not the doer of it. "It may be he did it unwillingly, or by chance. It was a trick put upon him, or he was forced to it. He did it for reward perhaps, not hatred; nor of his own accord, but he was urged on to it." Nay, some regard must be had to the age of the person, or to fortune; and we must consult humanity and candor in the case. One does me a *great mischief* at *unawares*; another does me a very *small* one by *design*, or peradventure none at all, but intended me one. The latter was more in fault, but I will be angry with neither. We must distinguish betwixt what a man cannot do and what he will not. "It is true he has once offended me; but how often has he pleased me! He has offended me often, and in other kinds; and why should not I bear it as well now as I have done?" Is he my friend? why then, "It was against his will." Is he my enemy? It is "no more than I looked for." Let us give way to wise men, and not squabble with fools; and say thus to ourselves, "We have all of us our errors." No man is so circumspect, so considerate, or so fearful of offending, but he has much to answer for.

A generous prisoner cannot immediately comply with all the sordid and laborious offices of a slave. A footman that is not breathed cannot keep pace with his master's horse. He that is over-watched may be allowed to be drowsy. All these things are to be weighed before we give any ear to the first impulse. If it be my duty to love my country, I must be kind also to my countrymen; if a veneration be due to the whole, so is a piety also to the parts: and it is the common interest to preserve them. We are all members of one body, and it is as natural to help one another as for the hands to help the feet, or the eyes the hands. Without the love and care of the parts, the whole can never be preserved, and we must spare one another because we are born for society, which cannot be maintained without a regard to particulars. Let this be a rule to us, never to deny a pardon, that does no hurt either to the giver or receiver. That may be well enough in one which is ill in another; and therefore we are not to condemn anything that is common to a nation; for custom defends it. But much more pardonable are those things which are common to mankind.

It is a kind of spiteful comfort, that whoever does me an injury may receive one; and that there is a power over him that is above me. A man should stand as firm against all indignities as a rock does against the waves. As it is some satisfaction to a man in a mean condition that there is no security in a more prosperous; and as the loss of a son in a corner is borne with more patience upon the sight of a funeral carried out of a palace; so are injuries and contempts the more tolerable from a meaner person, when we consider, that the greatest men and fortunes are not exempt. The wisest also of mortals have their failings, and no man living is without the same excuse. The difference is, that we do not all of us transgress the same way; but we are obliged in humanity to bear one with another.

We should, every one of us, bethink ourselves, how remiss we have been in our duties, how immodest in our discourses, how intemperate in our cups; and why not, as well, how extravagant we have been in our passions? Let us clear ourselves of this evil, purge our minds, and utterly root out all those vices, which upon leaving the least sting, will grow again and recover. We must think of everything, expect everything, that we may not be surprised. It is a shame, says Fabius, for a commander to excuse himself by saying, "I was not aware of it."

XI

TAKE NOTHING ILL FROM ANOTHER MAN, UNTIL YOU HAVE MADE IT YOUR OWN CASE

It is not prudent to deny a pardon to any man, without first examining if we stand not in need of it ourselves; for it may be our lot to ask it, even at his feet to whom we refuse it. But we are willing enough to do what we are very unwilling to suffer. It is unreasonable to charge public vices upon particular persons; for we are all of us wicked, and that which we blame in others we find in ourselves. It is not a paleness in one, or a leanness in another, but a pestilence that has laid hold upon all.

It is a wicked world, and we make part of it; and the way to be quiet is to bear one with another. "Such a man," we cry, "has done me a shrewd turn, and I never did him any hurt." Well, but it may be I have mischieved other people, or at least, I may live to do as much to him as that comes to. "Such a one has spoken ill things of me;" but if I first speak ill of him, as I do of many others, this is not an injury, but a repayment. What if he did overshoot himself? He was loth to lose his conceit perhaps, but there was no malice in it; and if he had not done me a mischief, he must have done himself one. How many good offices are there that look like injuries! Nay, how many have been reconciled and good friends after a professed hatred!

Before we lay anything to heart, let us ask ourselves if we have not done the same thing to others. But where shall we find an equal judge? He that loves another man's wife (only because she is another's) will not suffer his own to be so much looked upon. No man is so fierce against calumny as the evil speaker; none so strict exactors of modesty in a servant as those that are most prodigal of their own. We carry our neighbors' crimes in sight, and we throw our own over our shoulders. The intemperance of a bad son is chastised by a worse father; and the luxury that we punish in others, we allow to ourselves. The tyrant exclaims against homicide; and sacrilege against theft. We are angry with the persons, but not with the faults.

Some things there are that cannot hurt us, and others will not; as good magistrates, parents, tutors, judges; whose reproof or correction we are to take as we do abstinence, bleeding, and other uneasy things, which we are the better for, in which cases, we are not so much to reckon upon what we suffer as upon what we have done. "I take it ill," says one; and, "I have done nothing," says another: when, at the same time, we make it worse, by adding arrogance and contumacy to our first error. We cry out presently, "What law have we transgressed?" As if the letter of the law were the sum of our duty, and that piety, humanity, liberality, justice, and faith, were things beside our business. No, no; the rule of human duty is of a greater latitude; and we have many obligations upon us that are not to be found in the *statute-books*. And yet we fall short of the exactness event of that *legal innocency*. We have intended one thing and done another; wherein only the want of success has kept us from being criminals. This very thing, methinks, should make us more favorable to delinquents, and to forgive not only ourselves, but the gods too; of whom we seem to have harder thoughts in taking that to be a particular evil directed to us, that befalls us only by the common law of mortality. In fine, no man living can absolve himself to his conscience, though to the world, perhaps, he may. It is true, that we are also condemned to pains and diseases, and to death too, which is no more than the quitting of the soul's house. But why should any man complain of bondage, that, wheresoever he looks, has his way open to liberty? That precipice, that sea, that river, that well, there is freedom in the bottom of it. It hangs upon every crooked bow; and not only a man's throat, or his heart, but every vein in his body, opens a passage to it.

To conclude, where my proper virtue fails me, I will have recourse to examples, and say to myself, Am I greater than Philip or Augustus, who both of them put up with greater reproaches? Many have pardoned their enemies, and shall not I forgive a neglect, a little freedom of the tongue? Nay, the patience but of a second thought does the business: for though the first shock be violent; take it in parts, and it is subdued. And, to wind up all in one word, the great lesson of mankind, as well in this as in all other cases, is, "to do as we would be done by."

XII

CRUELTY

There is so near an affinity betwixt *anger* and *cruelty*, that many people confound them; as if *cruelty* were only the *execution* of *anger* in the payment of a *revenge*: which holds in some cases, but not in others. There are a sort of men that take delight in the spilling of human blood, and in the death of those that never did them any injury, nor were ever so much suspected for it; as Apollodorus, Phalaris, Sinis, Procrustus, and others, that burnt men alive; whom we cannot so properly call *angry* as *brutal*, for *anger* does necessarily presuppose an injury, either *done*, or *conceived*, or *feared*, but the other takes *pleasure* in *tormenting*, without so much as pretending any *provocation* to it, and *kills* merely for *killing sake*. The *original* of this *cruelty* perhaps was *anger*, which by frequent *exercise* and *custom*, has lost all sense of *humanity* and *mercy*, and they that are thus affected are so far from the countenance and appearance of men in *anger*, that they will *laugh*, *rejoice*, and *entertain themselves* with the most *horrid spectacles*, as *racks*, *jails*, *gibbets*, several sorts of *chains* and *punishments*, *dilaceration* of *members*, *stigmatizing*, and *wild beasts*, with other exquisite inventions of torture; and yet, at last the cruelty itself is more horrid and odious than the means by which it works. It is a bestial madness to *love* mischief; beside, that it is *womanish* to *rage* and *tear*. A generous beast will scorn to do it when he has any thing at his mercy. It is a vice for wolves and tigers, and no less *abominable* to the *world* than *dangerous* to itself.

The Romans had their *morning* and their *meridian spectacles*. In the *former*, they had their combats of *men* with *wild beasts*; and in the *latter*, the *men* fought *one with another*. "I went," says our author, "the other day to the *meridian spectacles*, in hope of meeting somewhat of mirth and diversion to sweeten the humors of those that had been entertained with blood in the *morning*; but it proved otherwise, for, compared with this inhumanity, the former was a mercy. The whole business was only murder upon murder: the combatants fought naked, and every blow was a wound. They do not contend for *victory*, but for *death*; and he that kills one man is to be killed by another. By wounds they are forced upon wounds which they take and give upon their bare *breasts. Burn that rogue*, they cry *What! Is he afraid of his flesh? Do but see how sneakingly that rascal dies.* Look to yourselves, my masters, and consider of it: who knows but this may come to be your own case?" Wicked examples seldom fail of coming home at last to the authors. To destroy a *single* man may be dangerous; but to murder whole nations is only a more *glorious wickedness. Private avarice* and *rigor* are condemned, but *oppression*, when it comes to be *authorized* by an act of state, and to be publicly *commanded*, though particularly forbidden, becomes a point of *dignity* and *honor*. What a shame is it for men to interworry one another, when yet the fiercest even of beasts are at peace with those of their own kind? This brutal fury puts philosophy itself to a stand. The drunkard, the glutton, the covetous, may be reduced; nay, and the mischief of it is that no vice keeps itself within its proper bounds. Luxury runs into avarice, and when the reverence of virtue is extinguished, men will stick at nothing that carries profit along with it; man's blood is shed in wantonness — his death is a spectacle for entertainment, and his groans are music. When Alexander delivered up Lysimachus to a lion, how glad would he have been to have had nails and teeth to have devoured him himself: it would have too much derogated, he thought, from the dignity of his wrath, to have appointed a *man* for the execution of his friend. Private cruelties, it is true, cannot do much mischief, but in princes they are a war against mankind.

C. Caesar would commonly, for *exercise* and *pleasure*, put *senators* and *Roman knights* to the *torture*; and *whip* several of them like *slaves*, or put them to *death* with the most acute *torments*, merely for the satisfaction of his *cruelty*. That Caesar that "wished the people of Rome had but one neck, that he might cut it off at one blow;" — it was the employment, the study, and the joy of his life. He would not so much as give the expiring leave to groan, but caused their mouths to be stopped with sponges, or for want of them, with rags of their own clothes, that they might not breathe out so much as their last agonies at liberty; or, perhaps, lest the tormented should speak something which the tormentor had no mind to hear. Nay, he was so impatient of delay, that he would frequently rise from supper to have men killed by *torch-light*, as if his life and death had depended upon their dispatch before the next morning; to say nothing how many *fathers* were put to death in the same night with their *sons* (which was a kind of mercy in the prevention of their mourning). And was not Sylla's cruelty prodigious too, which was only stopped for want of enemies? He caused seven thousand *citizens* of Rome to be slaughtered at once; and some of the senators being startled at their cries that were heard in the *senate-house*, "Let us mind our business," says Sylla; "this is nothing but a few mutineers that I have ordered to be sent out of the way." A *glorious spectacle*! says Hannibal, when he saw the trenches flowing with human blood; and if the rivers had run blood too, he would have liked it so much the better.

Among the famous and detestable speeches that are committed to memory, I know none worse than that impudent and *tyrannical maxim*, "Let them hate me, so they fear me;" not considering that those that are kept in obedience by fear, are both malicious and mercenary, and only wait for an opportunity to change their master. Beside that, whosoever is terrible to others is likewise afraid of himself. What is more ordinary than for a tyrant to be destroyed by his own guards? which is no more than the putting those crimes into practice which they learned of their masters. How many slaves have revenged themselves of their cruel oppressors, though they were sure to die for it! but when it comes once to a *popular tyranny*, whole nations conspire against it. For "whosoever threatens all, is in danger of all," over and above, that the cruelty of the prince increases the *number* of his enemies, by destroying some of them; for it entails an hereditary hatred upon the friends and relations of those that are taken away. And then it has this misfortune, that a man must be wicked upon necessity; for there is no going back; so that he must betake himself to arms, and yet he lives in fear. He can neither trust to the faith of his friends, nor to the piety of his children; he both dreads death and wishes it; and becomes a greater terror to himself than he is to his people. Nay, if there were nothing else to make cruelty detestable, it were enough that it passes all bounds, both of custom and humanity; and is followed upon the heel with sword or poison. A private malice indeed does not move whole cities; but that which extends to all is every body's mark. One sick person gives no great disturbance in a family; but when it comes to a depopulating plague, all people fly from it. And why should a prince expect any man to be good whom he has taught to be wicked?

But what if it were *safe* to be *cruel*? Were it not still a sad thing, the very state of such a *government*? A *government* that bears the image of a *taken city*, where there is nothing but *sorrow*, *trouble*, and *confusion*. Men dare not so much as trust themselves with their friends or with their pleasures. There is not any entertainment so innocent but it affords pretence of crime and danger. People are betrayed at their *tables* and in their *cups*, and drawn from the very *theatre* to the *prison*. How horrid a madness is it to be still *raging* and *killing*; to have the rattling of *chains* always in our *ears; bloody spectacles* before our *eyes*; and to carry *terror* and *dismay* wherever we go! If we had *lions* and *serpents*, to rule over us, this would be the manner of their *government*, saving that they agree better among themselves. It passes for a mark of greatness to burn cities, and lay whole kingdoms waste; nor is it for the honor of a prince, to appoint this or that single man to be killed, unless they have whole *troops*, or (sometimes) *legions*, to work upon. But it is not the spoils of *war* and *bloody trophies* that make a prince *glorious*, but the *divine power* of preserving *unity* and *peace*. *Ruin* without *distinction* is more properly the business of a general *deluge*, or a *conflagration*. Neither does a fierce and inexorable *anger* become the *supreme magistrate*; "Greatness of mind is always meek and humble; but cruelty is a note and an effect of weakness, and brings down a governor to the level of a competitor."

CLEMENCY

The humanity and excellence of this virtue is confessed at all hands, as well by the men of *pleasure*, and those that think every man was made for himself, as by the Stoics, that make "man a sociable creature, and born for the common good of mankind:" for it is of all dispositions the most *peaceable* and *quiet*. But before we enter any farther upon the discourse, it should be first known what *clemency* is, that we may distinguish it from *pity*; which is a *weakness*, though many times mistaken for a *virtue*: and the next thing will be, to bring the mind to the *habit* and *exercise* of it.

"Clemency is a favorable disposition of the mind, in the matter of inflicting punishment; or, a moderation that remits somewhat of the penalty incurred; as *pardon* is the total remission of a deserved punishment." We must be careful not to confound *clemency* with *pity*; for as *religion worships* God, and *superstition profanes* that worship; so should we distinguish betwixt *clemency* and *pity*; *practicing* the *one*, and *avoiding* the *other*. For *pity* proceeds from a *narrowness of mind*, that respects rather the *fortune* than the *cause*. It is a kind of moral sickness, contracted from other people's misfortune: such another weakness as laughing or yawning for company, or as that of sick eyes that cannot look upon others that are bleared without dropping themselves. I will give a shipwrecked man a plank, a lodging to a stranger, or a piece of money to him that wants it: I will dry up the tears of my friend, yet I will not weep with him, but treat him with constancy and humanity, as *one man* ought to treat *another*.

It is objected by some, that *clemency* is an insignificant virtue; and that only the bad are the better for it, for the good have no need of it. But in the first place, as physic is in use only among the sick, and yet in honor with the sound, so the innocent have a reverence for clemency, though criminals are properly the objects of it. And then again, a man may be innocent, and yet have occasion for it too; for by the accidents of fortune, or the condition of times, virtue itself may come to be in danger. Consider the most populous city or nation; what a solitude would it be if none should be left there but those that could stand the test of a severe justice! We should have neither judges nor accusers; none either to grant a pardon or to ask it. More or less, we are all sinners; and he that has best purged his conscience, was brought by errors to repentance. And it is farther profitable to mankind; for many delinquents come to be converted. There is a tenderness to be used even toward our slaves, and those that we have bought with our money: how much more then to free and to honest men, that are rather under our protection than dominion! Not that I would have it so general neither as not to distinguish betwixt the good and the bad; for that would introduce a confusion, and give a kind of encouragement to wickedness. It must therefore have a respect to the quality of the offender, and separate the curable from the desperate; for it is an equal cruelty to pardon all and to pardon none. Where the matter is in balance, let mercy turn the scale: if all wicked men should be punished, who should escape?

Though mercy and gentleness of nature keeps all in peace and tranquillity, even in a *cottage*; yet it is much more beneficial and conspicuous in a *palace*. *Private men* in their *condition* are likewise *private* in their *virtues* and in their *vices*; but the words and the actions of *princes* are the subject of *public rumor*; and therefore they had need have a care, what occasion they give people for discourse, of whom people will be always a talking. There is the *government* of a *prince* over his *people*, a *father* over his *children*, a *master* over his *scholars*, an *officer* over his *soldiers*. He is an unnatural father, that for every trifle beats his children. Who is the better master, he that rages over his scholars for but missing a word in a lesson, or he that tries, by admonition and fair words, to instruct and reform them? An outrageous officer makes his men run from their colors. A skilful rider brings his horse to obedience by mingling fair means with foul; whereas to be perpetually switching and spurring, makes him vicious and jadish: and shall we not have more care of *men* than of *beasts*? It breaks the hope of generous inclinations, when they are depressed by servility and terror. There is no creature so hard to be pleased with ill usage as man.

Clemency does *well* with *all* but *best* with *princes*; for it makes their power comfortable and beneficial, which would otherwise be the pest of mankind. It establishes their greatness, when they make the good of the public their particular care, and employ their power for the safety of the people. The prince, in effect, is but the soul of the community, as the community is only the body of the prince; so that being merciful to others, he is tender of himself: nor is any man so mean but his master feels the loss of him, as a part of his empire: and he takes care not only of the lives of his people, but also of their reputation. Now, giving for granted that all virtues are in themselves equal, it will not yet be denied, that they may be more beneficial to mankind in one person than in another. A beggar may be as magnanimous as a king: for what can be greater or braver than to baffle ill fortune? This does not hinder but that a man in authority and plenty has more matter for his generosity to work upon than a private person; and it is also more taken notice of upon the bench than upon the level.

When a gracious prince shows himself to his people, they do not fly from him as from a tiger that rouses himself out of his den, but they worship him as a benevolent influence; they secure him against all conspiracies, and interpose their bodies betwixt him and danger. They guard him while he sleeps, and defend him in the field against his enemies. Nor is it without reason, this unanimous agreement in love and loyalty, and this heroical zeal of abandoning themselves for the safety of their prince; but it is as well the interest of the people. In the breath of a prince there is life and death; and his sentence stands good, right or wrong. If he be angry, nobody dares advise him; and if he does amiss, who shall call him to account? Now, for him that has so much mischief in his power, and yet applies that power to the common utility and comfort of his people, diffusing also clemency and goodness into their hearts too, what can be a greater blessing to mankind than such a prince? *Any man* may *kill* another *against* the law, but only a *prince* can *save* him so. Let him so deal with his own subjects as he desires God should deal with him. If Heaven should be inexorable to sinners, and destroy all without mercy, what flesh could be safe?

But as the faults of great men are not presently punished with thunder from above, let them have a like regard to their inferiors here upon earth. He that has revenge in his power, and does not use it, is the great man. Which is the more beautiful and agreeable state, that of a calm, a temperate, and a clear day; or that of lightning, thunder, and tempests? and this is the very difference betwixt a moderate and turbulent government. It is for low and vulgar spirits to brawl, storm, and transport themselves: but it is not for the majesty of a prince to lash out into intemperance of words. Some will think it rather slavery than empire to be debarred liberty of speech: and what if it be, when government itself is but a more illustrious servitude?

He that uses his power as he should, takes as much delight in making it comfortable to his people as glorious to himself. He is affable and easy of access; his very countenance makes him the joy of his people's eyes, and the delight of mankind. He is beloved, defended, and reverenced by all his subjects; and men speak as well of him in private as in public. He is safe without guards, and the sword is rather his ornament than his defence. In his duty, he is like that of a good father, that sometimes gently reproves a son, sometimes threatens him; nay, and perhaps corrects him: but no father in his right wits will disinherit a son for the first fault; there must be many and great offences, and only desperate consequences, that should bring him to that decretory resolution. He will make many experiments to try if he can reclaim him first, and nothing but the utmost despair must put him upon extremities.

It is not flattery that calls a prince *the father of his country*; the titles of *great* and *august* are matter of compliment and of honor; but in calling him *father*, we mind him of that moderation and indulgence which he owes to his children. His subjects are his members; where, if there must be an amputation, let him come slowly to it; and when the part is cut off, let him wish it were on again: let him grieve in the doing of it. He that passes a sentence *hastily*, looks as if he did it *willingly*; and then there is an injustice in the excess.

It is a glorious contemplation for a prince, first to consider the vast multitudes of his people, whose seditious, divided, and impotent passions, would cast all in confusion, and destroy themselves, and public order too, if the hand of government did not restrain them; and thence to pass the examination of his conscience, saying thus to himself, "It is by the choice of Providence that I am here made God's deputy upon earth, the arbitrator of life and death; and that upon my breath depends the fortune of my people. My lips are the oracles of their fate, and upon them hangs the destiny both of cities and of men. It is under my favor that people seek either for prosperity or protection: thousands of swords are drawn or sheathed at my pleasure. What towns shall be advanced or destroyed; who shall be slaves, or who free, depends upon my will; and yet, in this arbitrary power of acting without control, I was never transported to do any cruel thing, either by anger or hot blood in myself or by the contumacy, rashness, or provocations of other men; though sufficient to turn mercy itself into fury. I was never moved by the odious vanity of making myself terrible by my power, (that accursed, though common humor of ostentation and glory that haunts imperious natures.) My sword has not only been buried in the scabbard, but in a manner bound to the peace, and tender even of the cheapest blood: and where I find no other motive to compassion, humanity itself is sufficient. I have been always slow to severity, and prone to forgive; and under as strict a guard to observe the laws as if I were accountable for the breaking of them. Some I pardoned for their youth, others for their age. I spare one man for his dignity, another for his humility; and when I find no other matter to work upon, I spare myself. So that if God should at this instant call me to an account, the whole world agree to witness for me, that I have not by any force, either public or private, either by myself or by any other, defrauded the commonwealth; and the reputation that I have ever sought for has been that which few princes have obtained, the conscience of my proper innocence. And I have not lost my labor neither; for no man was ever so dear to another, as I have made myself to the whole body of my people." Under such a prince the subjects have nothing to wish for beyond what they enjoy; their fears are quieted, and their prayers heard, and there is nothing can make their felicity greater, unless to make it perpetual; and there is no liberty denied to the people but that of destroying one another.

It is the interest of the people, by the consent of all nations, to run all hazards for the safety of their prince, and by a thousand deaths to redeem that one life, upon which so many millions depend. Does not the whole body serve the mind, though only the one is exposed to the eye and the other not, but thin and invisible, the very seat of it being uncertain? Yet the hands, feet, and eyes, observe the motions of it. We lie down, run about and ramble, as that commands us. If we be covetous, we fish the seas and ransack the earth for treasure: if ambitious, we burn our own flesh with Scaevola; we cast ourselves into the gulf with Curtius: so would that vast multitude of people, which is animated but with one soul, governed by one spirit, and moved by one reason, destroy itself with its own strength, if it were not supported by wisdom and government. Wherefore, it is for their own security that the people expose their lives for their prince, as the very bond that ties the republic together; the vital spirit of so many thousands, which would be nothing else but a burden and prey without a governor.

When this union comes once to be dissolved, all falls to pieces; for empire and obedience must stand and fall together. It is no wonder then if a prince be dear to his people, when the community is wrapt up in him, and the good of both as inseparable as the body and the head; the one for strength, and the other for counsel; for what signifies the force of the body without the direction of the understanding? While the prince watches, his people sleep; his labor keeps them at ease, and his business keeps them quiet. The natural intent of monarchy appears even from the very discipline of bees: they assign to their master the fairest lodgings, the safest place; and his office is only to see that the rest perform their duties. When their king is lost, the whole swarm dissolve: more than one they will not admit; and then they contend who shall have the best. They are of all creatures the fiercest for their bigness; and leave their stings behind them in their quarrels; only the king himself has none, intimating that kings should neither be vindictive nor cruel.

Is it not a shame, after such an example of moderation in these creatures, that men should be yet intemperate? It were well if they lost their stings too in their revenge, as well as the other, that they might hurt but once, and do no mischief by their proxies. It would tire them out, if either they were to execute all with their own hands, or to wound others at the peril of their own lives.

A prince should behave himself generously in the power which God has given him of life and death, especially towards those that have been at any time his equals; for the one has his revenge, and the other his punishment in it. He that stands indebted for his life has lost it; but he that receives his life at the foot of his enemy, lives to the honor of his preserver: he lives the lasting monument of his virtue; whereas, if he had been led in triumph, the spectacle would have been quickly over. Or what if he should restore him to his kingdom again? would it not be an ample accession to his honor to show that he found nothing about the conquered that was worthy of the conqueror? There is nothing more venerable than a prince that does not revenge an injury. He that is gracious is beloved and reverenced as a common father; but a tyrant stands in fear and in danger even of his own guards. No prince can be safe himself of whom all others are afraid; for to spare none is to enrage all. It is an error to imagine that any man can be secure that suffers nobody else to be so too. How can any man endure to lead an uneasy, suspicious, anxious life, when he may be safe if he please, and enjoy all the blessings of power, together with the prayers of his people? Clemency protects a prince without a guard; there is no need of troops, castles, or fortifications: security on the one side is the condition of security on the other; and the affections of the subject are the most invincible fortress. What can be fairer, than for a prince to live the object of his people's love; to have the vows of their heart as well as of their lips, and his health and sickness their common hopes and fears? There will be no danger of plots; nay, on the contrary, who would not frankly venture his blood to save him, under whose government, justice, peace, modesty, and dignity flourish? under whose influence men grow rich and happy; and whom men look upon with such veneration, as they would do upon the immortal gods, if they were capable of seeing them? And as the true representative of the ALMIGHTY they consider him, when he is gracious and bountiful, and employs his power to the advantage of his subjects.

When a prince proceeds to punishment, it must be either to vindicate himself or others. It is a hard matter to govern himself in his own case. If a man should advise him not to be credulous, but to examine matters, and indulge the innocent, this is rather a point of justice than of clemency: but in case that he be manifestly injured, I would have him *forgive*, where he may *safely* do it: and be *tender* even where he cannot *forgive*; but far more exorable in his own case, however, than in another's.

It is nothing to be free of another man's purse, and it is as little to be merciful in another man's cause. He is the great man that masters his passion where he is stung himself, and pardons when he might destroy. The end of punishment is either to comfort the party injured, or to secure him for the future. A prince's fortune is above the need of such a comfort, and his power is too eminent to seek an advance of reputation by doing a private man a mischief. This I speak in case of an affront from those that are below us; but he that of an equal has made any man his inferior, has his revenge in the bringing of him down. A *prince* has been *killed* by a *servant*, destroyed by a serpent: but whosoever preserves a man must be greater than the person that he preserves. With citizens, strangers, and people of low condition, a prince is not to contend, for they are beneath him: he may spare some out of good will, and others as he would do some little creatures that a man cannot touch without fouling his fingers: but for those that are to be pardoned or exposed to public punishment, he may use mercy as he sees occasion; and a generous mind can never want inducements and motives to it; and whether it be *age* or *sex*, *high* or *low*, nothing comes amiss.

To pass now to the vindication of others, there must be had a regard either to the amendment of the person punished, or the making others better for fear of punishment, or the taking the offender out of the way for the security of others. An amendment may be procured by a small punishment, for he lives more carefully that has something yet to lose — it is a kind of *impunity* to be incapable of a *farther punishment*. The corruptions of a city are best cured by a few and sparing severities; for the multitude of offenders creates a custom of offending, and company authorizes a crime, and there is more good to be done upon a *dissolute age* by *patience* than by *rigor*; provided that it pass not for an *approbation* of *ill-manners*, but only as an *unwillingness* to proceed to *extremities*. Under a merciful prince, a man will be ashamed to offend, because a punishment that is inflicted by a gentle governor seems to fall heavier and with more reproach: and it is remarkable also, that "those sins are often committed which are very often punished." Caligula, in five years, condemned more people to the *sack* than ever were before him: and there were "fewer parricides before the law against them than after;" for our ancestors did wisely presume that the crime would never be committed, until by law for punishing it, they found that it might be done. *Parricides* began with the *law* against them, and the punishment instructed men in the crime. Where there are few punishments, innocency is indulged as a public good, and it is a dangerous thing to show a city how strong it is in delinquents. There is a certain contumacy in the nature of man that makes him oppose difficulties. We are better to follow than to drive; as a generous horse rides best with an easy bit. People *obey willingly* where they are *commanded kindly*.

When Burrhus the prefect was to sentence two malefactors, he brought the warrant to Nero to sign; who, after a long reluctancy came to it at last with this exclamation: "I would I could not write!" A speech that deserved the whole world for an auditory, but all princes especially; and that the hearts of all the subjects would conform to the likeness of their masters. As the head is well or ill, so is the mind dull or merry. What is the difference betwixt a *king* and a *tyrant*, but a *diversity* of *will* under one and the *same power*. The one destroys for his pleasure, the other upon necessity; a distinction rather in fact than in name.

A gracious prince is armed as well as a tyrant; but it is for the defence of his people and not for the ruin of them. No king can ever have faithful servants that accustoms them to tortures and executions; the very guilty themselves do not lead so anxious a life as the persecutors: for they are not only afraid of justice, both divine and human, but it is dangerous for them to mend their manners; so that when they are once in, they must continue to be wicked upon necessity. An universal hatred unites in a popular rage. A temperate fear may be kept in order; but when it comes once to be continual and sharp, it provokes people to extremities, and transports them to desperate resolutions, as wild beasts when they are pressed upon the *toil*, turn back and assault the very pursuers. A turbulent government is a perpetual trouble both to prince and people; and he that is a terror to all others is not without terror also himself. Frequent punishments and revenges may suppress the hatred of a few, but then it stirs up the detestation of all, so that there is no destroying one enemy without making many. It is good to master the *will* of being *cruel*, even while there may be cause for it, and matter to work upon.

Augustus was a gracious prince when he had the power in his own hand; but in the *triumviracy* he made use of his sword, and had his friends ready armed to set upon Antony during that dispute. But he behaved himself afterwards at another rate; for when he was betwixt forty and fifty years of age he was told that Cinna was in a plot to murder him, with the time, place and manner of the design; and this from one of the confederates. Upon this he resolved upon a revenge, and sent for several of his friends to advise upon it. The thought of it kept him waking, to consider, that there was the life of a young nobleman in the case, the nephew of Pompey, and a person otherwise innocent. He was off and on several times whether he should put him to death or not. "What!" says he, "shall I live in trouble and in danger myself, and the contriver of my death walk free and secure? Will nothing serve him but that life which Providence has preserved in so many civil wars — in so many battles both by sea and land; and now in the state of an universal peace too — and not a simple murder either, but a sacrifice; for I am to be assaulted at the very altar — and shall the contriver of all this villainy escape unpunished?" Here Augustus made a little pause, and then recollecting himself: "No, no, Caesar," says he, "it is rather Caesar than Cinna that I am to be angry with: why do I myself live any longer after that my death is become the interest of so many people? And if I go on, what end will there be of blood and of punishment? If it be against my life that the nobility arm itself, and level its weapons, my single life is not worth the while, if so many must be destroyed that I may be preserved."

His wife Livia gave him here an interruption, and desired him that he would for once hear a woman's counsel. "Do," says she, "like a physician, that when common remedies fail, will try the contrary: you have got nothing hitherto by severity — after Salvidianus there followed Lepidus — after him Muraena — Caepio followed him, and Egnatius followed Caepio — try now what mercy will do — forgive Cinna. He is discovered, and can do no hurt to your person; and it will yet advantage you in your reputation." Augustus was glad of the advice, and he gave thanks for it; and thereupon countermanded the meeting of his friends, and ordered Cinna to be brought to him alone; for whom he caused a chair to be set, and then discharged the rest of the company. "Cinna," says Augustus, "*before I go any farther*, you must promise not to give me the interruption of one syllable until I have told you all I have to say, and you shall have liberty afterwards to say what you please. You cannot forget, that when I found you in arms against me, and not only made my *enemy*, but *born* so, I gave you your life and fortune. Upon your petition for the priesthood, I granted it, with a repulse to the sons of those that had been my fellow-soldiers; and you are at this day so happy and so rich, that even the conquerors envy him that is overcome; and yet after all this, you are in a plot, Cinna, to murder me." At that word Cinna started, and interposed with exclamations, "that certainly he was far from being either so wicked or so mad." "This is a breach of conditions, Cinna," says Augustus, "it is not your time to speak yet: I tell you again, that you are in a plot to murder me;" and so he told him the time, the place, the confederates, the order and manner of the design, and who it was that was to do the deed. Cinna, upon this, fixed his eye upon the ground without any reply: not for his word's sake, but as in a confusion of conscience: and so Augustus went on. "What," says he, "may your design be in all this? Is it that you would pretend to step into my place? The commonwealth were in an ill condition, if only Augustus were in the way betwixt you and the government. You were cast the other day in a cause by one of your own *freemen*, and do you expect to find a weaker adversary of Caesar? But what if I were removed? There is aemilius Paulus, Fabius Maximus, and twenty other families of great blood and interest, that would never bear it." To cut off the story short; (for it was a discourse of above two hours; and Augustus lengthened the punishment in *words*, since he intended that should be all;) "Well, Cinna," says he, "the life that I gave to you once as an enemy, I will now repeat it to a *traitor* and to a *parricide*, and this shall be the last reproach I will give you. For the time to come there shall be no other contention betwixt you and me, than which shall outdo the other in point of friendship." After this Augustus made Cinna *consul*, (an honor which he confessed he durst not so much as desire) and Cinna was ever affectionately faithful to him: he made Caesar his *sole heir*; and this was the *last conspiracy* that ever was formed against him.

This moderation of Augustus was the excellency of his mature age; for in his youth he was passionate and sudden; and he did many things which afterward he looked back upon with trouble: after the battle of Actium, so many navies broken in Sicily, both *Roman* and *strangers*: the *Perusian altars*, where 300 *lives* were *sacrificed* to the *ghost* of Julius; his frequent *proscriptions*, and other severities; his *temperance* at last seemed to be little more than a *weary cruelty*. If he had not *forgiven* those that he *conquered*, whom should he have *governed*? He chose his very *life-guard* from among his *enemies*, and the *flower* of the Romans owed their *lives* to his *clemency*. Nay, he only punished Lepidus himself with *banishment*, and permitted him to wear the *ensigns* of his *dignity*, without taking the *pontificate* to himself so long as Lepidus was living; for he would not possess it as a *spoil*, but as an *honor*. This *clemency* it was that secured him in his greatness, and ingratiated him to the people, though he laid his hand upon the government before they had thoroughly submitted to the yoke; and this clemency it was that made his *name famous* to *posterity*. This is it that makes us reckon him *divine* without the authority of an *apotheosis*. He was so tender and patient, that though many a bitter jest was broken upon him, (and *contumelies* upon princes are the most *intolerable* of all *injuries*) yet he never punished any man upon that subject. *It is*, then, generous *to be* merciful, *when we have it in our* power to *take* revenge.

A son of Titus Arius, being examined and found guilty of *parricide*, was banished Rome, and confined to Marseilles, where his father allowed him the same annuity that he had before; which made all people conclude him guilty, when they saw that his father had yet *condemned* the son that he could not *hate*. Augustus was pleased to sit upon the fact in the house of Arius, only as a *single member* of the *council* that was to examine it: if it had been in Caesar's palace, the judgment must have been Caesar's and not the *father's*. Upon a full hearing of the matter, Caesar directed that every man should write his opinion whether *guilty* or *not*, and without declaring of his own, for fear of a partial vote. Before the opening of the books, Caesar passed an oath, that he would not be Arius's *heir*: and to show that he had no interest in his sentence, as appeared afterward; for he was not condemned to the ordinary *punishments* of *parricides*, nor to a prison, but, by the mediation of Caesar, only banished Rome, and confined to the place which his father should name; Augustus insisting upon it, that the father should content himself with an easy punishment: and arguing that the young man was not moved to the attempt by *malice*, and that he was but half resolved upon the fact, for he wavered in it; and, therefore, to remove him from the city, and from his father's sight, would be sufficient. This is a glorious mercy, and worthy of a prince, to make all things gentler wherever he comes.

How miserable is that man in himself, who, when he has employed his power in rapines and cruelty upon others, is yet more unhappy in himself! He stands in fear both of his domestics and of strangers; the faith of his friends and the piety of his children, and flies to actual violence to secure him from the violence he fears. When he comes to look about him, and to consider what he *has* done, what he *must*, and what he is *about* to do; what with the *wickedness*, and with the *torments* of his *conscience*, many times he fears death, oftener he wishes for it; and lives more odious to himself than to his subjects; whereas on the contrary, he that takes a care of the public, though of one part more perhaps than of another, yet there is not any part of it but he looks upon as part of himself. His mind is tender and gentle; and even where punishment is necessary and profitable, he comes to it unwillingly, and without any rancor or enmity in his heart. Let the authority, in fine, be what it will, clemency becomes it; and the greater the power, the greater is the glory of it. "It is a truly royal virtue for a prince to deliver his people *from other* men's anger, and not to oppress them *with his* own."

SENECA'S WRITINGS

It appears that our author had among the ancients three professed enemies. In the first place Caligula, who called his writings, sand without lime; alluding to the starts of his fancy, and the incoherence of his sentences. But Seneca was never the worse for the censure of a person that propounded even the suppressing of Homer himself; and of casting Virgil and Livy out of all public libraries. The next was Fabius, who taxes him for being too bold with the eloquence of former times, and failing in that point himself; and likewise for being too quaint and finical in his expressions; which Tacitus imputes, in part to the freedom of his own particular inclination, and partly to the humor of the times. He is also charged by Fabius as no profound philosopher; but with all this, he allows him to be a man very studious and learned, of great wit and invention, and well read in all sorts of literature; a severe reprover of vice; most divinely sententious; and well worth the reading, if it were only for his morals; adding, that if his judgment had been answerable to his wit, it had been much the more for his reputation; but he wrote whatever came next; so that I would advise the reader (says he) to distinguish where he himself did not, for there are many things in him, not only to be approved, but admired; and it was great pity that he that could do what he would, should not always make the best choice. His third adversary is Agellius, who falls upon him for his style, and a kind of tinkling in his sentences, but yet commends him for his piety and good counsels. On the other side, Columela calls him a man of excellent wit and learning; Pliny, the prince of erudition; Tacitus gives him the character of a wise man, and a fit tutor for a prince; Dio reports him to have been the greatest man of his age.

Of those pieces of his that are extant, we shall not need to give any particular account: and of those that are lost, we cannot, any farther than by lights to them from other authors, as we find them cited much to his honor; and we may reasonably compute them to be the greater part of his works. That he wrote several poems in his banishment, may be gathered partly from himself, but more expressly out of Tacitus, who says, "that he was reproached with his applying himself to poetry, after he saw that Nero took pleasure in it, out of a design to curry favor." St. Jerome refers to a discourse of his concerning matrimony. Lactantius takes notice of his history, and his books of Moralities: St. Augustine quotes some passages of his out of a book of Superstition; some references we meet with to his books of Exhortations: Fabius makes mention of his Dialogues: and he himself speaks of a treatise of his own concerning Earthquakes, which he wrote in his youth, but the opinion of an epistolary correspondence that he had with St. Paul, does not seem to have much color for it.

Some few fragments, however, of those books of his that are wanting, are yet preserved in the writings of other eminent authors, sufficient to show the world how great a treasure they have lost by the excellency of that little that is left.

Seneca, says Lactantius, that was the sharpest of all the Stoics, how great a veneration has he for the Almighty! as for instance, discoursing of a violent death; "Do you not understand?" says he, "the majesty and the authority of your Judge; he is the supreme Governor of heaven and earth, and the God of all your gods; and it is upon him that all those powers depend which we worship for deities." Moreover, in his Exhortations, "This God," says he, "when he laid the foundations of the universe, and entered upon the greatest and the best work in nature, in the ordering of the government of the world, though he was himself All in all, yet he substituted other subordinate ministers, as the servants of his commands." And how many other things does this Heathen speak of God like one of us!

Which the acute Seneca, says Lactantius again, saw in his Exhortations. "We," says he, "have our dependence elsewhere, and should look up to that power, to which we are indebted for all that we can pretend to that is good."

And again, Seneca says very well in his Morals, "They worship the images of the God," says he, "kneel to them, and adore them, they are hardly ever from them, either plying them with offerings or sacrifices, and yet, after all this reverence to the image, they have no regard at all to the workman that made it."

Lactantius again. "An invective," says Seneca in his

Exhortations, "is the masterpiece of most of our philosophers; and if they fall upon the subject of avarice, lust, ambition, they lash out into such excess of bitterness, as if railing were a mark of their profession. They make me think of gallipots in an apothecary's shop, that have remedies without and poison within."

Lactantius still. "He that would know all things, let him read Seneca; the most lively describer of public vices and manners, and the smartest reprehender of them."

And again; as Seneca has it in the books of Moral Philosophy, "He is the brave man, whose splendor and authority is the least part of his greatness, that can look death in the face without trouble or surprise; who, if his body were to be broken upon the wheel, or melted lead to be poured down his throat, would be less concerned for the pain itself, than for the dignity of bearing it."

Let no man, says Lactantius, think himself the safer in his wickedness for want of a witness; for God is omniscient, and to him nothing can be a secret. It is an admirable sentence that Seneca concludes his Exhortations withal: "God," says he, "is a great, (I know not what), an incomprehensible Power; it is to him that we live, and to him that we must approve ourselves. What does it avail us that our consciences are hidden from men, when our souls lie open to God?" What could a Christian have spoken more to the purpose in this case than this divine Pagan? And in the beginning of the same work, says Seneca, "What is it that we do? to what end is it to stand contriving, and to hide ourselves? We are under a guard, and there is no escaping from our keeper. One man may be parted from another by travel, death, sickness; but there is no dividing us from ourselves. It is to no purpose to creep into a corner where nobody shall see us. Ridiculous madness! Make it the case, that no mortal eye could find us out, he that has a conscience gives evidence against himself."

It is truly and excellently spoken of Seneca, says Lactantius, once again; "Consider," says he "the majesty, the goodness, and the venerable mercies of the Almighty; a friend that is always at hand. What delight can it be to him the slaughter of innocent creatures or the worship of bloody sacrifices? Let us purge our minds, and lead virtuous and honest lives. His pleasure lies not in the magnificence of temples made with stone, but in the pity and devotion of consecrated hearts."

In the book that Seneca wrote against Superstitions, treating of images, says St. Austin, he writes thus: "They represent the holy, the immortal, and the inviolable gods in the basest matter, and without life or motion; in the forms of men, beasts, fishes, some of mixed bodies, and those figures they call deities, which, if they were but animated, would affright a man, and pass for monsters." And then, a little farther, treating of Natural Theology, after citing the opinions of philosophers, he supposes an objection against himself: "Somebody will perhaps ask me, would you have me then to believe the heavens and the earth to be gods, and some of them above the moon, and some below it? Shall I ever be brought to the opinion of Plato, or of Strabo the Peripatetic? the one of which would have God to be without a body, and the other without a mind." To which he replies, "And do you give more credit then to the dreams of T. Tatius, Romulus, Hostilius, who caused, among other deities, even Fear and Paleness to be worshipped? the vilest of human affections; the one being the motion of an affrighted mind, and the other not so much the disease as the color of a disordered body. Are these the deities that you will rather put your faith in, and place in the heavens?" And speaking afterward of their abominable customs, with what liberty does he write! "One," says he, "out of zeal, makes himself an eunuch, another lances his arms; if this be the way to please their gods, what should a man do if he had a mind to anger them? or, if this be the way to please them, they do certainly deserve not to be worshipped at all. What a frenzy is this to imagine that the gods can be delighted with such cruelties, as even the worst of men would make a conscience to inflict! The most barbarous and notorious of tyrants, some of them have perhaps done it themselves, or ordered the tearing of men to pieces by others; but they never went so far as to command any man to torment himself. We have heard of those that have suffered castration to gratify the lust of their imperious masters, but never any man that was forced to act it upon himself. They murder themselves in their very temples, and their prayers are offered up in blood. Whosoever shall but observe what they do, and what they suffer, will find it so misbecoming an honest man, so unworthy of a freeman, and so inconsistent with the action of a man in his wits, that he must conclude them all to be mad, if it were not that there are so many of them; for only their number is their justification and their protection."

When he comes to reflect, says St. Augustine, upon those passages which he himself had seen in the Capitol, he censures them with liberty and resolution; and no man will believe that such things would be done unless in mockery or frenzy. What lamentation is there in the Egyptian sacrifices for the loss of Osiris? and then what joy for the finding of him again? Which he makes himself sport with; for in truth it is all a fiction; and yet those people that neither lost any thing nor found any thing, must express their sorrows and their rejoicings to the highest degree. "But there is only a certain time," says he, "for this freak, and once in a year people may be allowed to be mad. I came into the Capitol," says Seneca, "where the several deities had their several servants and attendants, their lictors, their dressers, and all in posture and action, as if they were executing their offices; some to hold the glass, others to comb out Juno's and Minerva's hair; one to tell Jupiter what o'clock it is; some lasses there are that sit gazing upon the image, and fancy Jupiter has a kindness for them. All these things," says Seneca, a while after, "a wise man will observe for the law's sake more than for the gods; and all this rabble of deities, which the superstition of many ages has gathered together, we are in such manner to adore, as to consider the worship to be rather matter of custom than of conscience." Whereupon St. Augustine observes, that this illustrious senator worshipped what he reproved, acted what he disliked, and adored what he condemned.

SENECA'S LIFE AND DEATH

It has been an ancient custom to record the actions and the writings of eminent men, with all their circumstances, and it is but a right that we owe to the memory of our famous author. Seneca was by birth a Spaniard of Cordova, (a Roman colony of great fame and antiquity.) He was of the family of Annaeus, of the order of knights; and the father, Lucius Annaeus Seneca, was distinguished from the son, by the name of the Orator. His mother's name was Helvia, a woman of excellent qualities. His father came to Rome in the time of Augustus, and his wife and children soon followed him, our Seneca yet being in his infancy. There were three brothers of them, and never a sister. Marcus Annaeus Novatus, Lucius Annaeus Seneca, and Lucius Annaeus Mela; the first of these changed his name for Junius Gallio, who adopted him; to him it was that he dedicated his treatise of Anger, whom he calls Novatus too; and he also dedicated his discourse of a Happy Life to his brother Gallio. The youngest brother (Annaeus Mela) was Lucan's father. Seneca was about twenty years of age in the fifth year of Tiberius, when the Jews were expelled from Rome. His father trained him up to rhetoric, but his genius led him rather to philosophy; and he applied his wit to morality and virtue. He was a great hearer of the celebrated men of those times; as Attalus, Sotion, Papirius, Fabianus, (of whom he makes often mention,) and he was much an admirer also of Demetrius the Cynic, whose conversation he had afterwards in the Court, and both at home also and abroad, for they often travelled together. His father was not at all pleased with his humor of philosophy, but forced him upon the law, and for a while he practiced pleading. After which he would needs put him upon public employment: and he came first to be quaestor, then praetor, and some will have it that he was chosen consul; but this is doubtful.

    Seneca finding that he had ill offices done him at court, and that Nero's favor began to cool, he went directly and resolutely to Nero, with an offer to refund all that he had gotten, which Nero would not receive; but however, from that time he changed his course of life, received few visits, shunned company, went little abroad; still pretending to be kept at home, either by indisposition or by his study. Being Nero's tutor and governor, all things were well so long as Nero followed his counsel. His two chief favorites were Burrhus and Seneca, who were both of them excellent in their ways: Burrhus, in his care of military affairs, and severity of discipline; Seneca for his precepts and good advice in the matter of eloquence, and the gentleness of an honest mind; assisting one another, in that slippery age of the prince (says Tacitus) to invite him, by the allowance of lawful pleasures, to the love of virtue. Seneca had two wives; the name of the first is not mentioned; his second was Paulina, whom he often speaks of with great passion. By the former he had his son Marcus.

In the first year of Claudius he was banished into Corsica, when Julia, the daughter of Germanicus, was accused by Messalina of adultery and banished too, Seneca being charged as one of the adulterers. After a matter of eight years or upwards in exile, he was called back, and as much in favor again as ever. His estate was partly patrimonial, but the greatest part of it was the bounty of his prince. His gardens, villas, lands, possessions, and incredible sums of money, are agreed upon at all hands; which drew an envy upon him. Dio reports him to have had 250,000 sterling[2] at interest in Britanny alone, which he called in all at a sum. The Court itself could not bring him to flattery; and for his piety, submission, and virtue, the practice of his whole life witnesses for him. "So soon," says he, "as the candle is taken away, my wife, that knows my custom, lies still, without a word speaking, and then do I recollect all that I have said or done that day, and take myself to shrift. And why should I conceal or reserve anything, or make any scruple of inquiring into my errors, when I can say to myself, Do so no more, and for this once I will forgive thee?" And again, what can be more pious and self-denying than this passage, in one of his epistles? "Believe me now, when I tell you the very bottom of my soul: in all the difficulties and crosses of my life, this is my consideration — since it is God's will, I do not only obey,

---

2   A comparison of the value of money then and now is completely mean-ingless. Because, even if we are able to calculate this 'value', they could not buy the goods of this time with their money and we cannot buy the goods of that time with our money.

but assent to it; nor do I comply out of necessity, but inclination."

"Here follows now," says Tacitus, "the death of Seneca, to Nero's great satisfaction; not so much for any pregnant proof against him that he was of Piso's conspiracy; but Nero was resolved to do that by the sword which he could not effect by poison. For it is reported, that Nero had corrupted Cleonicus (a freeman of Seneca's) to give his master poison, which did not succeed. Whether that the servant had discovered it to his master, or that Seneca, by his own caution and jealousy, had avoided it; for he lived only upon a simple diet, as the fruits of the earth, and his drink was most commonly river water.

"Natalis, it seems, was sent upon a visit to him (being indisposed) with a complaint that he would not let Piso come at him; and advising him to the continuance of their friendship and acquaintance as formerly. To whom Seneca made answer, that frequent meetings and conferences betwixt them could do neither of them any good; but that he had a great interest in Piso's welfare. Hereupon Granius Silvanus (a captain of the guard) was sent to examine Seneca upon the discourse that passed betwixt him and Natalis, and to return his answer. Seneca, either by chance or upon purpose, came that day from Campania, to a villa of his own, within four miles of the city; and thither the officer went the next evening, and beset the place. He found Seneca at supper with his wife Paulina, and two of his friends; and gave him immediately an account of his commission. Seneca told him, that it was true that Natalis had been with him in Piso's name, with a complaint that Piso could not be admitted to see him; and that he excused himself by reason of his want of health, and his desires to be quiet and private; and that he had no reason to prefer another man's welfare before his own. Caesar himself, he said, knew very well that he was not a man of compliment, having received more proofs of his freedom than of his flattery. This answer of Seneca's was delivered to Caesar in the presence of Poppaea, and Tigellinus, the intimate confidants of this barbarous prince: and Nero asked him whether he could gather anything from Seneca as if he intended to make himself away? The tribune's answer was, that he did not find him one jot moved with the message: but that he went on roundly with his tale, and never so much as changed countenance for the matter. Go back to him then, says Nero, and tell him, that he is condemned to die. Fabius Rusticus delivers it, that the tribune did not return the same way he came, but went aside to Fenius (a captain of that name) and told him Caesar's orders, asking his advice whether he should obey them or not; who bade him by all means to do as he was ordered. Which want of resolution was fatal to them all; for Silvanus also, that was one of the conspirators, assisted now to serve and to increase those crimes, which he had before complotted to revenge. And yet he did not think fit to appear himself in the business, but sent a centurion to Seneca to tell him his doom.

"Seneca, without any surprise or disorder, calls for his will; which being refused him by the officer, he turned to his friends, and told them that since he was not permitted to requite them as they deserved, he was yet at liberty to bequeath them the thing of all others that he esteemed the most, that is, the image of his life; which should give them the reputation both of constancy and friendship, if they would but imitate it; exhorting them to a firmness of mind, sometimes by good counsel, otherwhile by reprehension, as the occasion required. Where, says he, is all your philosophy now? all your premeditated resolutions against the violences of Fortune? Is there any man so ignorant of Nero's cruelty, as to expect, after the murder of his mother and his brother, that he should ever spare the life of his governor and tutor? After some general expressions to this purpose, he took his wife in his arms, and having somewhat fortified her against the present calamity, he besought and conjured her to moderate her sorrows, and betake herself to the contemplations and comforts of a virtuous life; which would be a fair and ample consolation to her for the loss of her husband. Paulina, on the other side, tells him her determination to bear him company, and wills the executioner to do his office. Well, says Seneca, if after the sweetness of life, as I have represented it to thee, thou hadst rather entertain an honorable death, I shall not envy thy example; consulting, at the same time, the fame of the person he loved, and his own tenderness, for fear of the injuries that might attend her when he was gone. Our resolution, says he, in this generous act, may be equal, but thine will be the greater reputation. After this the veins of both their arms were opened at the same time. Seneca did not bleed so freely, his spirits being wasted with age and a thin diet; so that he was forced to cut the veins of his thighs and elsewhere, to hasten his dispatch. When he was far spent, and almost sinking under his torments, he desired his wife to remove into another chamber, lest the agonies of the one might work upon the courage of the other. His eloquence continued to the last, as appears by the excellent things he delivered at his death; which being taken in writing from his own mouth, and published in his own words, I shall not presume to deliver them in any other. Nero, in the meantime, who had no particular spite to Paulina, gave orders to prevent her death, for fear his cruelty should grow more and more insupportable and odious. Whereupon the soldiers gave all freedom and encouragement to her servants to bind up her wounds, and stop the blood, which they did accordingly; but whether she was sensible of it or not is a question. For among the common people, who are apt to judge the worst, there were some of opinion, that as long as she despaired of Nero's mercy, she seemed to court the glory of dying with her husband for company; but that upon the likelihood of better quarter she was prevailed upon to outlive him; and so for some years she did survive him, with all piety and respect to his memory; but so miserably pale and wan, that everybody might read the loss of her blood and spirits in her very countenance.

"Seneca finding his death slow and lingering, desires Statius Annaeus (his old friend and physician) to give him a dose of poison, which he had provided beforehand, being the same preparation which was appointed for capital offenders in Athens. This was brought him, and he drank it up, but to little purpose; for his body was already chilled, and bound up against the force of it. He went at last into a hot bath, and sprinkling some of his servants that were next him, this, says he, is an oblation to Jupiter the deliverer. The fume of the bath soon dispatched him, and his body was burnt, without any funeral solemnity, as he had directed in his testament: though this will of his was made in the height of his prosperity and power. There was a rumor that Subrius Flavius, in a private consultation with the centurions, had taken up this following resolution, (and that Seneca himself was no stranger to it) that is to say, that after Nero should have been slain by the help of Piso, Piso himself should have been killed too; and the empire delivered up to Seneca, as one that well deserved it, for his integrity and virtue."